Contemp High Performance Computing

From Petascale toward Exascale

VOLUME TWO

Chapman & Hall/CRC
Computational Science Series

SERIES EDITOR

Horst Simon
Deputy Director
Lawrence Berkeley National Laboratory
Berkeley, California, U.S.A.

PUBLISHED TITLES

COMBINATORIAL SCIENTIFIC COMPUTING
Edited by Uwe Naumann and Olaf Schenk

CONTEMPORARY HIGH PERFORMANCE COMPUTING: FROM PETASCALE
TOWARD EXASCALE
Edited by Jeffrey S. Vetter

CONTEMPORARY HIGH PERFORMANCE COMPUTING: FROM PETASCALE
TOWARD EXASCALE, VOLUME TWO
Edited by Jeffrey S. Vetter

DATA-INTENSIVE SCIENCE
Edited by Terence Critchlow and Kerstin Kleese van Dam

THE END OF ERROR: UNUM COMPUTING
John L. Gustafson

FUNDAMENTALS OF MULTICORE SOFTWARE DEVELOPMENT
Edited by Victor Pankratius, Ali-Reza Adl-Tabatabai, and Walter Tichy

THE GREEN COMPUTING BOOK: TACKLING ENERGY EFFICIENCY AT LARGE SCALE
Edited by Wu-chun Feng

GRID COMPUTING: TECHNIQUES AND APPLICATIONS
Barry Wilkinson

HIGH PERFORMANCE COMPUTING: PROGRAMMING AND APPLICATIONS
John Levesque with Gene Wagenbreth

HIGH PERFORMANCE PARALLEL I/O
Prabhat and Quincey Koziol

HIGH PERFORMANCE VISUALIZATION:
ENABLING EXTREME-SCALE SCIENTIFIC INSIGHT
Edited by E. Wes Bethel, Hank Childs, and Charles Hansen

INTRODUCTION TO COMPUTATIONAL MODELING USING C AND
OPEN-SOURCE TOOLS
José M Garrido

PUBLISHED TITLES CONTINUED

Contemporary
High Performance
Computing
From Petascale toward Exascale
VOLUME TWO

Edited by

Jeffrey S. Vetter

CRC Press
Taylor & Francis Group
Boca Raton London New York

CRC Press is an imprint of the
Taylor & Francis Group, an **informa** business
A CHAPMAN & HALL BOOK

CRC Press
Taylor & Francis Group
6000 Broken Sound Parkway NW, Suite 300
Boca Raton, FL 33487-2742

First issued in paperback 2019

© 2015 by Taylor & Francis Group, LLC
CRC Press is an imprint of Taylor & Francis Group, an Informa business

No claim to original U.S. Government works

ISBN-13: 978-1-4987-0062-7 (hbk)
ISBN-13: 978-0-367-37775-5 (pbk)

Visit the Taylor & Francis Web site at
http://www.taylorandfrancis.com

and the CRC Press Web site at
http://www.crcpress.com

Contents

List of Figures

List of Tables

Preface

We are pleased to present you with this second volume of material that captures a snapshot of the rich history of practice in Contemporary High Performance Computing. As evidenced in the chapters of this book, High Performance Computing (HPC) continues to flourish, both in industry and research, both domestically and internationally. While much of the focus of HPC is on the hardware architectures, a significant ecosystem is responsible for this success. This book helps capture this broad ecosystem.

Why I Edited This Book

My goal with this series of books has been to highlight and document significant systems and facilities in HPC. With Volume 1, my main focus was proposed to be on the architectural design of important and successful HPC systems. However, as I started to interact with authors, I realized that HPC is about more than just hardware: it is an ecosystem that includes software, applications, facilities, educators, software developers, scientists, administrators, sponsors, and many others. Broadly speaking, HPC is growing internationally, so I invited contributions from a broad base of organizations including the USA, Japan, Germany, Sweden, and the United Kingdom. This second volume is a snapshot of these contemporary HPC ecosystems. Each chapter is typically punctuated with a site's flagship system.

My excitement about Volume 1 of this book grew as I started inviting authors to contribute: everyone said 'yes!' In fact, due to the limitations on hardback publishing, we had to create this second volume.

Topic Selection and Organization

For each contributed chapter, I asked the authors to provide snapshots of their contemporary HPC ecosystems, and to include the following content:

1. Program background and motivation

2. Applications and workloads

3. Keystone system overview

4. Hardware architecture

5. System software

6. Programming system

7. Storage, visualization, and analytics

8. Data center/facility

9. System statistics

Some of the authors followed this outline precisely while others found creative ways to include this content in a different structure. Once you read the book, I think that you will agree with me that most of the chapters have exceeded these expectations, and have provided a detailed snapshot of their HPC ecosystem, science, and organization.

Helping To Improve This Book

HPC and computing, in general, is a rapidly changing, large, and diverse field. If you have comments, corrections, or questions, please send a note to me at `vetter@computer.org`.

Chapter 1

Terascale to Petascale: The Past 17 Years in High Performance Computing

Jeffrey S. Vetter

Oak Ridge National Laboratory and Georgia Institute of Technology

High Performance Computing (HPC) is used to solve a number of complex questions in computational and data-intensive sciences. These questions include the simulation and modeling of physical phenomena, such as climate change, energy production, drug design, global security, and materials design; the analysis of large data sets, such as those in genome sequencing, astronomical observation, and cybersecurity; and, the intricate design of engineered products, such as airplanes and automobiles.

It is clear and well-documented that HPC is used to generate insight that would not otherwise be possible. Simulations can augment or replace expensive, hazardous, or impossible experiments. Furthermore, in the realm of simulation, HPC has the potential to suggest new experiments that escape the parameters of observability.

Although much of the excitement about HPC focuses on the largest architectures and on specific benchmarks, such as TOP500, there is a much deeper and broader commitment from the international scientific and engineering community than is first apparent. In fact, it is easy to lose track of history in terms of the broad uses of HPC and the communities that design, deploy, and operate HPC systems and facilities. Many of these sponsors and organizations have spent decades developing scientific simulation methods and software which serves as the foundation of HPC today. This community has worked closely with countless vendors to foster the sustained development and deployment of HPC systems internationally.

In this second volume of *Contemporary High Performance Computing* [4], we continue to document international HPC ecosystems including the sponsors and sites that host them. We have selected contributions from international HPC sites, which represent a combination of sites, systems, vendors, applications, and sponsors. Rather than focus on simply the architecture or the application, we focus on *HPC ecosystems* that have made this dramatic progress possible. Though the very word ecosystem can be a broad, all-encompassing term, it aptly describes HPC. That is, HPC is far more than one sponsor, one site, one application, one software system, or one architecture. Indeed, it is a community of interacting entities in this environment that sustains the community over time. Contributors were asked to address the following topics in their chapters:

1. Sponsor and site history

2. Highlights of applications, workloads, and benchmarks

3. Systems overview

4. Hardware architecture

5. System software

6. Programming systems

7. Storage, visualization, and analytics

8. Data center/facility

9. Site HPC statistics

By any measure, the past 17 years have witnessed dramatic increases in both the use and scale of HPC. Thinking back, it was 1997, only 17 years ago, when the ASCI Red system at Sandia National Laboratories in Albuquerque, New Mexico, broke the 1 Terascale barrier on TOP500 Linpack using 7,264 Pentium P6 processors over a proprietary interconnection network. In 2013, China's Tihane-2 system accelerated with Xeon Phi surpassed 33.8 Petaflops on the same benchmark: an increase of about 33,000 times in 17 years! It is impressive, indeed, when considering the well-known fact that the performance of commodity microprocessors has slowed due to power and thermal constraints [1, 2, 3].

Although much of the focus is on the #1 system on TOP500, and its architecture, it is important to promote the fact that there are dozens, in fact, hundreds of systems around the world in daily use for solving HPC problems. As Table 1.1 illustrates, we have seven chapters from contributing authors around the world describing their ecosystem. The architectures of these systems span the range from a fully customized processor and interconnection network to a complete commodity solution. A number of new sites have installed the new Cray XC30. Two sites have commodity clusters, where one is accelerated by Xeon Phi. Finally, Japan's K system is a specialized version of the SPARC64 processor, and the Tofu interconnection network.

In contrast to the hardware diversity we see in these systems, they share a tremendous amount of software as listed in Table 1.2. In fact, much of this software is open-source software that organizations can download, port, and install

TABLE 1.1: Significant systems in HPC.

System	Type	Organization	Location	Country
Archer	Cray XC30	University of Edinburgh	Edinburgh, Scotland	UK
HLRN-III	Cray XC30	Zuse Institute Berlin	Berlin	Germany
K	Fujitsu SPARC64 VIIIfx, Tofu	RIKEN Advanced Institute for Computational Science (AICS)	Kobe	Japan
Lindgren	Cray XE6	KTH Royal Institute of Technology	Stockholm	Sweden
Peregrine	HP Cluster with Xeon and Xeon Phi processors, and FDR Infiniband	National Renewable Energy Laboratory	Golden, Colorado	USA
Yellowstone	IBM Cluster with Xeon processors and FDR Infiniband	NCAR-Wyoming Supercomputing Center (NWSC)	Cheyenne, Wyoming	USA
Edison	Cray XC30	National Energy Research Scientific Computing Center at Lawrence Berkeley National Laboratory	Berkeley, California	USA

TABLE 1.2: HPC software summary.

Category	Item
Operating Systems	Linux (Multiple versions)
Languages	C, C++, FORTRAN (various)
Compilers	Cray Compiler Environment, GNU, Intel, PathScale, PGI
Scripting Languages	Java, Perl, Python (incl. mpipy, Numpy, Matplotlib, Anaconda), Ruby, Tcl/Tk
Distributed Memory Programming Models	Cray CCE (incl. Co-Array Fortran, UPC), Cray MPT, Global Arrays, MPI (OpenMPI, MVAIPICH, Intel MPI, Cray MPI, MPICH, IBM MPI), SHMEM
Shared Memory Programming Models	OpenMP, Pthreads
Heterogeneous Programming Models	Intel MIC Offload, OpenACC, PGI Accelerator
Performance Tools	Allinea MAP, Cray PAT, Cray Reveal, Darshan, Extrae/-Paraver, IPM, Intel Trace Analyzer, Vtune, ITAC MPIP, PAPI, Perftools, Perftools-lite, Scalasca, TAU, Vampir
Correctness Tools	Allinea DDT, Cray ATP, GNU GDB, LGDB, Totalview, Valgrind
Scientific Libraries and Frameworks	ACML, BLAS, Boost, Cray LibSci, FFTW, GNU GSL, GSL, HDF5, Hugetables, Intel MLK, LAPACK, NetCDF, PETSc, PETSc, ParMetis, SLEPc SPRNG, ScaLAPACK, SuiteSparse, Trilinos
Parallel Filesystems and Storage	IBM GPFS, Lustre, GridFtp
I/O Libraries and Software	ADIOS, CGNS, HDF5, Hercule, IOBUF, Silo, pnetCDF
Job Schedulers and Resource Managers	Cray ALPS, IBM LSF, PBSPro, Torque/Moab
System Management	Ganglia, HP Cluster Management Utility, xCAT
Visualization	Ferret, GNUPlot, GrADS SPlash, IDL, NcView R, VisIt
Integrated Problem Solving Environnments	MATLAB, Octave, R

on any system. In fact, although HPC systems share many hardware components with servers in enterprise and data centers, the HPC software stack is a distinguishing component of HPC. Generally speaking, the HPC software stack has multiple levels: system software, development environments, system management software, and scientific data management and visualization systems. Nearest to the hardware, system software typically includes operating systems, runtime systems, and low-level I/O software, like file systems. Next, the category of programming systems is a broad area that facilitates design and development of applications. In our framework, it includes programming models, compilers, scientific frameworks and libraries, and correctness and performance tools. Then, system management software coordinates, schedules, and monitors the system and the applications running on that system. Finally, scientific data management and visualization software provides users with domain specific tools for generating, managing, and exploring data for their science. This data may include output from simulations per se or empirically measured data from sensors in the real world, which can also be used to validate and calibrate simulation software.

Nevertheless, over the past 17 years, HPC software has had to adapt and respond to several challenges. First, the concurrency in applications and systems has grown over three orders of magnitude. The primary programming model, MPI, has had to grow and change to allow this scale. Second, the increase in concurrency has per core driven lower the memory and I/O capacity, and the memory, I/O, and interconnect bandwidth. Third, in the last five years, heterogeneity and architectural diversity have placed a new emphasis on application and software portability across programming environments.

Bibliography

[1] Jack Dongarra, Pete Beckman, Terry Moore, Patrick Aerts, Giovanni Aloisio, Jean-Claude Andre, David Barkai, Jean-Yves Berthou, Taisuke Boku, Bertrand Braunschweig, Franck Cappello, Barbara Chapman, Xuebin Chi, Alok Choudhary, Sudip Dosanjh, Thom Dunning, Sandro Fiore, Al Geist, Bill Gropp, Robert Harrison, Mark Hereld, Michael Heroux, Adolfy Hoisie, Koh Hotta, Zhong Jin, Yutaka Ishikawa, Fred Johnson, Sanjay Kale, Richard Kenway, David Keyes, Bill Kramer, Jesus Labarta, Alain Lichnewsky, Thomas Lippert, Bob Lucas, Barney Maccabe, Satoshi Matsuoka, Paul Messina, Peter Michielse, Bernd Mohr, Matthias S. Mueller, Wolfgang E. Nagel, Hiroshi Nakashima, Michael E Papka, Dan Reed, Mitsuhisa Sato, Ed Seidel, John Shalf, David Skinner, Marc Snir, Thomas Sterling, Rick Stevens, Fred Streitz, Bob Sugar, Shinji Sumimoto, William Tang, John Taylor, Rajeev Thakur, Anne Trefethen, Mateo Valero, Aad van der Steen, Jeffrey Vetter, Peg Williams, Robert Wisniewski, and Kathy Yelick. The international exascale software project roadmap. *International Journal of High Performance Computing Applications*, 25(1):3–60, 2011.

[2] Peter Kogge, Keren Bergman, Shekhar Borkar, Dan Campbell, William Carlson, William Dally, Monty Denneau, Paul Franzon, William Harrod, Kerry Hill, Jon Hiller, Sherman Karp, Stephen Keckler, Dean Klein, Robert Lucas, Mark Richards, Al Scarpelli, Steven Scott, Allan Snavely, Thomas Sterling, R. Stanley Williams, and Katherine Yelick. Exascale computing study: Technology challenges in achieving exascale systems. Technical report, DARPA Information Processing Techniques Office, 2008.

[3] Horst Simon, Thomas Zacharia, and Rick Stevens. Modeling and simulation at the exascale for energy and the environment. Technical report, US Department of Energy, Office of Science, 2007.

[4] Jeffrey S. Vetter, editor. *Contemporary High Performance Computing: From Petascale Toward Exascale*, volume 1 of *CRC Computational Science Series*. Taylor & Francis, Boca Raton, 1 edition, 2013.

Chapter 2

ARCHER

Xu Guo, David Henty, Chris Johnson, Alan Simpson, Lorna Smith, and Andrew Turner

EPCC, University of Edinburgh

2.1 Overview

2.1.1 Sponsor/Program Background

ARCHER is the latest UK national HPC service and is funded by two major UK research councils — the Engineering and Physical Sciences Research Council (EPSRC) and the Natural Environment Research Council (NERC). EPSRC users typically work on Chemistry, Materials, Physics, Computational Fluid Dynamics, and Engineering. NERC users work on Ocean Modelling, Atmospheric Science, and Mineral Physics. More details are given in Section 2.2.

EPSRC and NERC have contributed to a series of national HPC systems during the last 20 years.

Table 2.1 lists the series of overlapping national UK HPC services. Each service has lasted 7-8 years and has had a number of significant technology refreshes. There have also been overlaps between consecutive services to ensure smooth transitions for users.

EPCC took leading roles in all of the above services, apart from CSAR. However, EPCC's history of systems is significantly more extensive. In particular, the University of Edinburgh's first parallel systems were DAPs and Meiko transputer systems in the 1980s. These were followed by a Connection

TABLE 2.1: National parallel HPC systems in the UK.

Service	Vendor	Years
T3D/T3E	Cray	1994-2002
CSAR	SGI	1998-2006
HPCx	IBM	2002-2010
HECToR	Cray	2007-2014
ARCHER	Cray	2013-2017+

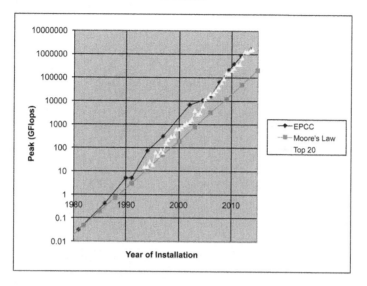

FIGURE 2.1: Peak performance of EPCC systems during the last 35 years.

Machine and a Meiko i860 system at the beginning of the 1990s; these systems marked the birth of EPCC.

The graph in Figure 2.1 shows the performance of the major systems at Edinburgh during the last 35 years. For comparison, the graph also includes a line reflecting Moore's Law and a plot of the peak performance of the systems at number 20 on the Top 500 list [4].

The graph shows an exponential increase in performance at EPCC, even somewhat ahead of Moore's Law. When we first plotted this graph about 10 years ago, we predicted that EPCC would have a Petaflop system in 2014; ARCHER met this prediction towards the end of 2013. The graph also shows that the leading systems within the UK are consistently within the top 20 largest systems in the world. The peak performance of ARCHER does not yet include any accelerators and so we are confident that it is one of the largest general-purpose HPC systems in the world and will deliver world-class research.

ARCHER will support more than 3000 users from throughout the UK working on a wide variety of applications areas. At this stage in the service, there are only limited statistics on usage, but the pattern is expected to be similar to the previous national service, HECToR. HECToR had more than 3000 users. Around half of the users were UK nationals, while the other half came from more than 80 different countries. These users came from more than 50 different UK universities and higher education institutes, including all of the major research institutions. The map in Figure 2.2 shows the distribution of users across the UK.

The map shows that UK national HPC systems attract users from throughout the UK, representing most of the major research universities. Although

FIGURE 2.2: Map of user distribution across the UK.*

there are significant groups of users associated with major centers of computational research (London, Manchester, Oxford, Cambridge, Edinburgh,...), there are noticeable similarities with the maps of population density produced by the UK's Office of National Statistics (http://www.ons.gov.uk/). The map indicates the broad importance of HPC across the UK.

2.1.2   Timeline

The procurement of ARCHER took exactly two years from the initial award of funding through to full user service. The key dates are shown in Table 2.2.

EPSRC, as managing agent for ARCHER, set up a technical procurement working group (PWG) consisting of representatives from both users and service providers. Their initial task was capturing the requirements of the users. The key elements of this process were a questionnaire circulated to users of the existing HECToR service and other interested parties, and a user meeting where the key issues were discussed; these occurred in March 2012. In

---

TABLE 2.2: Key dates for the ARCHER service.

Month	Key Event
December 2011	Funding secured
March 2012	User meeting and questionnaire
October 2012	Draft Statement of Requirements
November 2012	Initial responses from vendors
January 2013	Final bids from vendors
February 2013	Vendor bids evaluated
April 2013	Vendors informed of outcome
August 2013	Hardware delivered
September 2013	Installation
October 2013	Final acceptance tests
October 2013	Early access began
December 2013	Full service

parallel with this, there were also initial meetings with possible vendors. These meetings led to a slight delay in the procurement timeline so that the vendors would be able to offer the new Intel Ivy Bridge processors.

The draft Statement of Requirements was published in October 2012 and vendors were encouraged to submit initial responses. After minor changes to this Statement of Requirements, the final bids were submitted and evaluated in early 2013. Cray were told that they were the preferred bidder in April 2013.

There were then separate procurements for the Service Provision (operations and service desk) and in-depth Computational Science and Engineering support. Both of these were ultimately awarded to UoE HPCX Ltd, a wholly owned subsidiary of the University of Edinburgh.

The ARCHER system was built in the USA and then shipped to Edinburgh in August 2013. The on-site acceptance tests were completed in October and some users were offered early access. The full user service started in December 2013.

2.2 Applications and Workloads

ARCHER supports a broad range of scientific application areas within the remit of the UK Research Councils, particularly the Engineering and Physical Sciences Research Council (EPSRC) and the Natural Environment Research Council (NERC), where computational codes are frequently used to address current scientific research challenges. In particular, the following eight scientific application areas are dominant: Materials Science and Chemistry, Nanoscience, Earth Sciences, Plasma Physics, Soft Matter Physics, Computational Fluid Dynamics, Physical Life Sciences and Big Data/Data Intensive

Computing. The first six of these account for more than 80% of the time used on the UK's National HPC resources (ARCHER and its predecessor HECToR); the other two areas (Physical Life Sciences and Big Data/Data Intensive Computing) are both areas that are becoming increasingly important to UK computational science.

1. Materials Science and Chemistry

   Traditionally one of the largest areas of use on the UK's national HPC facilities, ARCHER is being exploited by a broad range of applications in this area, underpinned by research communities such as the Materials Chemistry Consortium and the UK Car-Parrinello Consortium. Key codes include CP2K and VASP, which account for around 25% of the total time usage. In addition CASTEP, ONETEP and NWChem all exploit the ARCHER service.

2. Nanoscience

   Significant use of ARCHER comes from Nanoscience applications. These are being used to exploit large-scale HPC facilities to model problems and phenomena that are simply not accessible using smaller-scale facilities. One of the largest of these is the GROMACS molecular dynamics package. This is primarily used for simulating biomolecules and is one of the most heavily used codes on our facilities. Other key applications in this area include GULP and LAMMPS.

3. Earth Sciences

   This NERC-funded area of science has traditionally been a large consumer of HPC time in the UK and is a key community on the ARCHER service. This community is notable in that many of the users exercise not just parallel compute capability, but also require the ability to effectively pre- or post-process simulation data and to handle the transfer of extremely large data sets onto or off the service. The Fluidity ocean modelling application and ECMWFs IFS application are two important applications in this area. NEMO, the Unified Model (UM) MicroMag are also long-term users of our services.

4. Plasma Physics

   The fusion community has been utilizing the UK HPC resources significantly over the past 5 years. The electromagenetic turbulence code Centori and the gyrokinetic simulation code GS2 codes are the main codes used in this area, with ELMFIRE and GENE also utilized on the system.

5. Soft Matter Physics

   The current simulation method of choice for soft-matter simulations is the Lattice-Boltzmann (LB) approach that shows excellent potential for scalability on current and next-generation HPC systems. The Ludwig code is being used by researchers on ARCHER to study soft materials using a coarse-grained approach based on solution of the Navier-Stokes equations via the LB method. The LB3D code is being used for the study of complex fluids such as oil/water mixtures, surfactant systems and porous media flows. Finally, HemeLB is being used to simulate blood flow in realistic geometries (e.g., arteries).

6. Computational Fluid Dynamics

   Computational Fluid Dynamics (CFD) simulations are being used on ARCHER in a range of scientific domains. Of particular importance is OpenFOAM, a widely used Open Source CFD framework. This is being used to study large turbine simulations within a hydroelectric power plant. The Gordon Bell winning Nek5000 code is also utilized on the system, as is the two-phase direct numerical simulation Navier-Stocks flow solver TPLS. Other codes include EBL, which is modelling a turbulence layer in the atmosphere, and FireGRID, a code being developed to model close-to-real-time modelling of fires.

7. Physical Life Sciences

   The use of ARCHER to model systems in the life science domain and to perform computationally demanding analyses of biological/medical data is increasingly important. This community often has extremely large amounts of data and are sophisticated in their data management and handling. Codes include SPRINT, a general purpose parallel framework for the R statistical language, and The Advanced Complex Trait Analysis (ACTA) open-source software which is being used to understand the role played by genetics in a range of diseases.

8. Big Data/Data Intensive Computing

   The amount of data produced by scientific instruments and simulations is expanding and supporting the management, analysis and transfer of huge data sets is a growing requirement of ARCHER. For example, the VERCE project - a pan-European FP7 project - is integrating the sharing and analysis of extremely large seismology data sets from disparate sources.

2.2.1 Highlights of Main Applications

ARCHER runs a wide variety of applications across multiple domains. The following are only a small selection of these.

1. CP2K performs atomistic and molecular simulations of solid state, liquid, molecular, and biological systems. Developments carried out on ARCHER's predecessor have allowed specific scientific examples

to achieve a 50% performance improvement. This work has involved improving the domain decomposition algorithms; introduced hybrid MPI/OpenMP parallelism; and improved the sparse linear algebra algorithms.

2. VASP is a plane wave electronic structure code which has been optimized for the use of the UK National systems. Work on VASP has been carried out to optimize the use of MPI collectives and the FFTW library in the application; and to introduce OpenMP parallelism to the exact-exchange part of the code. This has resulted in a 12x speedup for pure DFT calculations and the ability to exploit twice the number of cores effectively for exact-exchange calculations.

3. Fluidity is a multi-phase computational fluid dynamics code. Recent developments on ARCHER have included the addition of OpenMP to the matrix assembly routines; added threading to core functionality of the PETSc library, which is used as the linear solver engine; and optimized the mesh ordering using Hilbert space-filling curves.

4. GS2 — this gyrokinetic simulation code has been optimized to improve the FFT routines, to remove indirect addressing from core simulation routines, and to optimize the data decomposition using novel "unbalanced" decomposition ideas.

5. Ludwig is a lattice Boltzmann code being used to study soft materials. In particular it has been used to predict a new class of materials "bijels," which are now patented and under investigation for commercial applications.

6. SPRINT — this general purpose parallel framework for the R statistical language is being used to allow the computation of time-dependent correlations between 14,000 gene expressions in control and pathogen-infected systems.

2.3   System Overview

The ARCHER service is based around a Cray XC30 supercomputer that provides the central computational resource. This 3008 node MPP supercomputer is supported by a number of additional components including: high-performance parallel filesystems, pre- and post-processing facilities, external login nodes, and a large, resilient, long-term data facility (the UK Research Data Facility, UK-RDF).

TABLE 2.3: ARCHER hardware configuration.

Feature	Phase 1 (November 2013)
Node Architecture	Cray XC30
Processor	Intel Xeon E5-2697, 12-core
Processor microarchitecture	Ivy Bridge (x86_64)
Processor Frequency (GHz)	2.7
Processor Count per Node	2
Cores per Node	24
Hardware threads per Node	48
Node Memory Capacity (GB)	64/128
Node PCIe	Gen 3
Interconnection Network	Cray Aries
Interconnection Topology	Dragonfly
Latency	1.3 μs
Bisection Bandwidth	7200 GB/s
Compute Racks	26
Total number of nodes	4920
Peak FLOP Rate (TF)	2550.5

The Cray XC30 architecture itself consists of compute nodes connected together by the Aries interconnect and service nodes that act as interfaces for the file system, interfaces to external login nodes, and job launcher nodes.

The hardware that makes up the ARCHER service is summarized in Table 2.3 and described in more detail in Section 2.4.

The operating system is Cray Linux Environment, this consists of two components: fully featured Linux on the service nodes and an optimized version of Linux running on the compute nodes. This is described in more detail in the System Software section below.

Most standard compilers and tools are available along with the Cray Application Developer Environment to support the production of optimized parallel code. Table 2.4 provides details of the software installed on the system and the Section 2.5 describes the software in more detail.

In addition to the compute hardware, ARCHER comprises a number of different file systems and data analysis hardware. These include:

- NFS "home" filesystem — described in Section 2.4.

- Lustre "work" filesystem — described in Section 2.4.

- Post-processing nodes — high memory nodes for serial data processing. Described in Section 2.4.

- UK Research Data Facility — long-term data storage and data analytic hardware. Described in Section 2.7.

TABLE 2.4: ARCHER software configuration.

Feature	Phase 1
Login Node OS Compute Node OS Parallel Filesystem	Cray Linux Environment 5.1 Cray Linux Environment 5.1 Lustre/GPFS
Compilers	Intel 14/15 GCC 4.8/4.9 Cray Compiler Environment (CCE) 8.2/8.3
MPI SHMEM Coarray Fortran Unified Parallel C	Cray MPI Cray SHMEM via CCE via CCE
Notable Libraries	Cray LibSci Intel MKL PETSc NetCDF HDF5 Hugetables GSL SLEPc
Python	2.7.6, 3.3.3 mpi4py Numpy Matplotlib Anaconda
Job Scheduler Resource Manager	ALPS PBS Pro
Debugging Tools Performance Tools	Allinea DDT GDB Cray ATP CrayPAT Allinea MAP Scalasca Vampir Cray Reveal

2.4 Hardware Architecture

2.4.1 Compute Node Architecture

ARCHER compute nodes each contains two 2.7 GHz, 12-core E5-2697 v2 (Ivy Bridge) series processors. Each of the cores in these processors can support 2 hardware threads (Hyperthreads). Within the node, the two processors are connected by two QuickPath Interconnect (QPI) links.

Standard compute nodes on ARCHER have 64 GB of memory shared between the two processors. There are a smaller number of high-memory nodes with 128 GB of memory shared between the two processors. The memory is arranged in a non-uniform access (NUMA) form: each 12-core processor is a single NUMA region with local memory of 32 GB (or 64 GB for high-memory nodes). Access to the local memory by cores within a NUMA region has a lower latency than accessing memory on the other NUMA region.

There are 4544 standard memory nodes (12 groups, 109,056 cores) and 376 high-memory nodes (1 group, 9,024 cores) on ARCHER giving a total of 4920 compute nodes (13 groups, 118,080 cores).

At zero load the compute nodes on ARCHER draw approximately 700 kW of power and at full load they draw approximately 2000 kW of power.

2.4.2 Interconnect

The Cray Aries interconnect links all compute nodes in a Dragonfly topology. In the Dragonfly topology 4 compute nodes are connected to each Aries router; 188 nodes are grouped into a cabinet; and two cabinets make up a group. The interconnect consists of 2D all-to-all electric connections between all nodes in a group with groups connected to each other by all-to-all optical connections. The number of optical connections between groups can be varied according to the requirements of the system. ARCHER has 84 optical links per group giving a peak bisection bandwidth of over 11,090 GB/5 over the whole system. The MPI latency on Aries is 1.3 μs with an additional 100 ns of latency when communicating over the optical links. This additional latency is generally not visible to end users as it vanishes into the noise associated with the communications software stack.

2.4.3 Service Node Architecture

The ARCHER service nodes each contain two 2.6 GHz, 8-core Xeon E5-2650 v2 (Ivy Bridge) series processors.

The service nodes provide a number of different functions on ARCHER: PBS job launcher (MOM) nodes, LNET routers (for connecting to the filesystems) and others. The service nodes are internal to the XC30 hardware and are collocated in the cabinets with the compute nodes.

2.4.4 External Login Nodes (esLogin)

The ARCHER login nodes are external to the main XC30 system and are therefore available for use even when the compute portion of the facility is out of service. They have access to all the filesystems on ARCHER and also have the full Cray application development environment installed. This means that data can be accessed, programs compiled, and pre- and post-processing performed when the compute nodes are unavailable.

The esLogin nodes each has two 2.6 GHz, 8-core Xeon E5-2650 v2 (Ivy Bridge) series processors. There are eight login nodes provided to ARCHER users.

2.4.5   Pre- and Post-Processing Nodes

The two ARCHER post-processing (PP) nodes each contains four 2.0 GHz, 10-core Intel Xeon E7-4850 (Westmere) series processor giving a total of 40 physical cores (80 hyperthreads) available on each node. Each PP node has 1 TB physical memory available.

The PP nodes are available to users by two methods:

- Through the PBS Pro job submission system.

- By direct interactive access via the ARCHER login nodes.

As for the esLogin nodes, the PP nodes are usually available to use even when the compute portion of the system is unavailable. They also have the full Cray application development environment installed and mount all the ARCHER filesystems and the UK Research Data Facility (see below).

2.4.6   Storage Systems

ARCHER has a number of different storage systems with different purposes:

- "home" — NFS filesystems for small-scale storage of critical data such as source code. See below for more details.

- "work" — Lustre filesystems for high-performance IO operations. See below for more details.

- UK Research Data Facility — GPFS-based system for long-term storage of large amounts of data. Described in more detail in Section 2.7.

All of the group and user quotas on the ARCHER filesystems can be queried and managed by project managers and service staff through the SAFE web interface described at the end of this chapter.

The ARCHER filesystems collectively draw approximately 40 kW of power and the RDF draws approximately 120 kW of power.

2.4.6.1   "home" Filesystems

A set of four 50TB NFS filesystems designed to hold small amounts of critical project data such as source code and small input files. Each project on ARCHER is assigned space on one of the "home" filesystems and the allocation is balanced to try and achieve an even load across the full set.

The "home" filesystems are not available on the ARCHER compute nodes so any data that is required during simulations has to be stored on the "work" filesystems. The machine is specifically designed in this way to:

- avoid users seeing poor performance by mistakenly using the NFS filesystem for intensive IO operations;

- minimize the chances of the NFS filesystem becoming full with large output files from simulations.

The "home" filesystems are backed up, first to a second set of hard disks, and then to tape with a set of backups stored off-site for disaster recovery purposes.

2.4.6.2 "work" Filesystems

A collection of three high-performance, parallel Lustre filesystems with a total of around 4 PB of available storage. Each project is assigned space on a particular Lustre partition with the assignments chosen to balance the load across the available infrastructure.

The "work" filesystems are designed for use during simulations for high-performance IO operations. Users can choose how many of the available file servers they *stripe* the data over. For large files using parallel IO operations using the maximum number of stripes usually gives best performance.

The Lustre filesystems are not backed up in any way and are not a scratch filesystem (as they are not periodically cleaned up). It is up to individual projects and users to manage their own data.

2.5 System Software

2.5.1 Operating System

The operating system (OS) on ARCHER is the Cray Linux Environment (CLE) that in turn is based on SuSE Linux. CLE consists of two components: CLE and Compute Node Linux (CNL). The service nodes of ARCHER (for example, the esLogin nodes) run a full-featured version of Linux. The compute nodes of ARCHER run CNL. CNL is a stripped-down version of Linux that has been extensively modified to reduce both the memory footprint of the OS and also the amount of variation in compute node performance due to OS overhead.

2.5.2   Job Submission System: PBS Pro/ALPS

PBS Pro is used to schedule jobs. Users interact with PBS via job submission scripts and by using PBS commands on the esLogin nodes. All ARCHER job submission scripts run on Job Launcher Nodes rather than on the compute nodes themselves. These Job Launcher Nodes (sometimes also called MOM Nodes) are ARCHER Service Nodes that have permission to issue aprun commands to start jobs on the compute nodes. The Job Launcher Nodes are shared between users meaning that memory or CPU intensive serial commands are best placed in serial job submission scripts and run on the pre- and post-processing nodes.

Cray ALPS (Application Level Placement Scheduler) is used to launch and place parallel processes and threads. This provides fine grained control over which nodes and cores processes and threads run on. ALPS is initiated using the aprun command within a job submission script and is the only way to run jobs on the ARCHER compute nodes. Any commands launched within a script which are not launched with aprun will run on the Job Launcher Nodes. Options can be given to aprun to determine the total number of distributed processes, the number of distributed processes per compute node, the number of threads per distributed processes (i.e., the "stride" between processes) and the number of Intel Hyperthreads to use for each physical core (either 1 or 2).

ARCHER has queueing structure which allows for jobs of different lengths and sizes. Jobs can run for up to 24 hours any number of nodes (i.e., up to 118,080 processing cores with fully populated nodes) and up to 48 hours for jobs up to 128 nodes 3072 processing cores with fully populated nodes). Jobs are charged on completion according to the number of node-hours used. In addition, low priority jobs can run that are not charged but receive lower priority than charged jobs. The low priority access queue is only opened when the backlog in the queueing system drops below a certain threshold.

A typical job submission script contains just one aprun call to allow a parallel job to run. However, it is possible to run array style jobs on ARCHER using PBS allowing for multiple jobs to be run at once using the same submission script.

For jobs which do not fit into the above queue structure, users can apply to reserve a set of nodes for a fixed time period. This is particularly useful for occasional jobs running for more than 48 hours or for courses or demonstrations.

Pre- or post-processing jobs run on dedicated post-processing (PP) nodes. This is useful for long compilation, post-calculation analysis and data manipulation on single cores.

Interactive access to compute jobs and post-processing nodes is available via PBS allowing for the running and debugging of codes via the command line.

Tools such as bolt and checkScript have been developed to assist users in running scripts and checking their validity.

The bolt job submission script creation tool has been written by EPCC to simplify the process of writing job submission scripts for modern multicore architectures. Based on the options supplied by the user, bolt will try to generate a job submission script that uses ARCHER as efficiently as possible. This tool can generate job submission scripts for both parallel and serial jobs on ARCHER. MPI, OpenMP and hybrid MPI/OpenMP jobs are supported. If there are problems or errors in your job parameter specifications, then bolt will print warnings or errors. However, bolt cannot detect all problems so users can run the checkScript tool on any job submission scripts prior to running them to check for budget errors, etc.

2.6 Programming System

In this section we outline the parallel programming models that can be used on ARCHER, the various languages that support these models and the compilers that implement them. We also cover the major libraries and tools that we support to assist users in application development.

2.6.1 Programming Models

2.6.1.1 Message Passing

Like almost all petascale systems that do not employ accelerators, usage of ARCHER is dominated by message-passing applications written using MPI. A pan-European survey by the PRACE project [2] showed that 88% of applications on the largest systems could run using basic message-passing operations, although just over half of these could also exploit threaded parallelism using OpenMP (see Section 2.6.1.4). The vendor-supplied MPI library provides an implementation of the MPI-3.0 standard via the Cray Message Passing Toolkit (MPT). Although in principle this supports additional models such as single-sided puts and gets, and a unified memory model allowing exploitation of shared memory without the use of threads, almost all codes still use traditional two-sided message passing. The ARCHER network hardware and MPI software are optimized by Cray for HPC applications to such an extent that users can achieve low latency and high bandwidth simply by using traditional MPI send, receive and collective operations.

2.6.1.2 PGAS

Partitioned Global Address Space (PGAS) models, such as Unified Parallel C (UPC), Fortran Coarrays (CAF) and OpenSHMEM, have been the subject of much attention in recent years, in particular due to the exascale challenge. There is a widespread belief that existing message-passing approaches such as MPI will not scale to this level due to issues such as memory consumption and synchronization overheads. PGAS approaches offer a potential solution as they provide direct access to remote memory. This reduces the need for temporary memory buffers, and may allow for reduced synchronization and hence improved message latencies. Some modern distributed memory architectures allow for Remote Memory Access (RMA) directly over the interconnect, meaning the PGAS model maps directly onto the underlying hardware.

UPC extends the C language to allow for the declaration of logically shared data, even on a distributed memory system. UPC includes new data and work-sharing statements to give the user full control of how programs execute in parallel. Although typically classified as a PGAS language alongside CAF and OpenSHMEM, UPC takes quite a different approach to parallel data. In CAF and OpenSHMEM there are no data distribution directives: just as in MPI, accessing remote data requires the user to explicitly specify the remote processor. In UPC the user can reference a particular element of shared data and the compiler or runtime system works out if it is a local or remote access, and if remote which processor owns the data.

PGAS features have been introduced into the Fortran 2008 standard with coarrays. Programming using coarrays has many potential advantages compared to MPI. Amongst these are simplicity, compiler checking and scope for automatic optimization of communications by the compiler. Coarrays can also be introduced incrementally to existing MPI codes to improve performance-critical kernels.

Coarrays have a long history on Cray systems, with implementations dating back to 1998 on the Cray T3E. The original coarray extensions proposed by Bob Numrich and John Reid [9] were implemented as an option in Cray Fortran 90 release 3.1. The direct RMA capabilities of the T3E torus interconnect enabled this PGAS model to be implemented easily and efficiently.

The origins of OpenSHMEM, like Fortran coarrays, date back to the first Cray MPPs of the early 1990s. OpenSHMEM is a standardization of the various single-sided SHMEM models that evolved from the original Cray SHMEM. Unlike UPC and CAF, OpenSHEM is an API not a language extension. It includes single-sided puts and gets, various synchronization methods and collective operations.

The first generation of more modern Cray systems, the XT architecture, used the Seastar interconnect which had an underlying message-passing (i.e., two-sided) data-transfer model. As a result, PGAS approaches had to be implemented on top of some software layer such as GASNET [1] to emulate true RMA capabilities. However, ARCHER uses the ARIES interconnect which once again offers native RMA capabilities. UPC and CAF are supported natively by the Cray compilers, and OpenSHMEM is supplied as part of the Cray MPT. Studies of coarray performance on HECToR [7], a Cray XE6 system that was ARCHER's predecessor, showed that the GEMINI network performed very well. As ARCHER has the next-generation ARIES network,

PGAS performance is generally expected to be very good; initial studies of coarrays on ARCHER [8] support this.

2.6.1.3 Shared Memory

Each node of ARCHER is a 24-way shared-memory machine. Running pure MPI applications with one process per core does not take full advantage of this feature. Although intra-node messages will be very fast as the system software can exploit the shared memory, users cannot explicitly exploit it using MPI alone (other than using the very new and largely untested memory model supported by MPI 3.0). As is standard in HPC, OpenMP is the method used by most users since it provides higher-level abstractions than POSIX threads, and is tailored to parallel programming. However, a pure OpenMP code can only use 24 cores (less than 0.3% of ARCHER) so shared-memory approaches are only useful in combination with distributed-memory (e.g., message-passing) models.

An exception to this is for pre- and post-processing where we expect OpenMP to be used on ARCHER's large shared-memory "serial" nodes.

2.6.1.4 Hybrid Models

The standard way to run a parallel code on ARCHER is to run a single MPI process per core, i.e., 24 MPI processes per shared-memory node. However, there are a number of reasons in general why using a hybrid MPI/OpenMP model can be advantageous on modern systems:

- Replicated data;

- Poorly scaling MPI codes;

- Limitations of the MPI library for large process numbers;

- MPI implementation not tuned for SMP clusters.

The latter two reasons do not apply to ARCHER as Cray MPI easily scales to the full system size, and is well tuned for the SMP nature of the nodes. However, the first two reasons are features of the user application and may be relevant.

Running 24 separate processes can be wasteful in terms of memory as any replicated data (e.g., static lookup tables) needs to be stored 24 times on each node. With hybrid MPI/OpenMP, all the OpenMP threads can access a single copy of the data stored by the parent MPI process. In the limit of a single MPI process and 24 OpenMP threads, this means a single copy per node as opposed to 24 for pure MPI.

Although few HPC applications have large lookup tables, many have shared data in the form of halos round data arrays which store boundary values from neighboring processes. These halos can become a significant fraction of the total memory requirements, especially when local data volumes shrink with high core counts.

There are also situations where hybrid MPI/OpenMP can extend the scalability of existing MPI algorithms. For example, the simplest way to parallelize a 3D FFT on an $N \times N \times N$ array is to use a 1D "slab" domain decomposition across one of the array dimensions, giving entire $N \times N$ slices to each MPI process. However, this limits the scalability of the algorithm to N processes, which is likely to be in the hundreds rather than the thousands. Rather than changing the algorithm to a more complicated 2D "pencil" decomposition, another approach is to parallelize within each existing slab using OpenMP. This extends the scalability of the algorithm to one MPI process per core, or $24 \times N$ processes in total on ARCHER, which is a substantial improvement. Similar approaches have been used in the popular CP2K code [6], and these are expected to be useful on ARCHER.

Care always has to be taken with the way that MPI processes and OpenMP threads are placed on a node, but this is fairly simple to do using various options to Cray's aprun job launcher. Users have very fine-grained control over which cores the processes and threads are scheduled. However, the NUMA node architecture on ARCHER means that data locality may also need to be considered. As ARCHER only has two NUMA regions per node (corresponding to the two sockets), this is not a serious issue if more than one MPI processes are used per node. The processes can be allocated evenly between the sockets using aprun, so threads will always access data from the socket on which they are executing and no code changes are required. However, with a single MPI process per node threads can access data from both sockets so it is important to do NUMA-aware data allocation. Although this is quite easily done, as memory is allocated on a first-touch basis, it may require code changes. The easiest approach is to perform data initialization in parallel (even if this operation is not in itself time-critical) which can have significant performance benefits. Initial results on ARCHER show this clearly: NUMA-aware memory allocation doubles the performance of memory-bound OpenMP threaded codes running on 24 cores.

Although their inter-operation is not completely standardized, a few users have experimented with exotic hybrid models. For example, using MPI, OpenMP and Fortran coarrays all at the same time has given performance benefits in the IFS code [5].

2.6.2   Languages and Compilers

The fundamental HPC programming languages of Fortran, C and C++ are all supported by multiple compilers. On ARCHER, users can choose between the compilers listed in Table 2.5.

The default environment is the Cray one, although users can easily select an alternative by loading different modules. Compilers should always

TABLE 2.5: Supported compilers on ARCHER.

Module	Product	Specific Compilers
PrgEnv-cray	Cray Compilation Environment	crayftn, craycc, crayCC
PrgEnv-intel	Intel Composer Suite	ifort, icc, icpc
PrgEnv-gnu	GNU Compiler Collection	gfortran, gcc, g++

be referred to by their generic names (ftn, cc, CC), with the specific compiler being selected automatically depending on the currently loaded module. As mentioned previously, UPC and Fortran Coarrays are fully supported on ARCHER by the Cray compilers.

Python is becoming increasingly widely used in the scientific community, and is supported on ARCHER. At scale, importing python modules can be very slow so we are installing the Anaconda distribution to solve this problem.

2.6.3 Performance Tools

A number of performance tools are supported on ARCHER, including CrayPAT, Allinea MAP and Scalasca.

2.6.3.1 CrayPAT

The Cray Performance Analysis Tool (CrayPAT) is a Cray-specific tool that is designed to give performance data on very large and complicated parallel codes. Using CrayPAT has three distinct stages:

1. use the **pat_build** command to create an instrumented executable from an existing standard executable;

2. run the instrumented executable which produces various files which store the performance results;

3. use **pat_report** to produce summary text information, or more detailed reports which can be viewed with Cray's visualization tool Apprentice2.

At the **pat_build** stage, the user has very fine-grained control over what information is gathered from what portions of the code. However, to enable users easily to get a first impression of the overall performance of their code, this can be semi-automated as follows:

1. run an initial version instrumented using sampling;

2. feed the results of this sampling experiment back into **pat_build** by giving it the appropriate Automatic Profiling Analysis file (suffix .apa);

3. re-run the new executable which will be instrumented using a more detailed tracing approach, informed by the initial high-level sampling.

As it is provided by Cray, the CrayPAT tool is very closely integrated with the Cray compiler and runtime environment. For example, it is straightforward to find out the maximum amount of memory used by each process, or to find out how much time in an MPI collective call was spent in synchronization (which can be an indication of load imbalance).

2.6.3.2 Allinea MAP

Allinea MAP can be used to profile MPI code only - unlike CrayPAT, it does not support detailed profiling of OpenMP, SHMEM, CAF, or UPC. However, unlike CrayPAT it is a portable tool that is available on a wide variety of platforms. MAP is a commercial product, and on ARCHER we currently have license valid on up to 8192 cores.

Profiling using Allinea MAP consists of four steps:

1. set up a MAP profiling version of your MPI library (generally simple);

2. re-compile your code linking the MAP MPI profiling library;

3. run your code to collecting profiling information;

4. visualize the profiling using the MAP Remote Client.

MAP has been designed to have a small overhead, so results should generally be a good reflection of how the uninstrumented code actually behaves. Figure 2.3 shows a typical run viewed with the Allinea Remote Client.

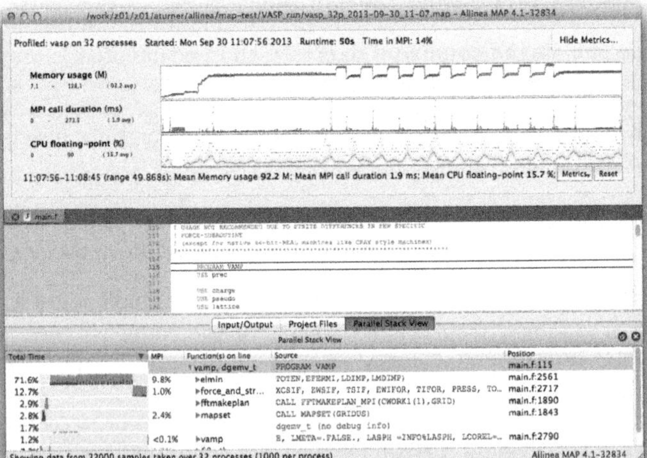

FIGURE 2.3: Typical MPI profiling output from Allinea MAP.

2.6.3.3 Scalasca

Scalasca [3] is "a software tool that supports the performance optimization of parallel programs by measuring and analyzing their runtime behavior. The analysis identifies potential performance bottlenecks - in particular those concerning communication and synchronization - and offers guidance in exploring their causes. It has been specifically designed for use on large-scale systems including IBM Blue Gene and Cray XC, but is also well-suited for small- and medium-scale HPC systems."

Scalasca is distributed free of charge and is available on ARCHER, and its design means that it scales well and can be used to do performance analyses of large production codes.

2.6.4 Debugging

The main debugging tool on ARCHER is Allinea DDT. DDT is a graphical debugging tool for scalar, multi-threaded and large-scale parallel applications. Running GUI-based applications on ARCHER and exporting the display is not recommended as network performance can severely limit the response time. The recommended way to use DDT on ARCHER is therefore to install the free DDT remote client on your workstation or laptop and use this to run DDT on ARCHER. As well as minimizing data transfer between ARCHER and the local machine, the client also enables job launching etc. to be controlled locally.

A typical view of the DDT debugging interface is shown in Figure 2.4.

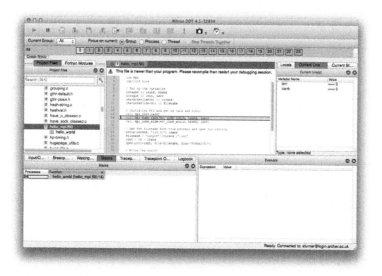

FIGURE 2.4: Typical debugging session using Allinea DDT.

2.7   Long-Term Storage and Data Analytics

As described in the Hardware Section, there are three filesystems available to ARCHER users: the "home" filesystems, the "work" filesystems, and the UK Research Data Facility (UK-RDF).

The "home" and "work" filesystems have been described in detail in the Hardware Section above so here we concentrate on the UK-RDF.

The UK Research Data Facility (UK-RDF) is external to the UK national HPC services, and is designed for long-term data storage. The RDF consists of 13.86 PB disk, with an additional 30 PB of offsite backup tape capacity. Data is backed up daily and the backup capability is managed via Tivoli Storage Manager.

2.7.1   UK Research Data Facility Overview

The UK-RDF, funded by EPSRC and NERC, is collocated with ARCHER and is housed at the ACF facility.

The Research Councils' vision behind the RDF includes:

- Provides a high capacity robust file store;

- Persistent infrastructure — will last beyond any one national service;

- Easily extensible in size and number of hosts — degree of future proofing and potential for increasing local post-processing activities;

- Operates independently of any one vendor's offering for compute;

- Remotely accessible via an Edinburgh host — not restricted to through login nodes;

- Removes end of service data issues — transfers at end of services have become increasingly lengthy;

- Ensures that data from the current ARCHER service is secured — this will ensure a degree of soft landing if there is ever a gap in National Services.

The RDF currently hosts a range of filesystems (see Table 2.6). We expect the range and type of fielsystems and data infrastructure to expand significantly as the facilty matures.

2.7.2   UK-RDF Technical Details

The disk storage is based on four DDN 10K storage arrays populated with near-line SAS 3 TB 72000 rpm HDDs. Metadata storage is based on two IBM DS3524s populated with SAS 300 GB 10 krpm HDDs.

TABLE 2.6: Current filesystems on the UK-RDF.

Filesystems on RDF	Disk capability	Primary use
/dirac	107 TB	Data storage from DiRAC Bluegene/Q system
/nerc	2.7 PB	Data storage, NERC projects on ARCHER
/epsrc	770 TB	Data storage, EPSRC projects on ARCHER
/general	171 TB	Data storage, other projects on ARCHER
/INDY	43 TB	Industrial data from INDY cluster
/roslin (RDF pilot)	193 TB	Data analytics for sequence data from Roslin Institute
/euclid (RDF pilot)	513 TB	Data analytics for University of Edinburgh gene sequencing service

In addition to the 13.86 PB disk, the RDF has 30 PB of offsite backup tape capacity. Data on the RDF is backed up daily using Tivoli Storage Manager, based on an IBM TS3500 tape library with 12 drives.

2.7.2.1 Connectivity

Table 2.7 summarizes the connectivity to the RDF both externally through JANET (the UK academic network backbone) and to different facilities.

The future plan for the network also includes plans to connect the RDF core switches directly to JANET at 40 Gb/s. The first stage of this 40 Gb/s to ACF routers will happen fairly soon.

2.7.2.2 Data Analytic Cluster

The RDF also includes a Data Analytic (DA) cluster with 24 nodes:

- 20 nodes have 2 10-core Intel E5-2660v2 (Ivy Bridge) 2.2 GHz processors, 128 GB RAM, 2 TB local disk

- 4 nodes have 4 8-core Intel E7-4830 (Ivy Bridge) 2.13 GHz processors and 2 TB RAM, 8 TB local disk

These nodes all have dedicated Infiniband links to the RDF storage with bandwidths of 2*56 Gb/s to each node to allow for large-scale data analysis.

2.7.3 Access to the UK-RDF and Moving Data

The RDF is directly mounted on ARCHER. Data transfer across from the "home" and "work" filesystems can be achieved by the standard commands

TABLE 2.7: Summary of UK-RDF Connectivity.

Connected to	Bandwidth	Notes
JANET (UK Academic Internet Backbone)	1 Gb/s	The DTNs and the compute nodes which ultimately become headnodes/vms are currently connected at 1 Gb/s.
PRACE	N/A	10 Gb/s connection to pan-European PRACE network planned for the near future.
JASMIN	1 Gb/s	Dedicated 1 Gb/s light path through JANET to JASMIN climate and earth system science data facility. Planned upgrade to 2 Gb/s in near future.
ARCHER	2*10 Gb/s	
Data Analytic Cluster	2*56 Gb/s	DAC nodes are connected directly to disk storage at 2*56 Gb/s.
Data Transfer Nodes	2*10 Gb/s	DTNs are connected to GPFS servers at 2*10 Gbs.
DiRAC BG/Q	N/A	No connection at the moment but is intended to have a bandwith of 10 Gb/s in the future.

such as cp. The native cp command was found to be able to give the best performance on transferring data from ARCHER filesystems to the RDF.

The RDF is also mounted on EPCC's industry-focused compute cluster: INDY and provides a long-term data store for data produced on this machine.

Access to data on the RDF is not restricted to HPC facilities. The four *Data Transfer Nodes* (DTN) have been configured on the RDF to enable access at times when facilities are unavailable such as during maintenance sessions, and provide direct 10 Gb/s Ethernet connections to the outside world. In addition to the normal Linux data transfer commands such as scp, the DTNs have been configured to use Grid-FTP, part of the Globus Toolkit, that provides a mechanism to efficiently move large volumes of data. Grid-FTP has been found to be able to give the best performance in transferring data from external sites to the RDF.

2.7.4   Data Analytic Workflows

The DA cluster has been set up to provide an extremely flexible resource for different scientific workflows. A number of modes of access are provided according to the needs and expertise of particular communities. These include:

- A standard linux build provided by ourselves including standard tools and a batch job submission system. Provided for communities with generic DA requirements and little/no expertise in building their own environments.

- Custom virtual data appliance managed by ourselves. Aimed at communities who have a custom DA requirement but who do not have all the expertise to manage their own virtual data appliance.

- Hosting of virtual data appliances managed by the community itself. We recognize that some user communities have the expertise and requirement to manage their own setup and we can host these instances on the DA cluster hardware.

For all of the above options we provide the ability to access data on the UK-RDF via direct connections to the disk at 2*56 Gb/s over dedicated Infiniband links. The DA hardware is configured to ensure the strict separation and security of data between different communities unless there is a requirement to share the data.

These data appliances can also be used to publically expose the data via, for example, a web interface if this is required by the community.

2.8   Data Center/Facility

2.8.1   Location and History

ARCHER is located at the Advanced Computer Facility (ACF) at the Bush Estate on the outskirts of Edinburgh. The center opened in 1976 as the Edinburgh Regional Computing Centre. The site has evolved through three development phases (2004, 2007 and 2012) and at each phase power and cooling systems were designed and installed to match the expected loads. Operating efficiencies were high on the design agenda, and this has been reflected in the increasing overall efficencies of the plant and infrastructure as the facility has evolved. During the most recent development in 2012 the center was enlarged as part of a £12 M extension to accommodate the ARCHER service bringing the total capacity to around 7 MW.

2.8.2   Infrastructure

The ACF now consists of three machines rooms, two having a floorspace of $280\,m^2$ and one larger room with a $500\,m^2$ floorspace which houses ARCHER. For ARCHER a new $760\,m^2$ plant room (see Figures 2.5 and 2.6) was constructed to supply cooling and power for ARCHER's machine room. This plant room supplies the ARCHER machine room with up to 4 MW of power. When idle, ARCHER draws 600 kW rising to 2 MW when the system is fully loaded. The RDF is also located in the larger machine room drawing around 100 kW of power.

FIGURE 2.5: The pipework for the ARCHER cooling system.

FIGURE 2.6: The high-voltage switchroom supplying ARCHER with power.

Each phase of the ACF plant has been designed to allow for an increasing amount of "free cooling" whereby final heat rejection to the atmosphere can be achieved with the minimum of mechanical overhead.

The Power Usage Effectiveness (PUE) is defined as the ratio of the total energy consumed by the facility (including cooling, etc.) to that consumed by the system itself. The PUE target for the ARCHER infrastructure is a mean value of 1.10, with expected seasonal variations between 1.05 and 1.15.

In addition to the power supplied to the plant from the UK National Grid, a 2 MW standby diesel generator is provided for essential services. The generator has an 8-hour running capacity and provides potential STOR (Short Term Operating Reserve) capability for the UK National Grid.

2.8.3 Innovations and Challenges

The increase in efficiency has been due to careful operational monitoring allowing optimization to be applied, with increasing efficiency being designed in at each upgrade phase. As computer systems have become power-hungry, the equipment suppliers have moved towards liquid-cooling with an increase in cooling water temperatures enabling the optimized plant to maximize efficiency and mimimize the cooling overhead. These trends seem set to continue.

However, since the overwhelming bulk of the energy required to operate large HPC systems is consumed by the computing equipment itself, the onus is on the computer manufacturers (and indeed chip designers) to design in operating efficiences (cores switching off, internal power management of fans, more efficient power supplies, enhanced cooling water temperature requirements and so forth).

Getting the plant right helps, but the problem is better tackled at the source.

2.9   System Statistics

The ARCHER system commenced production operation on the 16th December 2013. It currently has 3063 active users from 88 different nationalities and 1123 projects.

Figure 2.7 shows utilization of the service against time. ARCHER utilizes a metric called an allocation unit (AU), where 0.015 kAUs represent an hour on a single ARCHER core. Prior to production operation commencing, the service ran an early access program for users. As a result utilization was significant from the first few days of the production service, steadily increasing to a peak in January 2014. Usage has remained similar since then, averaging 75% utilization in 2014 1st January 2014–30th November 2014 (see Figure 2.8).

FIGURE 2.7: ARCHER's Aries interconnect.

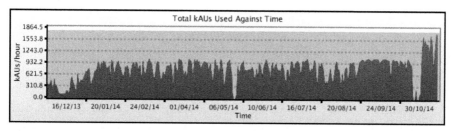

FIGURE 2.8: ARCHER usage against time for the 16th December 2013 to the 16th December 2014 in allocation units. The large increase in the end is due to the size increase with Phase 2 installation.

Breaking this down into subject area, Figure 2.9 shows that chemistry and environmental codes utilize the majority of the time (using 36% and 37% of the machine, respectively). Engineering codes also play a major role, utilizing 16% of the resources.

Within these areas, further analysis over the month of April 2014 shows that the dominant codes are VASP, CASTEP, CP2K, GROMACS and WRF are the most dominant codes. This is shown in Figure 2.10.

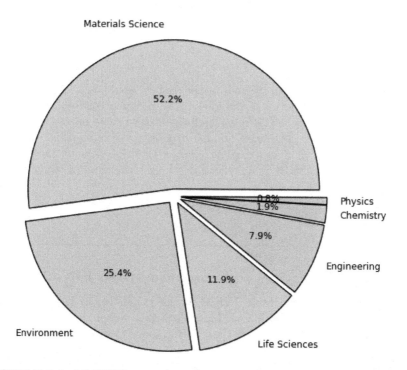

FIGURE 2.9: ARCHER usage by subject area for the period 16th December 2013 to the 16th December 2014.

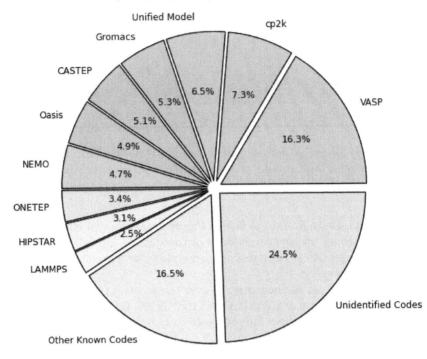

FIGURE 2.10: ARCHER usage by code for the period January–November 2014.

The range of job sizes utilized on the system are shown in Figure 2.11. It is clear that the majority of the jobs utilize between 1024 and 8192 cores, with a smaller percentage (12%) utilizing the highest core counts (larger than 8192). There is also a significant number of jobs in the range 129-1024 cores. These job sizes are, on average, slightly larger than job sizes on the previous UK National Service, HECToR, reflecting a long-term trend of increasing job size on these systems.

2.10   SAFE: Service Administration from EPCC

User management on the ARCHER service is handled by the SAFE (Service Administration from EPCC). This is a software system developed over the last decade by EPCC to manage High Performance Computing services such as ARCHER. It is a web-based system built using java-servlets and a SQL relational database. It is responsible for almost all aspects of user management ranging from user registration and service desk to resource management

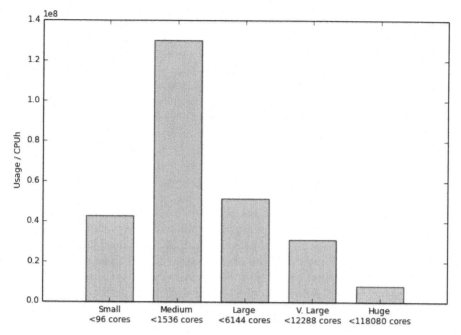

FIGURE 2.11: ARCHER usage by job size for the period January–November 2014.

and reporting. One of the particular challenges of this type of service is that it is often entirely stand-alone, rather than being embedded within the wider IT service provision of an existing organization. This means that there is no pre-existing database of users or support infrastructure that can be utilized; all these functions need to be provided from scratch. On the other hand this allows us to implement these functions in a single tool providing a focused and well-integrated solution.

One of the big advantages of this single integrated system is that it can easily be extended to allow many operations to be delegated to appropriate users. For example a project manager can approve access to, generate reports on, and manage resources within their projects. A similar level of integration would also have been possible with more traditional enterprise architectures where each function is implemented as a separate tool; however, a single code base allows for a more agile development process.

This ability to delegate operations to project managers is absolutely essential for ARCHER. Resource allocations are typically made to large projects. As these projects are large and complex there is often a need to support resource allocation to sub-groups within the project. These allocation decisions can only be made by the internal management within the project. In addition, the project membership is often quite fluid and decisions on membership of the sub-groups, and even membership of the project itself can also only be made by the project managers. It is therefore much more efficient to provide the project with the necessary management tools via a self-service web interface than to try and route all of these operations through a traditional help-desk as service requests. It provides a much better user interface for the project managers as requests can be validated for correctness in real time (for example ensuring that a disk quota request is not below the current usage within that quota). In addition, any requests that result in configuration changes to the service machine are mapped to a small set of well-defined change-tickets such as change-quota, new-user, password-reset, etc. For the ARCHER service, the implementation of these change-tickets has been largely scripted, though we choose to keep a manual approval step as part of the process rather than giving the SAFE the ability to make changes automatically.

The generation of reports and the analysis of system use is an important activity for any HPC service. There are many different groups that may require different levels of access to this data. Individual users need to be able to access information on their own use of the system. Project managers need to generate overview reports on the use by their project. System operators and funding agencies need reports on the overall use of the system. In addition reports need to be generated from a variety of different data sources. The reporting sub-system of the SAFE is capable of ingesting data from a variety of sources including most major batch systems. It uses a system of plug-in parsers to allow addition types of data source to be easily added to the system. The reporting system is not restricted to batch job information and can also handle such diverse information as project resource allocations, file-transfer activity or disk usage data. In addition, policy plug-ins can be used to trigger side effects such as job charging and to augment the raw information based on local site policies. For example, additional accounting properties can be derived based on the queue where the job runs, or additional log files can be parsed to add additional information such as executables used.

We chose to build a general purpose reporting system rather than focus solely on the generation of reports of jobs run on the HPC resource. This allows the same framework to be used to generate reports on disk utilization and helpdesk activity. The general nature of the reporting system has also allowed us to re-use the code in other unrelated software projects. There are three principle ways that the reporting system is used:

1. *Integrated reports:* these are charts and tables generated in-line in SAFE web pages as part of the fixed user interface, and generated using direct calls to the reporting programming interface.

2. *Dynamic reports:* these are defined dynamically using an XML-based report generation language. This allows new reports to safely be added dynamically to the running SAFE without requiring any changes to the application code. The report generation language is quite flexible and can generate a wide variety of charts and tables. The reporting language contains elements that support access-control rules, allowing

reports to be restricted to particular groups of users. Dynamic reports can be parameterized, in which case a form is presented to users allowing them to select the appropriate parameters, such as the reporting period.

3. *Custom analysis:* for those cases where the analysis is too intensive to run against the live database or sufficiently complex that it needs to use the programming interface rather than the XML reporting language, then small custom analysis applications can easily be built and run against an offline copy of the SAFE database.

SAFE is an invaluable tool that allows access to all of the data associated with a service, such as ARCHER. This helps PIs track the CPU and data usage of their users, as well as providing easy access to the raw data for the regular reports produced by the Service Provider.

However, in addition to this, SAFE allows us to answer a wide variety of questions about the service. In this section, as an example of the kinds of questions it lets us answer, we discuss another analysis performed in response to discussions with EPSRC and at the Scientific Advisory Committee using data from ARCHER and its predecessor service HECToR.

Historically, there have been regular discussions about the appropriate level of utilization for a major capability service. It was widely believed that at high utilization, the job wait times increased significantly. However, as SAFE contains information about when all jobs were queued and then run, we were able to analyze this to provide quantitative information about the relationship between utilization and wait time. Figure 2.12 shows this information for the various phases of HECToR, as well as for the initial months of ARCHER.

Each point on the graph represents an analysis of a calendar week of the service. The vertical axis is a measure of the average amount of work queued during the week normalized by the maximum performance of the machine during that phase to give a drain time in hours. The horizontal axis is average

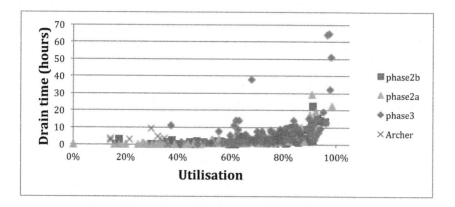

FIGURE 2.12: Drain time as a function of utilization.

percentage utilization of the machine during the week. The strong similarity between data from four generations of Cray hardware and four different sizes of machine suggest the results represent a universal relation between utilization and waiting work.

The graph shows that the likely wait time for a job grows relatively slowly up to around 80% utilization. However, thereafter, the wait time grows rapidly. This in turn suggests that a target utilization of around 80-85% is a good balance between effective use of the system and modest wait times.

SAFE is a single integrated tool to manage the wide variety of service functions and service data, including user management, service desk, resource management and reporting. It has proven extremely valuable for a number of major UK-HPC services, providing a high quality service to users. In addition, SAFE allows custom analyses to address key questions about the service; these analyses are invaluable for tailoring the service to best match the needs of users, and for planning future services.

Bibliography

[1] GASNET. http://gasnet.lbl.gov.

[2] PRACE. http://www.prace-ri.eu.

[3] Scalasca. http://www.scalasca.org.

[4] Top500 list. http://www.top500.org.

[5] A PGAS implementation by co-design of the ECMWF integrated forecasting system (IFS). *High Performance Computing, Networking, Storage and Analysis (SCC), 2012 SC Companion:*, pages 652–661, 2012.

[6] Iain Bethune. Improving the scalability of CP2K on multi-core systems: A DCSE project. http://www.hector.ac.uk/cse/distributedcse/reports/cp2k02/cp2k02_final_report.pdf. Accessed 4 December 2014.

[7] David Henty. Performance of Fortran coarrays on the Cray XE6. *Proceedings of Cray User Group 2012*, 2012.

[8] David Henty. Fortran coarrays: PGAS performance on Cray XE6 and Cray XC30 platforms, 2014. Presentation at EASC 2014. Details from author on request.

[9] Numrich and Reid. Co-array Fortran for parallel programming. *ACM Fortran Forum*, 17(2):1–31, 1998.

Chapter 3

Edison: Enabling Extreme Scale Science at NERSC

Sudip Dosanjh, Jeff Broughton, Katie Antypas, Brent Draney, Jason Hick, Tina Declerck, and Nicholas Wright

NERSC

The National Energy Research Scientific Computing Center (NERSC) at Lawrence Berkeley National Laboratory (Berkeley Lab) is the primary scientific production computing facility for the Department of Energy's (DOE) Office of Science (SC). With 5,000 users from universities, national laboratories, and industry, NERSC supports the largest and most diverse research community of any computing facility within the DOE complex. NERSC provides large-scale, state-of-the-art computing, storage, and networking for DOE's unclassified research programs in high energy physics, biological and environmental sciences, basic energy sciences, nuclear physics, fusion energy sciences, mathematics, and computational and computer science.

NERSC – originally called the Controlled Thermonuclear Research Computer Center – was founded in 1974 to support the fusion energy research community, the first time such a powerful computing resource was used for unclassified scientific computing. Located at Lawrence Livermore National Laboratory from 1974 to 1996, the center was renamed the National Magnetic Fusion Energy Computing Center in 1976, and in 1983 began providing a fraction of its computing cycles to other research areas.

To reflect its increasingly broad scientific mission, the Center was christened the National Energy Research Supercomputer Center in 1990. The facility moved to Berkeley Lab in 1996 and, while keeping the acronym NERSC, was renamed the National Energy Research Scientific Computing Center. NERSC is currently housed in Berkeley Lab's Oakland Scientific Facility, but will relocate to the new Computational Research and Theory facility on Berkeley Lab's main campus in 2015.

Over the years, NERSC has installed and operated many of the world's fastest supercomputers. In fact, NERSC's history is a reflection of the evolution of high-performance computing (HPC) over the last four decades. In 1974, the Center began operation with a borrowed Control Data Corporation (CDC) 6600 computer. In 1975, a CDC 7600 replaced the 6600, but the new machine was rapidly filled to capacity, and for a while NERSC had to purchase additional 7600 time from Berkeley Lab.

The Center acquired a Cray-1 in 1978 and soon became known as an innovator in the management and operation of supercomputers. The world's first Cray-2, a four-processor system, was installed at the Center in 1985. In 1992, with its user base growing steadily, NERSC added Cray's newest supercomputer, the Y-MP C90 – the first C90 to be installed in the U.S. at a non-classified customer site. In 1997, the facility deployed a Cray T3E-900 supercomputer and named it MCurie in honor of Marie Curie, a physicist who was the first woman to win a Nobel Prize. MCurie was followed two years later by Seaborg, an IBM RS/6000 SP system named for Berkeley Lab Nobel Laureate Glenn Seaborg.

In 2003, NERSC put its first 10 teraflops per second IBM supercomputer – the Seaborg II – into service, providing researchers with the most powerful computer for unclassified research in the U.S. at the time. From 2005 to 2009, NERSC further expanded its supercomputing resources to include DaVinci, an SGI Altix system; Jacquard, a Linux computing cluster; Bassi, an IBM p575; and Franklin, a Cray XT4 that was one of NERSC's most prolific supercomputers before being retired in 2012. And in 2010, NERSC broke the quadrillions-of-calculations-per-second mark with its Hopper system, a Cray XE6 named for pioneering computing scientist Grace Murray Hopper.

NERSC also has a history of collaborating with users to migrate their codes to next-generation architectures. These code changes are often evolutionary, but sometimes significant modifications are needed. During the late 1990s, NERSC worked very closely with its users to successfully transition their codes to massively parallel architectures. This was a daunting task due to the large number of teams computing at NERSC and the complexity of the changes that were required. A similar transition is now under way with the emergence of manycore processors. NERSC is launching an application readiness effort aimed at preparing our users for energy-efficient processors that will be used in NERSC systems going forward.

A paradigm shift for NERSC has been the growing importance of data-intensive computing. Almost every month more than a petabyte of data is transferred to the Center from experimental facilities around the world. The Center currently deploys data-intensive systems to analyze this deluge of data. Many generations of the Parallel Distributed Systems Facility (PDSF) at NERSC have served the high energy physics and nuclear physics communities for over a decade. In 2010, NERSC collaborated with the Joint Genome Institute to deploy a data-intensive system, Genepool, for DOE's genomics community. Several architectural features in NERSC's next supercomputer – announced in May 2014 and named Cori for American scientist Gerty Cori – are aimed at further supporting this data-intensive workload. Cori will have a significant data partition that will contain latency optimized processors with more memory per core and will run a software stack aimed at data-intensive computing. Cori will also contain a layer of nonvolatile memory to accelerate I/O, which is often a bottleneck for these applications.

From its earliest days, NERSC's mission has remained consistent: to accelerate the pace of scientific discovery by providing high-performance computing, information, data, and communications services to the DOE SC community. Today, typically over 300 users are logged into each of NERSC's supercomputers during daytime hours, with tens or hundreds of jobs simultaneously active. Batch queues run continuously, with each system typically running at 95% or higher utilization. The NERSC workload reflects the variety of the research performed by its users, including many simulations that span a large fraction of NERSC's supercomputers. In addition to capability calculations, high-throughput data analysis and massive datasets are becoming increasingly important at NERSC in support of SC experimental facilities.

3.1 Edison Supercomputer—NERSC-7

During 2009-2011, the DOE SC Advanced Scientific Computing Research (ASCR) office commissioned a series of workshops to characterize the computational resource requirements for current and future science programs [7, 8, 9, 10, 11, 12, 13, 14]. A careful analysis of these requirements demonstrated a critical mission need for an order-of-magnitude increase in high performance production computing platform capability by 2014 to address the computational needs of projects sponsored by SC Program Offices and avoid creating an unacceptable gap between needs and available computing resources.

As a result, NERSC initiated the NERSC-7 program, with a goal of procuring and installing a next-generation supercomputer that could meet this computing criteria and enable NERSC to continue to support the research activities of SC. Through NERSC-7, NERSC acquired the very first Cray

FIGURE 3.1: Edison, NERSC's newest supercomputer, is a Cray XC30 with a peak performance of 2.57 petaflops/sec, 133,824 compute cores, 357 terabytes of memory, and 7.4 petabytes of disk.

XC30 system (serial #1) and named it Edison in honor of American inventor Thomas Alva Edison (Figure 3.1). The XC30 [1] is the first all-new Cray design since Red Storm, a supercomputer architecture designed for the DOE's National Nuclear Security Administration Advanced Simulation and Computing Program, which was first deployed in 2005.

Edison was the first Cray XC30 supercomputer, which was developed in part with the Defense Advanced Research Projects Agency's (DARPA) High Productivity Computing Systems (HPCS) program. Run by the U.S. Department of Defense, DARPA formed the HPCS program to foster development of the next generation of high productivity computing systems for both national security and industrial user communities. Program goals were to develop more broadly applicable, easier-to-program, and failure-resistant high performance computing systems. The Cray XC30 system represents the last phase of the three-phase HPCS program, and the DARPA HPCS prototype became the first cabinet of Edison.

As part of the program, DARPA and its mission partners were to have up to 20 million hours of computing time on an XC30 for testing, evaluation, and machine characterization. In a collaboration with Cray and DARPA, NERSC hosted mission partners from DARPA, DOE, and universities. Forty-four mission partner users were integrated into the NERSC community of users, with full access to NERSC training, consulting, and other user benefits. To ensure the mission partners had adequate access to the machine for their runs, NERSC implemented a fair-share schedule on the pre-production Edison system to give DARPA its promised 25% share of the system until the 20 million hour usage level was reached. Mission partners concluded their testing when Edison went into production in January 2014.

With the addition of Edison, NERSC was able to retire Franklin (NERSC-5). Hopper will continue in operation through 2015. Having two systems available to users is a fundamental operational and procurement strategy at NERSC. (See Section 3.2.4.)

The Edison system has a peak performance of 2.57 petaflops/s, 133,824 compute cores, 357 terabytes of memory, and 7.4 petabytes of online disk storage with a peak I/O bandwidth of 168 GB/s (Table 3.1). To enable this performance, Edison features a large number of high-performance compute nodes and a high-bandwidth, low-latency inter-node communications network that offers very high levels of sustained performance on real user codes. It incorporates Intel Xeon E5–2695 v2 "Ivy Bridge" processors and the next-generation Aries interconnect, which uses a dragonfly topology instead of a torus.

Edison was designed to optimize data motion, which is a key bottleneck for many of our applications. Many applications are unable to take advantage of more floating point operations per second unless there is a commensurate increase in memory bandwidth. Consequently, we did not deploy accelerators in Edison, which would have increased its peak speed but provide little average payoff to our very broad and diverse application base. By electing to deploy

TABLE 3.1: Edison hardware specifications.

System Type	Cray XC30
CPU Type	Intel Ivy Bridge
CPU Speed (GHz)	2.4
Compute Nodes	5,576
Service Nodes	118
SMP Size	24
Total Compute Cores	133,824
Flops/Core (Gflops/sec)	19.2
Peak Performance (Tflops/sec)	2569.4
Memory per Node	64 GiB
Aggregate Memory	349 TiB
Memory Speed	1,866
Avg. Memory/Core	2.67 GiB
Memory Bandwidth per Socket (STREAM)	105 GiB/s
Node Interconnect	Aries
Scratch Disk	7.56 PB (local) + 3.9 PB (global)
Disk Bandwidth	168 GB/s
Avg. Power (KW)	1,600

Intel Ivy Bridge processors with 1866 Mhz memory, we were able to provide more than a 2X increase in performance per node compared with Hopper (the previous generation NERSC-6 system [2]). Some applications report as much as a 4X increase due to the much higher memory bandwidth.

Edison also utilizes a novel water-cooling mechanism that can operate with much warmer water temperatures than earlier supercomputers. The Cray XC30's hybrid water/air cooling system, transverse airflow, and high operating temperatures allow NERSC to use the moist, cool air that flows through the Golden Gate from the Pacific Ocean to help reduce cooling costs and increase energy efficiency. Using cooling towers only – without any mechanical refrigeration – Edison can be cooled for one-third the cost of earlier systems [6].

3.1.1 User Base and Science Areas

NERSC serves a broad range of science disciplines for the DOE SC and is the principal provider of HPC services to the six SC programs: Fusion Energy Sciences, High Energy Physics, Nuclear Physics, Basic Energy Sciences, Biological and Environmental Research, and Advanced Scientific Computing Research. Each year more than 5,000 researchers are working on 700 projects and running 600 different codes at NERSC across a broad range of disciplines [2], including:

- *Solar energy:* Understand the processes by which biological systems use solar energy, and design materials to efficiently convert solar energy to usable electricity or fuels.

- *Energy-efficient lighting:* Design highly efficient energy conversion processes for enhanced light emission in solid-state lighting devices.

- *Energy storage:* Design efficient and low-cost batteries and hydrogen storage devices.

- *Fusion science:* Understand and control instabilities that limit efficiency in fusion energy reactors.

- *Fundamental particles and interactions:* Supercomputer simulations are crucial to support DOE's "targeted outcomes" involving new facilities and experiments in quantum chromodynamics, the theory of the nuclear force, and the unification of the forces of nature.

- *Accelerator design and development:* Design cost- and energy-efficient particle accelerators, both for exploring the fundamental nature of the universe as well as for biomedical diagnoses and treatment.

- *Astrophysics:* Support DOE efforts in unraveling the origins of the universe, the nature of dark energy and matter, and astrophysical production of exotic nuclei. Another notable outcome will be the design and validation of a new generation of world-class telescopes and satellite.

- *Climate science:* Develop methods to predict extreme events. Support policy makers by providing accurate and precise understanding of relationships between climate change and Earth's ecosystems.

- *Biology:* Create predictive, systems-level understanding of complex biological systems in support of DOE missions in energy, the environment, and carbon sequestration. Understand how cells communicate, how proteins are created from DNA sequences, and how enzymes operate.

- *Bioinformatics*: Develop genome-scale microbial and plant system technologies for energy, the environment, and carbon sequestration.

- *Materials science:* Identify or design novel materials for energy capture, conversion, and storage; energy-efficient devices; carbon sequestration; bioremediation; desalination; radically faster computers; and information storage and communication devices.

- *Computer science:* Develop new high-efficiency, multi-physics simulation methods and codes to support research in combustion, porous media flow, astrophysics, cosmology, and engineering.

The number of NERSC science users has been growing almost 350 per year since 2008, and we expect this growth rate to continue. We have observed a usage trend in the past 10 years toward sciences with more potential for applied research applications, and we expect this trend to continue.

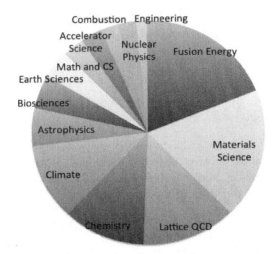

FIGURE 3.2: NERSC resource utilization by science area.

NERSC's primary focus is maximizing the scientific productivity of its users. To achieve high productivity, we balance computing, storage, and networking resources at our center. In addition, we deploy flexible resources to meet the wide-ranging needs of our users. For the last four years, NERSC has been a net importer of data. About a petabyte of data is typically transferred to NERSC every month for storage, analysis, and sharing.

Allocations of NERSC computer time are made on a yearly basis. Eighty percent of the DOE time is allocated by program managers in the DOE SC program offices; applicants must be part of a research project funded by the DOE SC or show that their work meets the DOE mission. Ten percent of DOE time is allocated through the ASCR Leadership Computing Challenge program. The final 10% of DOE time is the NERSC Director's reserve, allocated through the NERSC Initiative for Scientific Exploration program.

Figure 3.2 shows the allocation breakdown of NERSC supercomputing resources by science area.

3.2   Procurement Strategy

NERSC has nearly four decades of experience acquiring some of the largest supercomputers in the world, and as a result has developed a rigorous approach to procuring systems that has been widely adopted in the DOE community and elsewhere.

3.2.1 Requirements Gathering

As the primary provider of high performance scientific computing, storage, and services for the entire DOE SC, NERSC must support the mission of all six SC program offices as well as satisfy the operational needs of the scientists who use NERSC's resources. To ensure that it can meet these needs, NERSC regularly gathers requirements from the DOE SC program offices, other key HPC or domain experts, leading scientists in each research area, and its 5,000+ users. Requirements from the user community are obtained through regular meetings with the NERSC Users Group (NUG), an annual User Survey, allocations requests, one-on-one conversations with users, participation at community conferences and meetings, and a series of Computing and Storage Requirements Reviews with each program office within the DOE SC.

The requirements reviews are key to NERSC's strategy for gathering community requirements. This ongoing series of reviews, one for each program office, brings together DOE program managers, science leaders, and NERSC staff to derive future HPC needs for scientific communities. The results of the reviews include community requirements for computing, storage, and services five years in the future. Requirements for software and services are also captured in the review reports [14, 13, 11, 12, 10, 9, 8, 7]. Together these results help DOE and NERSC plan for future systems and HPC services.

In addition, NERSC holds regular monthly teleconferences with NUG and an annual face-to-face meeting with NUG where NERSC users are invited to discuss issues of interest or concern and make their needs known. NERSC users elect a 21-member Executive Committee (NUGEX) that plays an active role in making suggestions for improving NERSC systems, services, policies, and procedures (e.g., queue configurations). NUGEX members are given invitations to attend the requirements reviews in their area of research.

NERSC also collects satisfaction, importance, and usefulness scores on various systems and services via its annual User Survey. The survey responses help guide NERSC's choices for future systems and services offerings. Another important vehicle for collecting requirements is the allocations application process. When applying to use NERSC resources, projects are required to give detailed descriptions of their codes, data requirements, and software needs for the coming year.

3.2.2 Sustained Performance

The primary criteria for a NERSC system is sustained performance on scientific applications, not peak performance [16]. The required level of performance is based on the requirements gathering process and on available budget.

For Edison, as with several of its predecessors, NERSC used a suite of seven real applications carefully chosen to span important science areas and

TABLE 3.2: Seven real applications chosen to test sustained performance on NERSC supercomputers.

Science areas / Algorithm	Dense linear algebra	Sparse linear algebra	Spectral Methods (FFT)s	Particle Methods	Structured Grids	Unstructured or AMR Grids
Accelerator Science		X	IMPACT	IMPACT	IMPACT	X
Astrophysics	X	MAESTRO	X	X	MAESTRO	MAESTRO
Chemistry	GAMES	X	X	X		
Climate			CAM		CAM	X
Fusion	X	X		GTC	GTC	X
Lattice Gauge		MILC	MILC	MILC	MILC	
Material Science	PARATEC		PARATEC	X	PARATEC	

Note: Xs indicate algorithmic methods used by but not directly addressed for a particular science area.

algorithmic methods (Table 3.2). A specific input deck is defined for each benchmark, and a flop count is measured on a reference system. Each benchmark's time to solution is measured to get a flop/sec rate, and then divided again by the number of compute elements to get a flop/sec/compute element rate. The geometric mean of flop/sec/compute element is calculated across all the benchmarks. The average rate per compute element is then multiplied by the number of compute elements to get the final Sustained System Performance (SSP) [17]. Thus, SSP is a function of both performance of each compute element and the number of compute elements; it represents the throughput of the system. This matches the NERSC workload well as user-run applications at all scales.

Competing vendors must commit to an SSP target for a delivered system, and they must explain why they think they can meet that target. Vendors may be creative in meeting the target, balancing among such factors as processor and memory speed, core count, number of nodes, and compiler optimizations to determine the most competitive offering. The SSP target effectively establishes the "size" of the system for contractual purposes. If a delivered system with a particular number of processors, etc. does not meet the SSP requirement, the vendor is required to provide additional capacity to increase performance.

The SSP benchmark is updated for procurements of each successive generation of systems. This accounts for changes in computational methods and the introduction of new popular applications. However, the revised SSP is always calculated on earlier systems for comparison.

It is important to note that peak performance and microbenchmark performance (e.g., HPL or Stream) are considered at NERSC but are a minor factor in the center's evaluation of the system choice. As previously noted, NERSC primarily focuses on SSP. Recent "Top 10" systems have employed

GPUs to boost their peak performance, but such rates are difficult to achieve on most applications. As a result, the SSP for such systems as compared to the peak is a much lower ratio. NERSC chose not to list Edison on the Top 500 list because this increasing disparity between peak and sustained performance on real applications has rendered the ranking much less valuable.

3.2.3 Best Value

Because of the wide difference in the characteristics of systems offered by vendors, it is difficult to make direct comparisons between their systems. A decision based solely on price may not represent the optimal choice to meet the needs of NERSC's users. Instead, NERSC uses the "best value" process to make the selection [16]. Best value evaluates and compares non-price factors such as SSP, I/O performance, projected reliability, vendor reputation, and others, in addition to strict price. One of the most beneficial features of this approach is that it explicitly recognizes risk as a criteria, including technical schedule and business risks. Best value selection relies heavily on the judgment and experience of the buying team, as well as the various quantitative metrics available to describe machine performance.

3.2.4 Overlapping Systems

As the production computing facility for the DOE SC, it is critical that NERSC be able to provide substantial computing capability at all times. For this reason, we have adopted a strategy of acquiring a new system approximately every three years. Since systems have an expected lifetime of five to six years, this means we always have two large systems in operation concurrently.

Our overlapping system strategy has many benefits. Maintenance on the systems can be staggered, keeping one in operation at all times. Since 2008, it has been easy for users to move applications between systems, enabling them to realize this benefit. In addition, site preparation, installation, and testing of a new system take approximately one year (or more) following decommissioning of its predecessor. During this integration period, users still have access to a system of substantial capability.

The three-year cycle roughly approximates the timeline for new product introductions. For example, in Intel's tick-tock model, a complete cycle of new process technology (tick) and architecture (tock) takes roughly the same time period. Consequently, the newer system is closer to the state-of-the-art in performance and can address users' largest and most demanding applications, while the older system takes on volume processing of smaller jobs. By comparison, if NERSC were to acquire a system every 5-6 years, the Center could afford to purchase a system of approximately twice the size at the time of acquisition. But Moore's law (i.e., performance doubles every two years) would quickly render that system less performant than another newer system of half the price.

3.3   System Architecture

Edison is a highly scalable multiprocessor Cray XC30 that is built from multiple blades and connected by a flexible, high-bandwidth interconnect [15]. The system is packaged in 30 individually powered processing cabinets that provide an easily expandable and configurable environment. Each cabinet has three chassis; each chassis has 16 compute blades; each compute blade has four dual socket nodes.

3.3.1   Processor and Memory

Edison's 5,576 compute nodes are powered by 12-core Intel Xeon E5–2695 v2 "Ivy Bridge" processors running at 2.4 GHz. Each node has two sockets, each of which contains an Ivy Bridge processor, so that each node has 24 cores [3]. Each core runs at 19.2 Gflops/core, which equals 460.8 Gflops/node and 2.39 Pflops/s for the entire system. The Cray XC30 is the first time Cray has used Intel Xeon processors in a high-end supercomputer.

All memory used in service blades and compute blades is based on DDR3 Dual Rank Registered DIMMs (dual in-line memory modules) configured as two ranks of x4-based DDR3 SDRAM devices. The memory supports the Intel extended ECC algorithm, which allows the nodes to detect and correct 1- to 4-bit internal data and data pin failures within one memory device and detect up to 8-bit internal data and data pin failures within two memory devices. The Cray XC30 is designed to recover from faults that are contained within a single memory device that do not impact other memory devices in the memory system. The dual-rank configuration permits rank interleaving to help reduce memory access latency and improve performance.

3.3.2   Interconnect

Edison integrates Cray's HPC-optimized Aries interconnect to yield substantial improvements on all network performance metrics, including bandwidth, latency, and message rate. This network provides users with global access to all of the memory of parallel applications and supports demanding global communication patterns.

The Aries interconnect [1] uses a Dragonfly topology [15] for inter-node connections. This topology is a group of interconnected local routers connected to other similar router groups by high-speed global links. The groups are arranged such that data transfer from one group to another requires only one route through a global link.

This topology comprises circuit boards and copper and optical cables. Routers (represented by the Aries ASIC) are connected to other routers in the chassis via a backplane. Chassis are connected to form a two-cabinet group

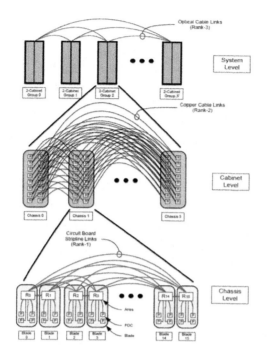

FIGURE 3.3: The Dragonfly Network.

(a total of six chassis, three per cabinet) using copper cables. Network connections outside the two-cabinet group require a global link. The system uses optical cables for all global links. All two-cabinet groups are directly connected to each other with these cables.

As shown in Figure 3.3, each router (Rx) in the Dragonfly Network is connected to four processor nodes (P). Sixteen blades, each with one router, are connected together at the chassis level by backplane links (Rank-1 Subtree). Six chassis are connected together to form the two-cabinet group by using copper cabling at the cabinet level (Rank-2 Subtree). Finally, the two-cabinet groups are connected to each other using optical cables for the global links (Rank-3 Subtree). A system may have as many as 482 cabinets.

3.3.2.1 Rank-1 Details

Within a chassis, the internal wiring of the backplane connects every Aries ASIC in the chassis to each other. As many as 16 Aries reside in each chassis (one per base board); there is one link between each ASIC. The interconnections of the chassis level ASICs require no cables. This set of interconnections is called the intra-chassis network (Figure 3.4).

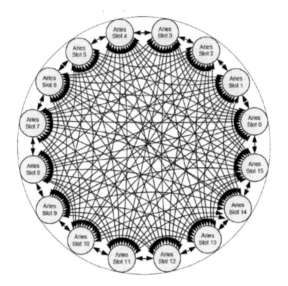

FIGURE 3.4: Intra-chassis connections (Rank-1).

3.3.2.2   Rank-2 Details

Copper cables connect each chassis in the two-cabinet group. Each cable contains three links that comprise a total of 18 differential pair wires (36 total). Each cable connects a blade router to a blade router in another chassis, in the same slot location. For example, the router in Slot 1, Chassis 0, Cabinet 0 would be connected to the five blades in the Slot 1 position in the five other chassis (two in the same cabinet and three in the neighboring cabinet). Two cabinet groups are always fully connected, which requires 240 cables.

3.3.2.3   Rank-3 Details

The Rank-3 network is used to interconnect two-cabinet groups. This level of the topology utilizes optical cables that are housed in integrated cable trays above the system cabinets.

The optical connection uses a 24-channel optical cable: 12 channels for transmit and 12 channels for receive. Each cable handles four links (six channels per link), two from each of two Aries ASICs. Up to five optical cables are associated with every pair of Aries ASICs, and a total of 40 optical connections are possible for each chassis. Thus a complete two-cabinet group has up to 240 optical connections.

The Rank-3 connections must form an all-to-all network between the two-cabinet groups. The width of these connections is variable and can be as few as 1 optical cable between two-cabinet groups and as many as INT(240/(N-1)), where N is the number of two-cabinet groups. For example, a system with 30 cabinets (or 15 two-cabinet groups) can utilize up to 17 optical cables (INT(240/(15-1))) between each pair of two-cabinet groups.

Since optical cables are the most expensive level of the interconnect, configurations are typically not fully populated in this dimension unless the application mix requires unusually high global bandwidth.

3.3.3   Cabinet and Chassis

The Cascade processing cabinet has three individual chassis that support a backplane and up to 16 blades. Configurations of up to 16 compute blades or up to eight I/O blades and the remaining compute blades are supported. The I/O and compute blades are installed in the front of the cabinet, and the high-speed internal network connections (cables) are installed in the rear. In addition, each cabinet is equipped with a power distribution unit (PDU) and a cabinet controller for power control, cooling control, and Ethernet communication with the System Management Workstation.

The chassis blade slots are divided into a left-hand side and a right-hand side. Blades designed for one side cannot be plugged into the other. I/O blades are left-side only. Right-side compute blades plug into the right side of the chassis and left compute blades plug into the left I/O. The compute blades are connected by the Aries ASICs. Processors communicate with the Aries ASIC Network Interface Core over a PCI-e x16 link. The Aries ASIC routers are connected together with links to form the high-speed network that provides communication between nodes on the compute blades.

3.3.3.1   Compute Blades

Compute blades are used only for user applications and have no direct external I/O connections. All I/O is routed through the Aries network. A compute blade is modular in nature and is composed of a base blade and two quad processor daughter cards (QPDCs) (Figure 3.5). The base blade has one Aries ASIC, a hardware supervisory system processor, connectors for the QPDCs, voltage regulator modules, connections for the copper interconnect cables, and a chassis backplane connector. Compute blades use QPDCs based on the Intel Socket R Xeon processor. Each QPDC contains two nodes, each composed of two processor chips and eight memory DIMMs. The QPDCs are designed to be upgradeable over time to accommodate new processing technologies as they become available. Compute blades are available with both a left- and right-hand version.

3.3.3.2   Service Blades

Service blades are used to provide operating system services and connectivity for the system. Functions include:

- Lustre LNET routing services

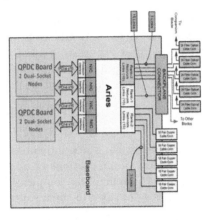

FIGURE 3.5: Compute blade block diagram.

- Connectivity to other file systems through the DVS facility

- Boot services and connectivity to the SMW and boot raid

- Connections to the login nodes

- Networking services

Service blades have one Aries ASIC, a hardware supervisory system processor, connectors for two node daughter cards, voltage regulator modules, connections for copper interconnect cables, and a chassis backplane connector (Figure 3.6). Service blades are based on the Sandy Bridge Xeon processor but contain only two nodes, each with one processor and four memory DIMMs. Each node is associated with two independent PCI-e busses (Gen3 x8), each

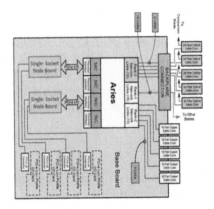

FIGURE 3.6: Service blade block diagram.

of which is associated with a slot designed to hold various host bus adapters (HBAs). Hence a single service blade supports up to four PCI-e HBAs. Service blades are only available with a left-hand personality.

3.3.3.3 Hardware Supervisory System

The Hardware Supervisory System (HSS) is a cabinet- and blade-level subsystem that controls and monitors the basic functions and health of the system. HSS also plays an important role in system debugging and diagnosis of system faults. The major functions of HSS include:

- Monitor and control the cabinet's power supplies and regulators

- Monitor and control the blade level power, including support of power management

- Monitor and control the cabinet and blade temperatures

- Conduct blade and node initialization sequences

- Provide monitoring and reporting services for nodes

- Support the In-Target Probe (ITP) test access port on the processors

- Report monitored device errors to the SMW

- Support processor memory dumps to the SMW through HSS network

- Support the diagnostic software for system analysis and diagnosis

The HSS consists of a SMW, cabinet controller (one for each cabinet), chassis host (one for each chassis), a blade controller (one for each blade), and various thermal and voltage sensors located throughout the cabinet (Figure 3.7). The cabinet controller, chassis host, and blade controllers are connected via a private Ethernet and a clocked serial sideband bus. In addition, the cabinet controller is connected to the SMW via a separate Ethernet network.

The processing cabinet includes the cabinet controller, PDU, and three chassis, with one chassis host each. Each chassis supports up to 16 compute or I/O blades. Each compute or I/O blade contains a blade controller for HSS control. Details are shown in Figure 3.8.

The cabinet controller is connected to the chassis host via Ethernet cables and sideband bus cables. Connection to the external Ethernet switch and SMW are via Ethernet cables only. The cabinet controller is directly connected to the cabinet controller backplane using standard backplane connectors. Connection of the cabinet controller to the blowers, rectifiers, and thermal sensors are through the environmental distribution board using various cables.

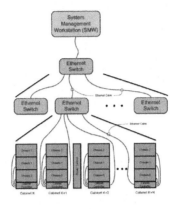

FIGURE 3.7: HSS cabinet level detail.

3.3.4 Storage and I/O

NERSC's systems are configured with local, scratch storage for fast I/O for the jobs running on the system. They also use a shared file system that is available on all NERSC systems for home directories, site provided software, shared areas for each project, and a shared scratch file system used to facilitate data sharing between all systems at NERSC (including Edison, Hopper, and smaller throughput-oriented clusters) by avoiding the need to move data between file systems.

3.3.4.1 Edison File Systems

The Edison system has access to several different file systems that provide different levels of disk storage and I/O performance (Table 3.3).

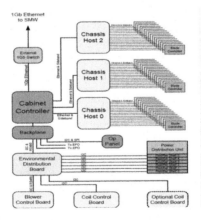

FIGURE 3.8: Cabinet controller diagram.

TABLE 3.3: Edison's file systems.

File System	Home	Local Scratch	Global Scratch	Project
Environment Variable Definition	$HOME	$SCRATCH	$GSCRATCH	None. Must use /project/projectdirs/
Purpose	• Global home file system shared with other NERSC systems. • All NERSC machines mount the same home directory. • GPFS file system. • Where users land when they log into the system.	• Three Lustre file systems, with 7.5 PB of total storage disk space. • Local means the files are not accessible on other NERSC systems.	• Large (3.9 PB) GPFS file system for temporary storage. • Currently mounted on all NERSC systems except PDSF.	• GPFS global file system mounted on all NERSC systems.
Default Quota	• 40 GB • 1 million inodes	• 10 TB* • 10 million inodes	• 20 TB • 2 million inodes	• 1 TB • 1 million inodes
Intended Purpose	• Shell initializations • Storing source code • Compiling codes • Not intended for IO intensive applications	• Running production applications • I/O intensive jobs • Temporary storage of large files	• Alternative file system to run production applications • Aid users whose workflow requires running on multiple platforms • Temporary storage of large files	• Running production applications • Groups needing shared data access • Projects running on multiple NERSC machines
Peak Performance	Low, ~100 MB/sec	168 GB/sec	15 GB/sec	40 GB/sec
Purged?	No	Yes, files older than 12 weeks are purged.	Yes, files older than 12 weeks are purged	No

Edison is configured with three local scratch file systems using the Lustre Parallel File System integrated into Cray Sonexion storage systems.

Two file systems provide 2.16 PB with a bandwidth of 37 GB/s, and one file system provides 3.24 PB file system with a bandwidth of 70 GB/s. The smaller file systems are used for user scratch directories and are assigned round robin the first time a user logs in. The third is provided on request for projects or users with a requirement for high-bandwidth applications.

Use of three file systems serves to improve metadata performance. At the time of Edison's installation, a single Lustre file system was able to achieve only roughly 20 thousand metadata operations per second. This is a relatively low number and led to frequently long waits for listing directories or other file operations such as create or delete. Subdividing the workload into three separate file systems increased overall metadata throughput by a factor of three. Future Lustre versions are expected to implement a clustered metadata server, in which case NERSC may elect to consolidate the two smaller file systems.

Having multiple file systems also improves system availability. In the relative rare event that a file system is damaged and has to be taken down for maintenance, the remaining file systems can continue to serve users without taking the whole system down.

3.3.4.2   Cray Sonexion 1600 Hardware

The Cray Sonexion 1600 [4] is a complete hardware and software solution housed in network-ready 42U racks (Sonexion rack). Each Sonexion file system includes two redundant Metadata Management Units (MMUs), multiple Scalable Storage Units (SSUs) providing modular expansion of disk storage and bandwidth, and 14 Data Rate (FDR) InfiniBand switches to connect to the compute nodes via Lnet routers.

The two 2.16 PB file systems occupy two racks with 12 SSUs. The 3.24 PB file systems occupy three racks with 18 SSUs.

Scalable Storage Unit Hardware

All SSUs are configured identically. Each SSU includes two embedded server modules (ESM) running the Lustre OSS, Cray Sonexion Storage Manager (CSSM) middleware, and back-end services. Each SSU is configured with identical hardware and software including 84 shared drives with shared access by the two ESMs.

Each of the ESMs in an SSU serves simultaneously as active/active Lustre OSS servers, each providing a secondary failover service for its peer in the event of a failure. On failure, the surviving ESM will take over the OSTs of the failed ESM. Both ESMs in an SSU can access the disks as shared storage through a common 6 GB SAS midplane to all drives in the SSU and shares a redundant high-speed interconnect across the midplane for failover services. The ESM runs Linux and has its own dedicated processor, memory, and network and storage connectivity.

At the front of each 5U SSU are two drawers; each drawer has 42 drive bays that support 3.5 inch dual-ported NL-SAS drives housed within carriers. The rear of the SSU houses the ESMs, two redundant power supplies, and five hot-swappable fans.

Each SSU contains 80 dual-ported 3.5 inch 3 TB NL-SAS 7,200 RPM disk drives, providing 180 TB of usable capacity. The disks are configured as eight RAID 6 arrays, each with eight data disks and two parity disks. Each array is configured as a single volume and each volume is formatted as a single LDFS (ext4) file system that is assigned to function as a single Lustre OST. Under normal operation access to the eight OSTs in each SSU is split equally between the ESMs. Thus each ESM/OSS instance will own and provide access to four of the Lustre OSTs. Two dual-ported 3.5 inch 100 GB SSDs drives are configured as a shared RAID 1 array. This array is partitioned and used for the MDRAID write intent bitmaps (WIBs) and the OST/ldiskfs file system journals. The remaining two 3 TB NL-SAS disk drives are used as hot standby spares.

Metadata Management Unit Hardware

Each MMU is configured with identical hardware and software components. Each MMU includes one 2U server with four Intel Metadata Servers (MDS), active and passive Management Servers (MGS), and active and passive Mouse servers and a Metadata Target (MDT) array with 22 450 GB 2.5 inch 6 GB SAS drives and two 100 GB SAS SSDs configured as RAID 1 for metadata journaling. The 450 GB SAS drives are configured as RAID10. The MMU connects to the FDR InfiniBand rack switches and to the 1 GbE management network.

Each Sonexion file system is configured with two MDS servers for redundancy and memory capacity. The primary, active MDS manages the name and directories in the file system and provides the network request handling for the metadata (filenames, directories, permissions and file layout) that is stored on the MDT. There is one MDT per file system. The MDT is also available to the backup, passive MDS, so that if the primary/active MDS fails, the passive MDS can serve the MDT and make it available to clients. Such an occurrence is referred to as "MDS failover."

Cray Sonexion 1600 Connection to Cray System Lustre Clients

Each Sonexion rack is connected to a host system via FDR InfiniBand cables and two director-class FDR InfiniBand switches to Lustre LNET router nodes in the system (Figure 3.9). The FDR InfiniBand switches are configured with enough ports to support the required Lustre file system bandwidth to the System and provide connectivity to the esLogin servers. Lustre client software on the Cray compute nodes are then able to communicate with the Cray Sonexion 1600 MMU and SSUs via the LNET routing capability. The Cray Sonexion 1600 supports communication with Lustre 1.8.6 and higher client versions.

Each file system requires two LNET routers to connect from the compute system to the MMU. SSUs are always deployed in groups of three, and require 4 LNET routers. Thus, there is a 2:1 ratio of LNETs to MMUs and 4:3 for SSUs.

Cray Sonexion Software

Edison utilizes the Cray Sonexion System Manager (CSSM), the management software used for installation, configuration, and baseline testing in the factory and management and monitoring at the customer's site. CSSM features a graphical user interface (GUI) that provides a unified system management view, presenting all necessary information from the various sources on the platform including hardware, Lustre, and the storage. The GUI is accessible through a direct connection between the NERSC designated network and the Management Server (MGS).

Each Sonexion file system is configured with an active and a passive MGS to run CSSM and store information for all the resources in the file system. The Lustre MDS and OSS servers contact the MGS to post this information, and the Lustre clients interact with the MGS to discover location and configuration information for the file system components. Within a Sonexion 1600 the MGS runs in an active-passive configuration on a pair of server nodes that are connected to shared storage. This shared storage is referred to as the Management Target (MGT) that is provisioned as a discrete storage volume, dedicated for use by the MGT. The MGT and the underlying file system are hosted on a dedicated RAID 1 volume. In the event the active MGS fails, the failover process ensures that the passive MGS is activated, taking control of the MGT and all MGS functions.

Each Sonexion rack provides a dedicated local network on a 1 GbE switch that is used for configuration management and health monitoring of all components in the Cray Sonexion. The management network is private and not used for data I/O in the cluster. This network is also used for IPMI traffic to the MMU's MDSs and the SSU's OSSs, enabling them to be power-cycled by the CSSM.

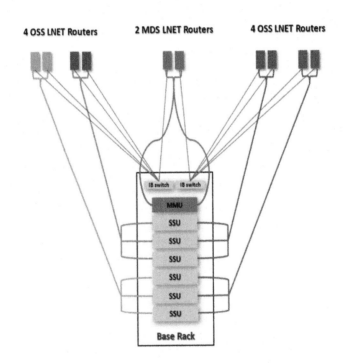

FIGURE 3.9: Logical Cray Cascade LNET routing.

Software and firmware upgrades across an entire Cray Sonexion system are executed through CSSM. CSSM interacts with the enclosure firmware in the SSUs and MMU for each file system to provide the following:

- Failover and failback of primary and secondary I/O modules

- Thermal monitoring and automatic fan speed control

- Drive power control

- Drive fault/identity LEDs

- I/O controller fault/identity LEDs

- Enclosure LEDs and audible alarm control

- Device presence detection

- Power supply monitoring via PSMI

- Communications bus fault detection

- Data and fault logging

CSSM monitors and manages the entire Sonexion storage system and will provide administrative control to the Lustre file system and nodes. In addition to the GUI, CSSM supports the administrative functions to be run from a command line interface (CLI) using a terminal session.

3.3.4.3 Global File System

The NERSC global file system (NGF) is a collection of centerwide file systems, based on IBM's GPFS, available on nearly all systems at the facility. The file systems that comprise NGF include one providing a common login user environment for all our systems, one for sharing data among collaborators on a science project or team and one for high bandwidth short term storage across systems at the facility. The main focus of NGF is data sharing, ease of workflow management (i.e., not moving data around or maintaining unnecessary copies of data), and data analysis.

The NERSC global file system is available to the Edison nodes through the data virtualization service (DVS). The Cray DVS is a network service that provides compute nodes transparent access to file systems mounted on a reduced number of service nodes. Through DVS, applications use a remote file system that appears to be mounted on and local to a compute node. This solves several common problems, including:

- Provides access to existing file systems in the data center

- Reduces resource overhead of file system clients on the compute nodes

- Enables file system access scaling to many thousands of compute nodes

Edison is configured with 16 DVS nodes and is capable of providing 80 GB/sec of total bandwidth to all NERSC global file systems.

Global Scratch

The global scratch file system uses Data Direct Networks (DDN) Storage Fusion Architecture 12000 Embedded (SFA12KE). The storage hardware essentially combines file system servers with the disk array controllers, thereby embedding file system functionality into disk arrays. Advantages of this approach are reduced complexity and better hardware efficiency. The disk controllers are connected directly to a centerwide IB network. The centerwide IB network connects storage to the Edison DVS nodes and other computational systems at NERSC.

The GPFS file system is tuned for large sequential I/Os and thus has an 8 MB block size. Applications on Edison are capable of achieving 80 GB/sec of sustained sequential I/O on the file system. Data in the file system is highly active as it is purged regularly of files that have not been used in the past 12 weeks.

Global Project

The global project file system uses more than a single type of storage in order to reduce the effect or risk that problems with a single type of storage would cause the file system. Currently, the file system uses Nexsan E-series storage (E60s) and DDN Silicon Storage Architecture 9900s (S2A9900s). The file system uses traditional GPFS Network Storage Device servers with the aforementioned disk arrays to provide more than 5PB of capacity at over 40GB/sec sustained aggregate bandwidth using the same centerwide IB network mentioned in the Global Scratch section.

This file system is tuned for smaller I/Os with a 4 MB block size, with its primary focus being enabling users to share their data with collaborators or the broader scientific community through science gateway nodes. As a result, the file system is not purged and generally requires better data management in order to prevent overuse. High-speed access to global project exists from the data transfer nodes at the facility that aid importing or exporting large amounts of data to or from the facility.

Global Home and Common

Global home and common file systems are primarily higher availability storage and are built on a combination of Netapp E-series and Hitachi AMS model hardware. The file systems are tuned for very small I/Os with a 128 KB block size. They are not purged, and users are discouraged from using the file systems for computational system job I/O so that they remain reasonable for interactive I/O. The major advantage of using the global home and common file systems on Edison and other computational systems at NERSC are that users benefit from having a common login and software environment across systems.

3.3.4.4   Data Management Platform and Login Nodes

The Cray Data Management Platform (DMP) integrates Cray XC30 systems into a customer environment using 1U and 2U commodity rack-mounted service nodes. DMP nodes run a combination of commercial off-the-shelf Linux software and Cray proprietary software to replicate the Cray Linux Environment for application development and testing. These specialized external login and service nodes expand the role of the Cray system internal login nodes and provide a development platform for shared externalized file systems, data movers, or high-availability configurations. A Cray Integrated Management Services node runs the commercially available Bright Cluster Manager software (Bright). Bright software enables administrators to manage many DMP nodes using the Bright CMDaemon (cmd), cluster management shell (cmsh), or the cluster management GUI (cmgui).

Edison's external service nodes consist of 12 eslogin nodes, each with four quad-processor Intel Sandy Bridge CPUs and 512 GB of RAM. Each node has two dual port 10 GE network cards with two ports bonded that connect to the external network (which allows connections from outside the facility) and the other two ports bonded to connect with the NERSC internal networks used primarily for GPFS access. In addition, two dual port FDR infiniband HCAs are used for access to the lustre scratch file systems and GPFS. Two additional nodes are used to manage the login nodes (esms – external services management server) with a primary and backup server for redundancy. Bright cluster management software is used to configure and manage the login nodes.

3.3.5   System Software

The NERSC user community is focused on the continuing development of highly parallel application codes. The resource management facility for scheduling, submitting, and executing user jobs must be efficient, flexible, robust, and capable of handling the various scientific workflows of NERSC users. The production environment requires mature software and tools that are well integrated with the operating system software (Table 3.4).

Cray systems at NERSC use a variant of SuSE Linux. The configuration of the compute nodes uses what is called CNL (compute node Linux). This is a scaled-down version of Linux that runs in memory on each compute node. This keeps as much memory as possible available for user applications. Since some applications require libraries that are not available in CNL, CCM (cluster compatibility mode) provides a fuller version of Linux using DVS through DSL (dynamic shared library) nodes. These jobs require some additional setup, which is provided through the job prologue. To allow users to build code for the Cray systems, the login nodes are configured with the same levels of software and tools needed on the Cray to ensure compatibility. To ensure nodes are in a good state, a node health check is run at the completion of each job to verify that no user processes are still on the system, along with

TABLE 3.4: Major system software, applications, and libraries on Edison.

Software Area	Application Area	Representative Software
Operating Systems		SUSE Linux, CLE
Batch System		Torque/Moab
Storage Systems		Lustre, GPFS
Communication Stack		OFED, Aries
Applications	Math	Matlab
	Chemistry	G09, NWChem, GAMESS, NAMD, AMBER, Molpro
	Material Sciences	VASP, QE, LAMMPS, CP2K, BerkeleyGW, GROMACS, SIESTA
Compiler/Languages		GCC, Intel, Cray Compiler/Fortran, C, C++, PGAS, Python, Java, Shell
Development Tools	General	CVS, SVN, CMAKE, MySQL, Craypkg-gen
	Debugging	DDT, Totalview, LGDB, CCDB, GDB, Valgrind
	Profiling	Perftools, perftools-lite, PAPI, IPM, TAU, Darshan
Programming Libraries	Math	LibSci, MKL, PETSc, GSL, Cray-tpsl, FFTW, SPRNG
	I/O	HDF5, NetCDF, ADIOS, IOBUF, Silo
	Graphics	NCAR
	Communication	Cray-mpich, cray-shmem, uGNI, DMAPP, cray-onesided, OpenMPI
	Other	Trilinos, Boost, Global Array
Analytics/Visualization		Visit, IDL, R

other checks to ensure node health. If a node is found to be in a bad state, it is put into an *admindown* state so new jobs will not be started on it.

In addition to a rich set of software libraries supplied by Cray, NERSC builds, installs, and supports a number of popular applications, including VASP, BerkeleyGW, Quantum Espresso, NWChem, and NAMD. NERSC also augments the Cray code development tools with third-party debuggers from Allinea Software (DDT) and Rouge Wave Software (totalview).

The batch system software is configured to support a mix of extreme scale parallel applications and large numbers of ensemble runs at a more modest parallel concurrency [5].

Edison's development and runtime environment was configured to be remarkably similar to the environment on Hopper, which eased the porting and transition effort required by application scientists. As a result, system utilization was effectively 100 percent on the first day all NERSC users were granted access to the system.

3.4   Physical Infrastructure

Edison was installed at the University of California Oakland Scientific Center (OSF) in Oakland, CA. However, in 2015 NERSC and Edison will move to the new Computational Research and Theory (CRT) facility, on the Berkeley Lab main campus in the hills of Berkeley, CA.

In order to be installed in CRT, it was critical that Edison operate with the higher temperature water and air provided by the "free cooling" mechanisms that are key elements of the CRT design. The new cooling design of the XC30 meets this requirement. NERSC took advantage of this capability to modify OSF to mimic the CRT cooling mechanism and provide an early test of the CRT design [6]. Not only was this test successful, the Center saved enough electricity to earn a $435,000 energy efficiency rebate from our power utility.

3.4.1   Computational Research and Theory Facility

CRT has been designed to provide the kind of world-class energy efficiency necessary to support exascale systems. It will be a highly energy-efficient, state-of-the-art computing facility that can provide over 40 MW of power and 30,000 square feet of space for computing and storage (Figure 3.10). The additional power and space within CRT will allow NERSC to deploy pre-exascale

FIGURE 3.10: Artist's rendering of the new Computational Research and Theory facility at Berkeley Lab.

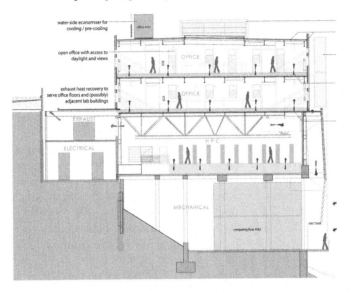

FIGURE 3.11: A cross-section of NERSC's CRT data center, opening in 2015. The bottom mechanical floor houses air handlers, pumps and heat exchangers. The second floor is the data center; the top two floors are offices.

and exascale systems that are usable by the broad scientific community and meet the exponentially growing data needs of DOE.

The San Francisco Bay Area climate is strongly moderated by the bay itself. Temperatures remain relatively cool year-round, and on those occasions when temperatures rise above the 70s, humidity stays low. The design of CRT leverages this benign environment to provide year-round cooling without mechanical chillers, which consume large amounts of power (Figure 3.11).

On the air side, the building is designed to "breathe," taking in outside air to cool systems and expelling the hot exhaust generated by the systems. Hot air can be recirculated to temper and dehumidify the inlet air. (Heat is also harvested to warm office areas.) On the water side, evaporative cooling is used to dissipate heat from systems. Water circulates through cooling towers, where it is cooled by evaporation. This outside, open water loop is connected by a heat exchanger to a closed, inside water loop that provides cool water directly to the systems. The water loop additionally provides cooling for air on hot days.

Many data centers utilize free cooling when the conditions are amenable, and fall back on chillers when temperatures and humidity rise. For example, free cooling may be used in the winter but not in summer, or at night but not during the day. In the Bay Area conditions are favorable all year. In the worst conditions, which occur only a few hours per year, CRT is designed to provide 74°F air and 75°F water. For this reason, NERSC has decided to attempt to forgo chillers altogether. As a result, the maximum PUE at CRT is predicted to be less than 1.1 for a likely mix of equipment.

NERSC's early experience with Edison was invaluable in understanding how to operate in a free-cooling environment, before we move into the CRT building. In addition, we have increased pump capacity in CRT and have added requirements for flow rate, differential pressure, and water quality to requests for proposals (RFPs) for future systems.

3.4.2 Cray XC30 Cooling Design

The Cray XC30 system has an innovative cooling mechanism that uses a side-to-side airflow where the exhaust air from one rack becomes the intake air of the next (Figure 3.12). Each cabinet contains a water intercooler (radiator) on the outlet side. This transfers heat from the air blowing through the cabinets to the water loop and cools air delivered to the next cabinet in the row. Fan cabinets are placed at the intake and outlet ends of the row as well as interspersed between pairs of two compute racks.

Flowing the air from side to side has unique advantages. First, additional cabinets in a row do not require more air from the computer room than was supplied to the first rack. Less overall air requirements means fewer building air handlers and greater overall center efficiency.

Additionally, the surface area of the side of the rack is greater than the front and the width of the rack is less than the depth. Both of these contribute to less fan energy required to move the same volume of air through a compute rack. With the air moving more slowly across an intercooler, a greater amount of heat is extracted per volume. This leads to a closer temperature approach between the water used to cool the system and the air that is being cooled, and a greater change in temperature of both the air (cooling) and the water (warming) through the system.

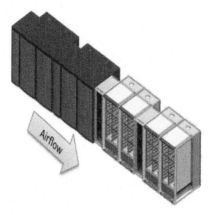

FIGURE 3.12: The Cray XC30 side-to-side airflow design.

Approach is the difference between the water temperature and the exiting air temperature. The slower the air moves through the coil (more time to transfer the heat) and the more efficient the coil is, the smaller the approach will be. Approach can get to a few degrees on a very efficient system but can never be zero. Depending on the direction of water flow through the intercooler, the approach can be the difference between the exiting water and the exiting air (parallel flow) or the entering water and the exiting air (counter flow). Since the entering water is always colder than the exiting water, it is more efficient to have the water flow in the opposite direction of the air. Counter-flow is required for efficient free cooling, and is included in the XC30 design.

Since the OSF and CRT sites are nearby and share the same climate, the free cooling approach was also implemented at OSF as a way to prototype the CRT design and understand system requirements. In addition, power cost savings were calculated at 80%, or 216 kW per year [6].

3.5   User Services

NERSC users have access to a wide array of consulting and support services designed to increase their scientific productivity through technical support, education, advocacy, and the development and deployment of new computational and data technologies. NERSC provides problem management and consulting, help with user code optimization and debugging, strategic project support, web documentation and training, and third-party applications and library support for its diverse set of users.

NERSC's User Services group comprises 12 consultants, including nine HPC experts, six with Ph.D. degrees. NERSC's two account support personnel each has 10+ years of experience. NERSC's consultants and account support staff are available to users via email, a web interface, and on the phone during business hours (8 a.m.-5 p.m. Pacific Time). Account support is available via the NERSC operations staff 24 x 7, 365 days a year, with many capabilities also available online.

When users contact NERSC, they immediately are in contact with highly trained HPC specialists who can usually solve issues directly or immediately route the request to the appropriate systems engineers. NERSC's policy is to respond to all inquiries within four business hours, and either solve the problem or communicate a work plan to the user within three business days for all reported incidents.

Each month, NERSC's consulting and support staff field about 140 user questions related to Edison. Users most often ask for assistance on how to run parallel jobs more efficiently, how to use software libraries and applications, how to debug and optimize code, and how to read and write data files at high performance. NERSC also helps users with data analytics and visualization related to their computations run on Edison.

3.6 Early Application Results on Edison

Since Edison Phase I first came online in early 2013, a number of NERSC users have been running very large data projects on the system. Here are some of their initial results [18, 3].

3.6.1 Sequestered CO_2

Edison's 64 gigabytes of memory per node and faster processors are critical to the data-rich research of David Trebotich, a Berkeley Lab scientist who is studying the effects of sequestering carbon dioxide (CO_2) deep underground to better predict the physical and chemical changes it will cause and where all the CO_2 will wind up. Trebotich is modeling the physical and chemical changes sequestered CO_2 causes in the rocks and saline reservoirs it is pumped into deep underground. Such "geologic sequestration" is already in use at some sites, but scientists still cannot predict its behavior using flow simulations that zoom in no closer than meters.

To get the detail necessary for accurate predictions, Trebotich's models calculate the physical and chemical reactions at a resolution of 1 micron, generating datasets of one terabyte for a single, 100 microsecond time-step – 16 seconds for the full simulation (Figure 3.13). Edison's high memory-per-node means that more of each calculation (and the resulting data) can be stored close to the processors working on it. As a result, the simulations run 2.5 times faster than on the previous flagship system, reducing the time it takes him to get a solution from months to weeks.

3.6.2 Large-Scale Structure of the Universe

Zarija Lukic, a cosmologist with Berkeley Lab's Computational Cosmology Center (C3), models mega-parsecs of space in an attempt to understand the large-scale structure of the universe. Working with 2 million early hours on Edison, Lukic and collaborators performed the largest Lyman alpha forest simulation to date: the equivalent of a cube measuring more than 300 million light years on each side (Figure 3.14). Such large-scale simulations will be key to interpreting the data from many upcoming observational missions, including the Dark Energy Spectroscopic Instrument (DESI). The work supports the Dark Universe project, part of the DOE's Scientific Discovery through Advanced Computing (SciDAC) program.

FIGURE 3.13: Simulation showing computed pH on calcite grains at 1 micron resolution. (Image: David Trebotich.)

3.6.3 Graphene and Carbon Nanotubes

Vasilii Artyukhov, a post-doctoral researcher in materials science and nanoengineering at Rice University, used 5 million processor hours during Edison's testing phase to simulate how graphene and carbon nanotubes are

FIGURE 3.14: Using the Nyx code on Edison, scientists were able to run the largest simulation of its kind (370 million light years on each side) showing neutral hydrogen in the large-scale structure of the universe. (Image: Casey Stark.)

"grown" using chemical vapor deposition. His goal is to develop a theory for the growth of carbon nanotubes to be able to selectively grow the ones that are most needed.

Edison's Aries interconnect wired in the Dragonfly configuration allowed Artyukhov to run his code on twice as many processors, at speeds twice as fast as before. Artyukhov is also running codes that work at the molecular level that are not as computationally demanding, but because Edison is so large, he is able to run many of them at once.

3.6.4 Better Combustion for New Fuels

Jackie Chen of Sandia National Laboratory (SNL) is investigating how to improve combustion using new engine designs and new fuels – such as biodiesel, hydrogen-rich "syngas" from coal gasification, and alcohols like ethanol. She models the behavior of burning fuels by simulating the conditions found in these combustion engines, using a direct numerical simulation code developed at SNL (Figure 3.15).

During Edison's early science period, she and post-doctoral researchers Hemanth Kolla and Sgouria Lyra modeled hydrogen and oxygen mixing and burning in a transverse jet configuration commonly employed by turbine combustors in aircraft engines and industrial power plants.

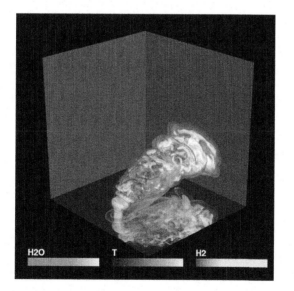

FIGURE 3.15: This volume rendering shows the reactive hydrogen/air jet in crossflow in a combustion simulation. (Image: Hongfeng Yu, University of Nebraska.)

Chen was able to run her direct numerical simulation code, S3D, on 100,000 processors at once and observed a 4x-5x performance improvement over the Cray XE6 (Hopper). They were also pleased with the I/O performance on file systems, with a write performance of about 6-10 GB/s and read performance of around 2.5 GB/s.

3.7 Exascale Computing and the Future of NERSC

A critical strategic objective at NERSC is to meet the ever growing computing and data needs of our users by providing usable exascale computing and storage systems, transitioning SC codes to execute effectively on many-core architectures, and influencing the computer industry to ensure that future systems meet the mission needs of SC.

The aggregate computing needs of SC science teams at NERSC will be well into the exascale regime by the end of the decade. Users need to run simulations at hundreds of petaflops, and they need to run thousands to millions of petascale simulations to achieve their goals. Following Edison (NERSC-7), NERSC will deploy pre-exascale systems in 2016 (NERSC-8) and 2019 (NERSC-9), and we anticipate deploying our first exascale system, NERSC-10, in 2022. Our goal is to provide our users a consistent path to exascale, particularly in the evolution of the programming model.

NERSC will continue to support MPI into the foreseeable future so that our codes can execute, albeit at less than optimal performance, on future systems with little or no modifications. We anticipate that many of our codes will transition to MPI for interprocessor communication plus OpenMP for on-node concurrency in the NERSC-8 time frame.

3.7.1 NERSC-8 as a Pre-Exascale System

The NERSC-8 system will be a Cray XC system delivered in 2016 that will provide over 10 times the sustained performance of NERSC's Hopper system, a 1.2 peak petaflop Cray XE6 system. In addition to increasing the computational capability available to DOE computational scientists, the NERSC-8 system will also begin to transition DOE scientific applications to more energy-efficient, manycore architectures.

The system, named Cori in honor of bio-chemist and Nobel Laureate Gerty Cori, will be composed of over 9300 single-socket compute nodes using Intel's next-generation Xeon Phi processor, code-named "Knights Landing." The Knights Landing processor used in NERSC-8 will have over 60 cores, each with multiple hardware threads with improved single thread performance over the current generation Xeon Phi co-processor. The Knights Landing processor is "self-hosted," meaning that it is not an accelerator or dependent on a host processor. With this model, users will be able to retain the MPI/OpenMP programming model they have been using on NERSC's Hopper and Edison systems. The Knights Landing processor also features on-package high bandwidth memory that can be used as a cache or explicitly managed by the user.

Additionally, Cori will provide over 400 GB/s of I/O bandwidth and 28 PB of disk space. The Cray XC features the Aries high-bandwidth, low latency network for inter-node communication. The system will be installed directly into the new CRT facility in 2016.

3.7.1.1   Burst Buffer

Included in the NERSC-8 contract is an option for a Burst Buffer, a layer of solid-state flash storage meant to address the persistent and growing gap between memory performance and disk performance. The initial design for the Burst Buffer was focused on check-point restart, a means for applications to restart in case of interruption. However, NERSC's use cases are much broader, including the need to quickly access large datasets generated at DOE experimental facilities.

By using solid-state flash storage, a Burst Buffer can provide many times the bandwidth of a similarly priced pure disk solution as well as significantly better random, small-block I/O characteristics. Thus, leveraging the capabilities of solid-state flash and traditional disk-based parallel file systems into a single HPC system can provide both higher bandwidth and larger capacity than either solid-state flash or disk could provide alone for a given price.

While promising, the Burst Buffer technology is immature and the software to support it undeveloped. For this reason, the NERSC-8 system was designed to achieve the mission goals without a Burst Buffer. The Burst Buffer software will be developed through a separate Non-Recurring Engineering contract. Depending on Burst Buffer software development progress, NERSC may execute the option for a Burst Buffer.

3.7.1.2   Collaboration with ACES

NERSC has been and is continuing to collaborate with ACES (Alliance for Computing at the Extreme Scale, an HPC partnership between Los Alamos National Laboratory and Sandia National Laboratories) to procure the next generation systems for each organization: NERSC-8 and the Trinity system. NERSC and ACES collaborated informally in the past and, in 2010, independently procured very similar systems: Hopper, a Cray XE6 for NERSC, and Cielo, a Cray XE6 for ACES. The Office of Science and the National Nuclear Security Administration have been working together for many years, and most recently the two programs began partnering on DesignForward and FastForward, with the goal of developing critical technologies needed for extreme-scale computing.

There were numerous reasons that motivated the decision to work together on the NERSC-8 and Trinity projects. Principally, the collaboration supports

TABLE 3.5: NERSC systems roadmap.

System	PF	Memory (TB)	Storage (PB)	BW (GB/s)
Franklin	0.35	77.4	0.93	28
Hopper	1.3	216.6	2.4	70
Edison	2.6	358.9	7.4	168
Cori (planned)	>27.9	893.2	28.5	432
NERSC-9	250-500	10 PB	300	4,000
NERSC-10	1,000	30 PB	700	12,000

the strategy of each program's headquarters (SC and NNSA), which seek to leverage each other's investments, provide a unified message to vendors during this time of rapidly changing technology in the HPC market, and build a broader coalition to overcome the challenges of transitioning the user communities to more energy efficient architectures.

The NERSC-8 and Trinity teams have been working together since the spring of 2012 and created joint technical requirements, developed a common set of application benchmarks, and jointly conducted vendor market surveys. The teams released a joint RFP for a single vendor to procure two independent systems in the 2015/2016 timeframe, one for NERSC-8 and one for Trinity. Staff from ACES and NERSC participated in the RFP response evaluation and selected the vendor's proposal that provided the best value system. After vendor selection, each team negotiated its own contract, though the teams were in close contact during negotiations, each observing the negotiations of the other. The Trinity and NERSC-8 teams will continue to collaborate through the delivery, integration, testing, and acceptance of the systems. While the two teams are collaborating, each project has its own mission drivers and contract.

The NERSC systems roadmap is shown in Table 3.5. Note that Memory and Storage figures are calculated using Base 10.

3.7.2 Application Readiness

Computing technology is undergoing major changes because chip hardware technologies are reaching physical scaling limits imposed by power constraints. Although transistor density continues to increase, chips are no longer yielding faster clock speeds; as a result, vendors are increasing the number of cores on a chip.

The HPC community at large is facing a challenge to prepare applications for these future architectures. From the most conservative architecture choice to the most exotic architecture choice a center like NERSC could adopt in the exascale time-frame, there are several common design elements. First, increased parallelism will be seen in increased core per node and threads per core, and increased vector lengths will also be prevalent. Second, memory per core/thread will decrease. Third, fast local memories will emerge and require explicit management by user programs.

These architecture innovations with vast increases in chip parallelism (referred to as "manycore") and new memory hierarchies are incorporated into the NERSC-8 Knight's Landing (KNL) processor, which will have more than 60 cores per node with multiple hardware threads each, and high bandwidth on-package memory. Although it will be straightforward to get applications running on the system, it is expected that many user applications will require code modifications to achieve high performance. The amount of code modification and restructuring will depend on many factors, including the extent to which users had begun transitioning to MPI+X programming models on existing, current-generation NERSC and DOE platforms. Achieving high performance on the KNL processor will likely require finer levels of parallelism, increased vector lengths, and utilization of on-package memory.

Well before the NERSC-8 architecture was selected, NERSC had assembled an Application Readiness team, comprising approximately 12 staff members, to examine how NERSC's approximately 600 applications would fare, performance wise, in light of these trends and estimate how much work it would take to optimize an application on an architecture with more on-node parallelism. With the NERSC-8 architecture identified, the Application Readiness effort will ramp up as a broad, multi-pronged effort that includes user training, access to early development systems, application analysis deep dives, and collaborations with vendors and other members of the HPC community who are facing the same transition to manycore architectures. Preparing users and their applications for advanced architectures is a long-term NERSC initiative and, as such, will last longer than the duration of the NERSC-8 project, well into NERSC-9 and beyond. NERSC plans to develop and deliver a rigorous and comprehensive training program to ensure that NERSC's end-user customers are adequately prepared for the new system.

NERSC has had substantial vendor support from Intel and Cray to aid in the transition of users to the KNL architecture. Before the NERSC-8 system arrives Intel will provide "white-box" test systems with early KNL processors. These single-node systems will provide NERSC staff and NERSC users an early opportunity to test and port codes to an early KNL architecture. Intel will also provide deep dive dungeon code sessions to help code teams transition to the KNL architecture.

NERSC will also form a partnership with Cray for a Center of Excellence (COE) comprising NERSC Application Readiness Staff and Cray staff. The COE was launched in the fall of 2014, and Cray staff will be tasked with helping to port and optimize key DOE SC applications to the KNL. As part of the Application Readiness effort, NERSC plans to create integrated code teams composed of NERSC principal investigators, Cray COE staff, NERSC Application Readiness staff, and newly hired postdoctoral researchers to aid in each application's transition.

NERSC has examined the top applications running on NERSC systems and has completed a preliminary analysis of each code's readiness for the NERSC-8 system. Several NERSC top application codes run on the Leadership Computing Facilities at Oak Ridge and Argonne, and many of them are already well prepared for the NERSC-8 system. Other application teams will need more guidance and help making the transition. NERSC will leverage best practices from the LCFs, ACES, and others in the HPC community to prepare its users for the NERSC-8 architecture. Additionally, because the Edison system will overlap with the NERSC-8 system, users who need to make substantial code changes will still be able to compute productively on the Edison (NERSC-7) system.

While transitioning the NERSC workload to manycore architectures presents several challenges, NERSC has developed a comprehensive plan and acquired the necessary resources to make it a success. Making this transition as smoothly and effectively as possible will allow our science teams to meet their goals in the 2015-2023 timeframe.

3.8 Conclusion

Edison is the first all-new Cray supercomputer design in nearly a decade. It features Intel processors and a new, higher performance interconnect (Aries) that uses a Dragonfly topology. The system can execute nearly 2.57 quadrillion floating-point operations per second (petaflop/s) at peak theoretical speeds. While theoretical speeds are impressive, however, NERSC's longstanding approach is to evaluate proposed systems based on sustained performance on real applications to increase the scientific productivity of our users.

As a result, Edison was designed to optimize data motion – the primary bottleneck for many applications at NERSC – rather than peak speed. It has very high memory bandwidth, interconnect speed, and bisection bandwidth relative to its floating point operation speed. In addition, each node has twice the memory of many leading systems. This combination of fast data motion and large memory per node makes it well suited for NERSC's traditional HPC workload and newly emerging data-intensive applications.

Acknowledgments

The authors wish to thank the Advanced Scientific Computing Research Program in the U.S. Department of Energy's Office of Science, which supports

NERSC under contract No. DE-AC02-05CH11231. The authors would also like to thank Cray Inc. for their numerous contributions to this document, notably the description and drawings of the Aries interconnect and Sonexion I/O system.

Bibliography

[1] Bob Alverson, Edwin Froese, Larry Kaplan, and Duncan Roweth. "the cray xc series network". http://www.cray.com/Assets/PDF/products/xc/CrayXC30Networking.pdf. Cray Inc.

[2] K. Antypas, J. Shalf, and H. Wasserman. NERSC6 workload analysis and benchmark selection process. *LBNL Technical Report - LBNL 1014E*, August 13, 2008.

[3] Katie Antypas, Nicholas Wright, and Zhengji Zhao. Effects of hyperthreading on the NERSC workload on Edison. *Cray Users Group (CUG)*, 2013.

[4] Nicholas P. Cardo. Sonexion 1600 I/O performance. *Cray Users Group (CUG)*, 2013.

[5] Tina Declerck and Iwona Sakrejda. External torque/MOAB and fairshare on the Cray XC30. *Cray Users Group (CUG)*, 2013.

[6] Brent Draney, Jeff Broughton, Tina Declerck, and John Hutchings. Saving energy with free cooling and the Cray XC30. *Cray Users Group (CUG)*, 2013.

[7] Richard Gerber, Harvey Wasserman et al. Large scale computing and storage requirements for biological and environmental research. https://www.nersc.gov/assets/HPC-Requirements-for-Science/NERSC-BER-WorkshopReport.pdf, May 7-8, 2009.

[8] Richard Gerber, Harvey Wasserman et al. Large scale computing and storage requirements for high energy physics. https://www.nersc.gov/assets/HPC-Requirements-for-Science/NERSC-HEP-WorkshopReport.pdf, November 12-13, 2009.

[9] Richard Gerber, Harvey Wasserman et al. Large scale computing and storage requirements for basic energy sciences. https://www.nersc.gov/assets/HPC-Requirements-for-Science/NERSC-BES-WorkshopReport.pdf, February 9-10, 2010.

[10] Richard Gerber, Harvey Wasserman et al. Large scale computing and storage requirements for fusion energy sciences. https://www.nersc.gov/assets/HPC-Requirements-for-Science/NERSC-FES-WorkshopReport.pdf, August 3-4, 2010.

[11] Richard Gerber, Harvey Wasserman et al. Large scale computing and storage requirements for advanced scientific computing research. https://www.nersc.gov/assets/HPC-Requirements-for-Science/NERSC-ASCR-WorkshopReport.pdf, January 5-6, 2011.

[12] Richard Gerber, Harvey Wasserman et al. Large scale computing and storage requirements for nuclear physics research. https://www.nersc.gov/assets/HPC-Requirements-for-Science/NERSC-NP-WorkshopReport.pdf, May 26-27, 2011.

[13] Richard Gerber, Harvey Wasserman et al. Large scale computing and storage requirements for biological and environmental research - target 2017. https://www.nersc.gov/assets/HPC-Requirements-for-Science/BER2017/BER2017FinalJune7.pdf, September 11-12, 2012.

[14] Richard Gerber, Harvey Wasserman et al. Large scale computing and storage requirements for high energy physics - target 2017. https://www.nersc.gov/assets/pubs_presos/NERSC-PRR-HEP-2017.pdf, November 27-28, 2012.

[15] John Kim, Wiliam J. Dally, Steve Scott, and Dennis Abts. Technology-driven, highly-scalable dragonfly topology. *SIGARCH Comput. Archit. News*, 36(3):77–88, June 2008.

[16] William Kramer. Percu: A holistic method for evaluating high performance computing systems. *Technical Report No. UCB/EECS-2008-143*, November 5, 2008.

[17] William Kramer, John Shalf, and Erich Strohmaier. The NERSC sustained system performance (SSP) metric. *LBNL tech report*, 2005.

[18] Zhengji Zhao. Comparing compiler and library performance in material science applications on Edison. *Cray Users Group (CUG)*, 2013.

Chapter 4

HLRN-III at Zuse Institute Berlin

**Wolfgang Baumann, Guido Laubender, Matthias Läuter,
Alexander Reinefeld, Christian Schimmel, Thomas Steinke,
Christian Tuma, and Stefan Wollny**

Zuse Institute Berlin

4.1   Introduction

4.1.1   Scientific Computing and Computer Science at ZIB

The *Zuse Institute Berlin (ZIB)* is a research institute for applied mathematics and computer science. It was founded in 1984 by merging two computing centers in West Berlin, *Grossrechenzentrum Berlin (GRZ)* and *Wissenschaftliches Rechenzentrum Berlin (WRB)*. One important cornerstone in the foundation of ZIB was the observation that the tight collaboration of research and service is able to create a large amount of synergy. Today, internationally well-known researchers in applied mathematics and computer science closely collaborate with the HPC service providers to the mutual benefit of both parties. In fact, the idea of *HPC Consultants* was born at ZIB and quickly taken up by other centers as well. The HPC consultants at ZIB pursue their own domain specific research in fields such as chemistry, engineering, earth sciences or physics while providing consultancy to the supercomputer users. Our basic principle *"Fast Algorithms – Fast Computers,"* which was coined almost thirty years ago holds until today. We provide solutions for complex problems in science, engineering, environment, and society—solutions that often require innovative approaches implemented on latest HPC technology.

Berlin has a long tradition in joining forces to the benefit of its researchers and scientists in the three universities and non-university research institutes. As early as 1974, i.e., ten years before the foundation of ZIB, a state contract between the State of Berlin and the computer services departments of the two Berliner universities was signed to organize the joint operation and usage of the Telefunken TR 440 owned by the State of Berlin, the CD 6500 owned by the Technical University Berlin, and the CD Cyber 72 owned by the Free University Berlin. Because of its location behind the Iron Curtain in East Berlin the third university, the Humboldt-Universität zu Berlin, could only join after Germany's reunification. Today, ZIB is tightly linked to the three universities, not only through project cooperations and long-term collaborations, but also because of the joint professorships that each of the three ZIB directors holds with one of the Berlin universities.

In 1984 a state contract between the three states Lower Saxony, Schleswig-Holstein and Berlin was signed to create an alliance for the joint use of high-performance computers in North-West Germany [12]. At that time high-performance computing was synonymous to vector computing, and hence the alliance was named *North-German Vector Computer Association (NVV)*[1]. According to the contract, each of the three states was obliged to purchase a new supercomputer every six years and to give free access of 15% of the available computing time to each partner state. This pioneering approach had a tremendous impact on research and science in North Germany. From that

---

[1]NVV = Norddeutscher Vektorrechner-Verbund

time on, researchers could run their simulation codes on the most advanced supercomputers. Every second year a new system was available, which greatly fuelled the advance of the state-of-the-art in scientific computing.

4.1.2 Supercomputers at ZIB: Past to Present

The major supercomputers that were operated at ZIB are listed in Table 4.1. All systems up to the Cray T3E were exclusively owned by ZIB (resp. the State of Berlin), whereas the systems after 2002 were jointly financed by the HLRN member states and operated at the two sites ZIB/Berlin and LUIS/Hanover (see next section). This was a necessary step, because no state had the financial capacity and political enforcement to finance the increasingly expensive HPC resources just by itself.

Figure 4.1 illustrates the increase of the systems' peak performance (solid curve) and memory capacity (dashed curve) as compared to Moore's law (dotted line). Over the years, ZIB had generally a system listed in the TOP500 list—despite the fact, that we did not focus on peak performance but rather on having well-balanced systems with powerful interconnects and sufficiently large main memories. Moreover, the supercomputers operated at ZIB do not comprise single monolithic systems, but rather a number of system components with complementary architectures for massively parallel processing (MPP) and shared-memory processing (SMP). The driving force on the selection of our system architectures has, of course, always been the user demand.

Apart from the high investment costs, the sharp increase in the operation costs became of major burden for HPC service providers. Today, Germany is probably among the most expensive European countries with respect to energy prices: Since the late 1990s we witnessed two major price leaps, the first one caused by the energy crisis and the second one due to the political goal to increasing the share of renewable energy. In combination with the increased taxes, the price per kWh more than doubled in the last fifteen

TABLE 4.1: Supercomputers in their final configuration at ZIB. The three most recent systems were financed by the HLRN Alliance and jointly operated at ZIB and LUIS.

Year	Main System	Cores	Peak Perf.	Memory	Disk
1984	Cray 1M	1	160 MFlops	8 MB	2.4 GB
1987	Cray X-MP/216	2	471 MFlops	128 MB	8 GB
1991	Cray Y-MP4D/464	4	1,3 GFlops	512 MB	40 GB
1994	Cray T3D SC, J90	256	38 GFlops	16 GB	126 GB
1997	Cray T3E LC	540	524 GFlops	86 GB	746 GB
2002	IBM p690	1024	5 TFlops	2 TB	52 TB
2008	SGI Altix	26,112	300 TFlops	128 TB	1.6 PB
2013	Cray XC30	85,000	2.5 PFlops	222 TB	7.2 PB

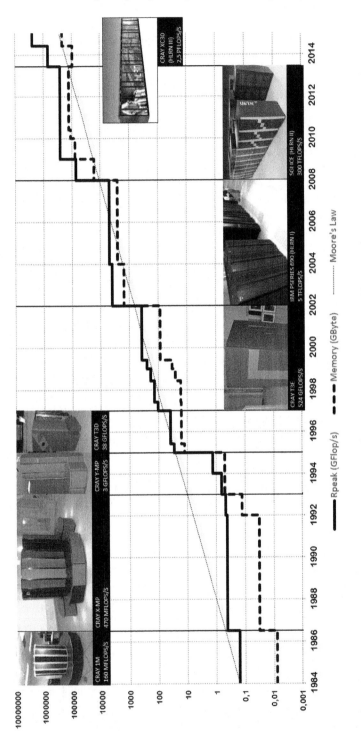

FIGURE 4.1: Evolution of high performance computing at ZIB.

years. Compared to North America with its more than 50% lower energy cost, Germany is a particularly difficult place for operating high-performance computing resources and we are therefore very grateful to the government authorities for their continuous support. As a rule of thumb, today the energy cost of an HPC system over five years almost matches the investment cost.

From the year 2013 on, this financial burden could no longer be carried by the two HLRN sites in Berlin and Hanover. Consequently the HLRN board decided to jointly finance the costs for system maintenance and energy, starting with the HLRN-III in 2013. Considering the current (2014) energy price of >0.17 Euros[2] per kWh, the operation cost for the computer and its cooling sums up to several million Euros per year.

4.2 HLRN Supercomputing Alliance

In 2001, six German States (Bundesländer) founded an alliance for the procurement and operation of high-performance computers, the *North-German Supercomputing Alliance HLRN*[3]. The founding member states Berlin, Bremen, Hamburg, Mecklenburg-Vorpommern, Niedersachsen, and Schleswig-Holstein signed the state contract in 2001, while the state of Brandenburg joined in 2012.

4.2.1 Bodies

The HLRN is today not only the largest HPC alliance in Germany and Europe, but also a unique science-political endeavour, as highlighted by the German Science Council. Almost half of the total 16 German states joined their forces for the operation of supercomputer resources to the benefit of the scientists. This outstanding (and sometimes delicate) construct was only possible by establishing a well-balanced system of bodies, ranging from science-politicians in the Administrative Council, IT experts in the Technical Council, domain-specific advisors in the Scientific Board to the network of HPC Consultants.

The systems owned by the HLRN are used by scientists from North-German universities and other scientific institutions of the seven member states. They cover the huge demand for computing resources in the domains of environmental research, climate and ocean modeling, engineering applications

---

[2]The cost for electrical power varies from state to state. It depends on the tariff of the local supplier of electric energy, the quantity of energy consumption, and on taxes, for e.g., the recently decided national green energy law and network concessions.

[3]Norddeutscher Verbund für Hoch- und Höchstleistungsrechnen, https://www.hlrn.de

like aerodynamics and naval engineering, as well as in fundamental research in physics, chemistry, and life sciences.

The *Administrative Council* comprises one member from each of the seven state science ministries. The administrative council decides about matters of strategic and financial relevance, including re-investments, usage fees, and the affiliation of new consortium members.

The *Technical Council* decides on the overall system operation and it organizes the procurements of new systems. It comprises one member from each of the seven states—usually a director of one of the computer service centers of the states' institutes or universities.

The *Scientific Board* comprises representative scientific stakeholders from various disciplines who decide on the allocation of compute resources to the users. All HLRN users are required to submit a proposal to the board, which then decides (supported by external reviewers) on the acceptance. All tasks for the application and administration of accounts and projects use web-based tools on the web server of the HLRN (www.hlrn.de).

The *HPC Consultants* are organized throughout the member states. They provide consultancy on the system access, the maintenance of software packages, and the optimization of application code as well as support in preparing HLRN project proposals.

4.2.2 Funding

Each member state funds a share of the HLRN systems and in turn gets access to the supercomputer facilities. The size of each state's contribution depends on the number of its inhabitants and its gross product. The states pay 50% of the investment cost, while the other 50% comes from the federal government.

Fortunately, the founders of the HLRN alliance recognized the need for continuous support. Today, HPC systems are outdated after about five years lifetime. This is not only because of Moore's Law which states an exponentially increasing performance of system components, but even more important (in Germany) because of improvements in the energy consumption, that is, a continuous reduction of electrical power per flop/s. Consequently, the HLRN alliance was designed right from the beginning as a continuous effort with a five-year system replacement rate.

4.2.3 Procurements

In Germany, all publicly funded supercomputer procurements are reviewed by the German Council of Science and Humanities (Wissenschaftsrat, WR), which decides on the science-political aspects and forwards the proposal to the German Science Council (DFG) for an in-depth review of the technical soundness, including an evaluation of the scientific need and the appropriateness of the proposed system architecture.

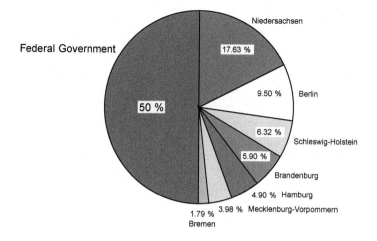

FIGURE 4.2: Financial contribution of the states to the HLRN-III investment costs.

Three supercomputer systems have been installed until today: HLRN-I (IBM p690) in 2002, HLRN-II (SGI Altix) in 2008, and HLRN-III (Cray XC30) in 2013. These systems are jointly operated at Zuse Institute Berlin (ZIB) and at Leibniz University IT Service (LUIS) in Hanover.

HLRN-I: The consortium had a late start with the HLRN-I, because in a competition situation, the German Science Council decided that Leibniz-Rechenzentrum Munich (LRZ) should install a national supercomputer in summer 2000 instead of HLRN. Thus the HLRN had to wait. When it finally started, the procurement was complicated by the fact that one of the bidders sued the consortium by claiming that the decision was biased. While this claim was never substantiated and eventually rejected by the court, the law case took almost one year of valuable time. Finally, the system was installed at the two HLRN sites in Berlin and Hanover in 2002. The HLRN-I was a 5 Tflop/s category supercomputer from IBM with 1024 Power 4 processors and a main memory of 2 TB.

HLRN-II: The procurement of the HLRN-II went more smoothly, despite the fact that the HLRN alliance had to submit two proposals in short succession to the German Science Council because of changes in the federal funding scheme. Again, a European call for tenders was issued. SGI won the competition and delivered a well-balanced supercomputer consisting of Altix ICE 8200 (Harpertown), Altix ICE 8200 Plus (Nehalem), Altix XE250, and UV 1000 system components. All components were connected by dual rail 4X DDR Infiniband. The system had a total of 26,112 cores and 128 TB of main memory.

FIGURE 4.3: Cray XC30 "Konrad" at ZIB in the first installation phase.

HLRN-III: With the long and time-consuming application process for HPC resources in Germany in mind, the HLRN consortium started the planning process for the HLRN-III already in the year 2009/2010, that is, shortly after the installation of the predecessor system. In spring 2011, the HLRN-III-proposal was submitted to the WR and DFG. After their positive decision, the HLRN alliance mandated ZIB to coordinate the Europe-wide procurement. All relevant HPC vendors were asked to participate. After several negotiation rounds Cray's bid was formally accepted and the competing bidders were informed. The contract was signed in December 2012 and the system was delivered in August 2013. From then on, it went very fast: Cray needed only a bit more than one week to install the XC30 from scratch at our premises. The more time-consuming and often underestimated part of such an installation is the overall system configuration with all the dependencies between the various support servers (login, batch, data mover, firewalls, monitoring, accounting, etc.). This is especially true for the HLRN system with its unique "single-system view" that provides a single user access to resource and project management, as well as accounting for a system that is operated at the two sites in Berlin and Hanover.

4.2.4 Benchmarks or How We Found "Mrs. Perfect"

This section is a short excursion on how we searched for "Mrs. Perfect"—the HLRN-III system. As in real life, finding the perfect system which matches the requirements of their users, administrators and – last but not least – the capabilities of the providers, is far from being an easy task. And yes – we found an almost "Mrs. Perfect" ...

We received proposals from many well-known HPC vendors on our European procurement (RFP). The selection process was primarily guided by the performance results of the *HLRN-III Benchmark Suite*. This benchmark suite aims to rate the overall compute and I/O performance of the two-site HLRN-III configuration over the operating time with optional two installation phases. Thus, the idea is to rate the performance of different HLRN-III configurations during the negotiation stage at the end by a single score.

The HLRN-III benchmark comprises the application benchmark as its major part and is complemented by an I/O benchmark section and the HPCC [15] benchmark to gain insight into low-level characteristics of the system architecture. Each of these benchmark sections are differently weighted with the major impact by results of the application benchmark.

Application Benchmark. The HLRN-III has to serve a broad range of HPC applications across various scientific disciplines in the North-German science community. Therefore, and not for the first time, our RFP and subsequent decision-making process was based on a balanced set of important applications running on HLRN resources. The balance here refers to cover a representative spectrum of traditional and foreseeable major applications across the HLRN users community.

The application benchmark is composed of eight program packages: BQCD [17], CP2K [23], PALM and PALM/particle [18], OpenFOAM [9], NEMO [8], FESOM [24], and FRESCO [4]. Workloads for the benchmark suite are defined by the HLRN benchmark team in close cooperation with major stakeholders from the different scientific fields. Reference benchmark results were obtained on the HLRN-II configuration with representative input data sets and possibly utilizing large portions of the HLRN-II resources.

I/O Benchmarks. The I/O benchmark suite include the IOR [6] and MDTEST [7] benchmark code, and is used (i) to measure the I/O bandwidth to the global file systems (HOME, WORK) and (ii) to evaluate the metadata performance of the parallel file system, i.e., the achievable file creation, remove, and stat operations per time interval.

Performance Rating Methodology. Our goal was to maximize the work that can be carried out on the computer system over its total operation time. With the *HLRN-III Benchmark Rating Procedure* (described below) this overall serviceable work is calculated.

Our rating procedure is based on the fundamental assumption that the work which can be carried out by the system is equally split across the various user communities – the HLRN policy implies no bias towards a specific science and engineering field. Each of the stakeholders is ideally represented by one of the application benchmarks. The achievable sustained performance of each of the application benchmarks determines the amount of work per community within the system's operating time. Together with the assumption described above the geometric mean of all application benchmarks gives an average performance of a system configuration – the *key performance indicator* – which then can be translated to the target value of work which can be delivered by the system.

To allow for flexibility in terms of up-to-date technology the vendors were allowed to offer a second installation phase with a technology-update or complete hardware exchange. In that case, the vendor has an additional degree of freedom in choosing an optimal point in time for a second installation phase. Again, the optimization target was to maximize the overall work which can be delivered by the system – now a time-weighted sum of each key performance indicator per installation phase.

For each of the application benchmarks a minimum performance was defined in the RFP making sure that the new system shows no performance degradation for a specific application case. Thus, the minimum performance serves as a strong penalty in the evaluation. The application performance is measured on a fully loaded system with as many application instances as possible. If necessary, the system is filled up with a HPL run. Application performance is either determined inside the application itself (if simple operation counts can be captured), or application wall-times are converted to performance numbers by predefined operations counts.

We did not want to leave the reader of this section without disclosing at least one benchmark number, that is the HPL performance. The two Cray XC30 systems of the first installation phase are rated with a Linpack performance (R_{max}) of 295.7 TFlop/s each. With that, the two MPP components of HLRN-III were ranked at position 120 and 121 in the November 2013 issue of the TOP500 list, respectively. A big leap in the ranking was achieved with the second installation phase of HLRN-III, which was ranked at position 51 in the November 2014 list.

4.3   Scientific Domains and Workloads

The projects at HLRN cover a wide variety of scientific areas and research topics with different computational demands. Therefore, the HLRN configuration with the Cray XC30 system and its additional resources like SMP nodes and the pre-/post-processing nodes constitutes a general-purpose HPC system. This poses a challenge to both, the system configuration and the operational parameters, e.g., of the batch system.

The CPU time usage breakdown on the HLRN-II system in the year 2013 across different scientific domains is shown in Figure 4.4. While the percentage of the various disciplines varies from year to year, the long-term average keeps almost the same. Note that there is some variation in the classification of

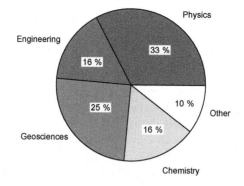

FIGURE 4.4: CPU time usage breakdown on the HLRN-II in 2013.

projects, e.g., in material sciences, since they can be either accounted under chemistry or physics, depending on their scientific focus or the users' home department.

The job sizes in terms of node counts, memory requirements and wall-time are determined by the problem sizes. First the problem has to fit into memory, and if parallel efficiency and scalability of the code and the problem allows, the number of used nodes can be increased to obtain a shorter time to solution.

The workload is a broad mix of all kinds of job types. Among the projects we observe two extremes.

The first type of projects submit hundreds or thousands of independent jobs ("job clouds") that themselves are either moderately or massively parallel computations. In principle, these workloads are able to adapt to the system utilization. Projects in particle physics domain are prominent representatives for this kind of workload.

Projects of the second type conduct only a small number of simulations that require a long total runtime until the desired solution is obtained. Here each computation should be performed in one long run, requiring several days, weeks or even months of wall-clock time. System stability considerations as well as fair-share aspects in the overall system usage have led us to the policy of limiting the maximum job run time. For the affected projects this implies the ability of application level checkpoint/restart capabilities. These projects may require special treatment by the batch system (e.g., special queues with longer wall-time limits, reservations). Climate development or long-term statistics for unsteady fluid-dynamic flow are typical examples for this type of work flow. The requirements of all other projects lies in between the extremes described above.

An increasing number of scientific workflows are impacted by the I/O capabilities. Massive data transfer to/from disk throughout the course of a simulation can occur. The I/O operations can be concentrated on one or very few files up to several files per MPI task, leading to a I/O management from several thousands to tens of thousands of files per job, sometimes written in each simulated time step. The overall amount of data transferred in one job can reach terabytes of data.

Especially those projects with big result data sets face the problem of demanding pre- and post-processing procedures. This part of their work flow can often be more time consuming than the computations themselves. Thus these projects need to carefully balance their data production with the capabilities of pre- and postprocessing their data.

In summary we can say that for many projects the available resources – not only on the computational side – determine the problem size they can tackle. The projects simply adapt to the given conditions, i.e., they focus on what is feasible.

4.4   Research Fields Exploiting the HLRN-III

Scientists from a broad spectrum of research fields exploit the HLRN-III resources to solve challenging questions. In the following, we briefly focus on the major scientific fields of chemistry and material science, earth sciences, engineering, and physics.

4.4.1   Chemistry and Material Sciences

The Chemistry and Materials Science projects range from high-level *ab initio* electronic structure calculations on systems of only few atoms in size to coarse-grained dynamics simulations of macromolecular systems. The simulation codes used here are mostly academic and were developed by community members, only few require license fees. Many of the current user projects at HLRN employ either empirical inter-atomic potential functions or density functional theory (DFT) for the description of their model systems. The former applies, for example, to molecular dynamics simulations of proteins, other biomolecules, and transport processes. DFT is the workhorse to perform electronic structure calculations on new materials for hydrogen storage, photoelectrolysis, molecular electronics, and spintronics. It is also employed at HLRN to describe properties of transition metal oxide aggregates, nanostructured semiconductors, functionalized oxide surfaces and supported graphene, as well as zeolite and metal-organic framework catalysts (Figure 4.5).

Plane wave DFT codes. Modern plane wave basis set DFT codes make use of several parallelization schemes. Most prominent is the distribution of plane wave coefficients and real-space grid points during fast Fourier transforms. Here the scaling behavior is limited by the size of both the model system and the plane wave basis set. The distribution of k-points for the Brillouin zone sampling and/or the replication of system images allows for a rather

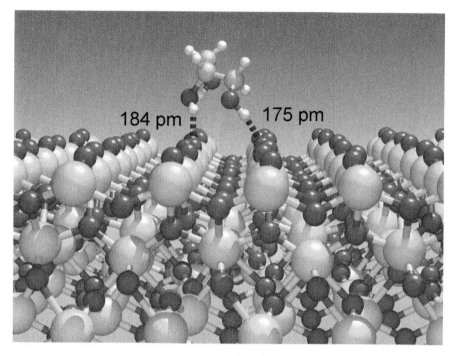

FIGURE 4.5: Hydrogen bond distances of a glycerol molecule adsorbed at the surface of a zirconia crystal.

simple extension of the code scalability. More advanced techniques involve the definition and distribution of task groups for a simultaneous treatment of electron orbitals. This can be of particular importance in hybrid functional DFT calculations where an efficient calculation of Fock exchange contributions is key to an improved code performance. Last but not least, distributed linear algebra and OpenMP threading can be applied on top. Overall, these measures allow for plane wave DFT calculations with acceptable scaling behavior over several thousands of CPU cores.

4.4.2 Earth Sciences

Because of its coastal location, the earth sciences domain plays an important role in the HLRN alliance. Projects are conducted in atmospheric sciences, meteorology, oceanography, and climate research. The HPC codes used in the projects are mostly developed within the community and can therefore be adapted from one computer generation to the next. As an important application in this field we present the PALM application which is used in a number of projects on the HLRN system.

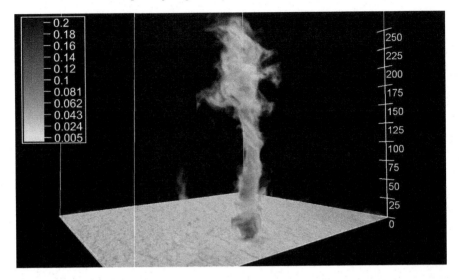

FIGURE 4.6: Dust devil simulated with PALM with height/diameter of about 250m/20m. The scale on the left shows dust concentration in g/m^3. The displayed area of 200x200 m^2 represents only a small part of the total simulated domain. (Image courtesy of PALM group, Inst. für Meteorologie und Klimatologie, Leibniz Universität Hannover.)

PALM, a *PArallelized Large-eddy simulation Model* (Figure 4.6) for atmospheric and oceanic flows [10], is a code that was especially designed for massively parallel computer architectures with a focus on highly scalable methods for all parts of the simulation process chain (numerics, I/O, and visualization). It is developed at the Institute of Meteorology and Climatology (IMUK) at the Leibniz Universität Hannover.

PALM exhibits excellent scaling and has been tested on up to 32,000 cores so far. Scalability has been proven on the Cray XC30 at HLRN-III by simulations with 4320^3 grid points that require about 13 TByte memory. The largest simulation conducted with PALM used 5600^3 (about $2 \cdot 10^{11}$) grid points.

Data analysis is done online in PALM (during model runs) in order to avoid I/O bottlenecks. The topography is realized on a cartesian grid which allows for steep topography. PALM uses non-cyclic horizontal boundary conditions including turbulent inflow. The code can be switched to an ocean version with salinity equation and equation of state for seawater. A parallelized Lagrangian particle model is embedded for various applications (e.g., footprint calculation, simulation of cloud droplet growth, and visualization). The PALM interface allows users to plug in their own code extensions without modifying the program core routines.

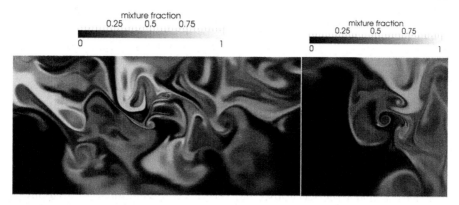

FIGURE 4.7: Large eddy simulation of passive scalar mixing at Reynolds number 10000 and Schmidt number 1000 along the centerline (left) and along the cross-section (right) of a mixing device. The volume of interest is 2x1x1 mm resolved with approximately 200 mio. cells using OpenFOAM on 2000 cores. (Images courtesy of Institute for Modeling and Numerical Simulation (LEMOS), Faculty of Mechanical Engineering and Marine Technology, University of Rostock.)

4.4.3 Engineering

The projects in engineering sciences cover an extreme wide range of scientific fields including fluid dynamics, combustion, aerodynamics, acoustics and (bio)mechanics. One focus of the typical North-German research profile at HLRN is on ship hydromechanics and naval technologies. Other research topics are flow optimization, aerodynamics and acoustics of planes, wings, cars, trucks, and trains, also in gas turbine engines, fans, and on propellers for higher flow efficiency. This area is also important in ship hull and propeller design with respect to drag and cavitation reduction and stability. Environmental aspects are important in research on fuel efficiency, pollutants and noise reduction in combustion processes. Some biomechanics projects use engineering codes and methods for their research on skeletal structures, bones and teeth. Our engineering projects use commercially licensed codes, community-developed and locally inhouse-developed codes.

OpenFOAM (Open Field Operation and Manipulation) [9] is a typical application from engineering sciences which is used in a number of projects at HLRN (Figure 4.7). The open source CFD toolbox OpenFOAM, written in C++, has a large user base across many areas of engineering and science, from both commercial and academic organizations. It has an extensive range of features to solve anything from complex fluid flows involving chemical reactions, turbulence and heat transfer, to solid dynamics and electro-magnetics. It includes tools for meshing and for pre- and post-processing. Almost everything (including meshing, and pre- and post-processing) runs in parallel as standard to take full advantage of the available computer hardware. At HLRN, OpenFOAM simulation runs are using up to 4000 cores (MPI tasks) per job.

4.4.4   Physics

Projects in physics cover elementary particle physics, astrophysics and aspects of material science. The simulation programs in use are in-house or community-developed codes.

As a key application for physics projects we present *PHOENIX* [11] developed by the Hauschildt group (Astrophysics Inst., University of Hamburg). PHOENIX is a general-purpose model atmosphere simulation package. It is designed to model the structures and spectra of a wide range of astrophysical objects, from extrasolar planets (both terrestrial and gas giant planets) to brown dwarfs and all classes of stars, extending to novae and supernovae (Figure 4.8). The main results from the calculations are synthetic spectra (and derived quantities, such as colors), these can be directly compared to observed spectra and, in 3D simulations, images. By adjusting the simulation parameters and comparing the results to the observed data, the physical parameters of the stars or planets can be determined.

Major physics features of the PHOENIX astrophysics code are 1D and 3D radiative transfer module based on a non-local operator splitting method; direct calculation of spectral line opacities with individual line profiles for atomic and molecular species (for a total of about 20 billion lines in a master

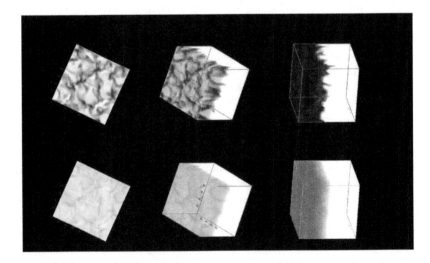

FIGURE 4.8: Visualization of the results for continuum 3D radiation transfer for a stellar convection model for pure absorption (top panel) and strong scattering (bottom panel). A total of about 1.5 billion intensities are calculated for each iteration with PHOENIX/3D.

database); and an operator splitting method for multi-level non-local thermodynamic equilibrium modeling of atoms and molecules (in 1D and 3D) with very large model atoms and molecules. The radiative transfer modules support special relativistic velocity fields in Lagrangian and Eulerian reference frames.

The PHOENIX package has been designed for parallel computers since 1993, the current version uses a hierarchical MPI based parallelization scheme. PHOENIX has in total 1.3 mio. lines of code (Fortran 2003, C/C++). Parallel PHOENIX/3D simulations show strong and weak scaling with 94% efficiency to at least 131,000 processes. 3D simulations which consider non-equilibrium thermodynamics produce a minimum of 2.6 TB spectra data, saving the complete imaging information would deliver about 11 PB raw data.

4.5 HLRN-III System Architecture

As its predecessors, the HLRN-III consists of two complexes each operated by the providers ZIB in Berlin and LUIS in Hanover, respectively. The two complexes, *"Konrad"* in Berlin and *"Gottfried"* in Hanover, are connected by a dedicated 10 Gbps fiber link. Figure 4.9 depicts the overall architecture of the HLRN-III system.

The HLRN-III system is the first one in the HLRN consortium which is not completely symmetrically configured across the two operational sites. With the installation of the second phase in October 2014, the MPP component in Berlin will provide more computational power whereas the installation in Hanover uniquely includes SMP nodes. The first installation phase comprises at *each site* a four cabinet Cray XC30 system with 744 nodes (Figure 4.11) with 24 Intel Ivybridge cores each, 46.5 TB distributed memory and 1.4 PB on-line disk storage (Lustre).

The Cray XC30 (Figure 4.12) is configured homogeneously in the first installation phase, that is, no accelerators are integrated into the compute nodes. A heterogeneous configuration may be considered for the second installation phase. For the evaluation of GPGPUs, ten of the SMP nodes at LUIS are equipped with Nvidia Kepler GPUs. To evaluate Intel's MIC architecture, a four-node Xeon Phi cluster is available at ZIB. This cluster is tightly integrated into the HLRN-III user management and the batch system and users have access to the shared HOME file system.

4.5.1 Hardware Configuration

All compute and service nodes are equipped with standard Intel x86 processors in the first installation phase. While the MPP system is built with dual-socket nodes the SMP nodes comprise a quad-socket solution (for details

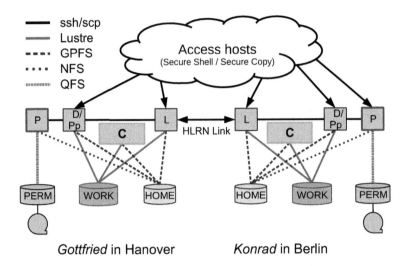

FIGURE 4.9: Schematic representation of the HLRN-III architecture with its two complexes. C: compute system consisting of XC30 and SMP nodes; L: login nodes, D: data nodes, Pp: post-processing nodes; P: archive servers.

see Table 4.2). Service nodes provide additional functionality for data movements, pre-/post-processing, and login (details are summarized in Table 4.3).

For the per site globally accessible on-line storage, two different technical solutions are chosen. The key characteristics are summarized in the following.

The HOME file system is realized as a network attached storage (NAS) with DDN SFA12K-20E GRIDScaler Appliances with a total capacity of 1.4 PB. For the XC30 compute nodes this file system is made visible via the Data Virtualization Service (DVS), which provides an aggregated I/O bandwidth of several GB/s. HOME is exported to the remaining clients (login nodes, data nodes, SMP nodes, and pre- and post-processing nodes) via General Parallel File System (GPFS) over a 10 Gbps Ethernet backbone.

The parallel file system WORK is implemented with a Cray Lustre File System (CLFS) based on DDN SFA 12K-40 block storage systems with a total capacity of 2.8 PB per site. The Lustre file system is configured with two metadata severs (MDS, active/passive) and eight object storage servers (OSS) per site. As illustrated in Figure 4.10 the Lustre servers are connected by Mellanox FDR InfiniBand to the storage system where the corresponding MDT and OST are located. Five I/O service nodes configured as LNET routers provide access to Lustre on the XC30. We measured an aggregated I/O bandwidth of more than 20 GB/s which more than doubled in the second installation phase.

These disk storage facilities are complemented by a tape library for archival storage (Oracle StorageTek) with a capacity of several PB and nearly 100 TB

TABLE 4.2: Compute nodes in the first installation phase (ZIB and LUIS).

	MPP	SMP
Total Number of Nodes	1488	32
Compute Racks	8	2
Peak FLOP Rate [TF]	686	22
Node Architecture	XC30 compute node	4 CPU sockets
	2 CPU sockets (diskless)	
CPU	Intel Xeon E5-2695v2	Intel Xeon E5-4650
CPU Microarchitecture	IvyBridge	SandyBridge
CPU Frequency [GHz]	2.4	2.7
Cores per CPU	12	8
CPU Count per Node	2	4
Memory Capacity [GB]	64	256
Memory Frequency [Mhz]	1866	1600
Node PCIe	Gen 3	Gen 3
Interconnection Network	Aries network	InfiniBand FDR
Data Network		10 Gbps Ethernet
Local Disk Space [TB]	-	10 (RAID6)
Global Disk Space [PB]	2.8 WORK	
	1.4 HOME	

TABLE 4.3: Service nodes in the first installation phase (ZIB and LUIS).

	Login	Data	Post-processing
Total Number of Nodes	4	8	4
Node Architecture	2 CPU sockets	4 CPU sockets	4 CPU sockets
CPU	Intel Xeon	Intel Xeon	Intel Xeon
	E5-2670	E5-2609	E5-4650
CPU Microarchitecture	SandyBridge	SandyBridge	SandyBridge
CPU Frequency [GHz]	2.6	2.4	2.7
Cores per CPU	8	4	8
CPU Count per Node	2	2	4
Memory Capacity [GB]	256	64	768
Memory Frequency [MHz]	1333	1600	1600
Node PCIe	Gen 3	Gen 3	Gen 3
GPU	-	-	NVIDIA K4000
GPU Count per Node	-	-	1
GPU Memory Capacity [GB]	-	-	3
Interconnection Network	InfiniBand FDR	InfiniBand FDR	InfiniBand FDR
Data Network	10 Gbps Ethernet	10 Gbps Ethernet	10 Gbps Ethernet
Local Disk Space [TB]	0.9 (RAID1)	2 (RAID1)	2 (RAID1)

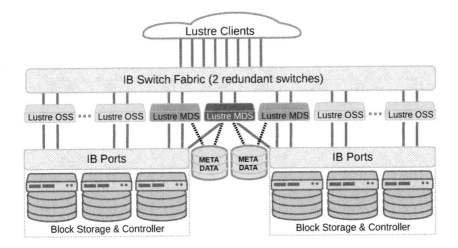

FIGURE 4.10: Architecture of the Lustre filesystem in the first installation phase of the HLRN-III system for one site.

online disk caches in the first installation phase. This hierarchical storage management system is based on Oracle's SAM-QFS which is run on two servers for fault tolerance.

For the second installation phase, additional nodes with Intel x86 processor technology and an extension of the storage capacity are planned (see Tables 4.4 and 4.5 for an overview of the final configuration).

4.6   Software Ecosystem

4.6.1   System Software

The XC30 is operated under the Cray Linux Environment (CLE), v. 5, which is based on the SUSE Linux Enterprise (SLES). As part of the CLE, the compute nodes are run under Compute Node Linux (CNL), a lightweight operating system which avoids the overhead of a full-fledged Linux kernel. The SMP nodes, the data nodes, and the pre- and post-processing nodes use SLES version 11. A third operating system, Sun Solaris, is used on the archive nodes, because they host the SAM-QFS software of the hierarchical storage management system.

System administration is performed by Cray's Hardware Supervisory System (HSS) with a System Maintenance Workstation (SMW) as a central point of control. The servers that are external to the XC30 (e.g., Lustre, SMP, data,

FIGURE 4.11: A Cray XC30 blade with four compute nodes with two sockets each (in the back) and the Aries router chip in the front.

TABLE 4.4: Compute nodes of the prospective final system (ZIB and LUIS).

	‖ MPP	│ SMP
Total Number of Nodes	3552	64
Compute Racks	19	4
Peak FLOP Rate [TF]	2589	44
Node Architecture	XC30 compute node	4 CPU sockets
	2 CPU sockets (diskless)	
CPU	Intel Xeon	Intel Xeon
CPU Microarchitecture	IvyBridge, Haswell	SandyBride, IvyBridge
CPU Count per Node	2	4
Memory Capacity [GB]	64	256, 512
Interconnect	Aries network	InfiniBand FDR
Data Network		10 Gbps Ethernet
Local Disk Space [TB]	-	10, 20 (RAID6)
Global Disk Space [PB]	8.4 WORK	
	1.4 HOME	

FIGURE 4.12: Cray XC30 Aries network cabling between two cabinets. (Image courtesy of Cray Inc.)

TABLE 4.5: Service nodes of the prospective final system (ZIB and LUIS).

	Login	Data	Post-processing
Total Number of Nodes	8	8	8
Node Architecture	2 CPU sockets	4 CPU sockets	4 CPU sockets
CPU	Intel Xeon	Intel Xeon	Intel Xeon
CPU Microarchitecture	SandyBridge, IvyBridge	SandyBridge, SandyBridge	SandyBridge, IvyBridge
CPU Count per Node	2	2	4
Memory Capacity [GB]	256	64	768, 1536
GPU	-	-	NVIDIA
GPU Count per Node	-	-	1
Interconnect	InfiniBand FDR	InfiniBand FDR	InfiniBand FDR
Data Network	10 Gbps Ethernet	10 Gbps Ethernet	10 Gbps Ethernet
Local Disk Space [TB]	0.9 (RAID1)	2 (RAID1)	2, 4 (RAID1)

TABLE 4.6: Overview of HLRN-III system software.

Cluster administration	Cray Hardware Supervisory System Bright Cluster Manager
Login Node OS *Compute Node OS* *Data Node OS* *Pre-/Post-processing Node OS* *Parallel Filesystem*	Cray Linux Environment 5 Cray Compute Node Linux SUSE Linux Enterprise Server 11 SUSE Linux Enterprise Server 11 Lustre 2.4 / CentOS 6
Job Scheduler *Resource Manager*	Moab HPC Suite Entreprise Edition Torque
Software management	Modules environment package

pre-/post-processing, login) are controlled by the Bright Cluster manager from Bright Computing [2] which runs on two dedicated servers configured as a high availability (HA) cluster.

For the system monitoring the Icinga tool [5] was configured by the HLRN system administrators. It is used to monitor the status of the various servers, including their utilization, power consumption, temperature, and other metrics.

The HLRN resources are managed by Moab/Torque from Adaptive Computing [1] in the HPC Entreprise Edition as batch system. Its stability in the former HLRN-II system and the possibility of fine-tuning the workflow via several parameters lead to the decision to use Moab on HLRN-III. Torque starts the user applications on the XC30 compute nodes via the Application Level Placement Scheduler (ALPS) running on the SDB node. The grid functionality of Moab allows to submit jobs from either side, Berlin or Hanover; see Section 4.9 on the single system view.

Other infrastructure for monitoring, license management, system and user support, mail service, and project management was taken from the installation of the predecessor systems. This site-specific software is vendor-independent and is therefore incrementally improved over the years. For hardware consolidation most of these services run in a virtualized environment based on KVM and oVirt.

We use the *Environment Modules* package from the environment modules project [3] to handle multiple compiler environments, libraries and the large number of installed applications in various versions.

4.6.2 Software for Program Development and Optimization

For the HLRN-III system, complete tool-chains for program development, runtime/performance analysis and debugging from Cray, Intel and the open source community (e.g., GNU project) are installed (see Table 4.7 for details).

TABLE 4.7: Software for program development and performance analysis.

Compilers	Cray Compiling Environment GNU Compiler Collection Intel C/C++ and Fortran compiler
PROGRAMMING MODELS *Distributed Memory* *Shared Memory*	 Cray Message Passing Toolkit (MPI, Shmem) Intel MPI Co-array Fortran, UPC, Co-array C++, Global Arrays OpenMP, OpenACC, pthreads
Debugging Tools *Performance Tools*	Allinea Distributed Debugging Tool TotalView Debugger Cray Performance Measurement & Analysis Tools Intel VTune, ITAC, Inspector PAPI
Scripting frameworks	Python, Perl, Java, Tcl/Tk

4.6.3　Application Software, Packages and Libraries

The HLRN HPC Consultants maintain a wide range of application software for scientific projects. The software is centrally installed by HLRN staff and available to all HLRN users, as far as license conditions permit. Table 4.8 lists the application software available for various general as well as special application areas. Aside from the open-source code OpenFOAM, the engineering software is available through commercially available licenses. The chemistry and material science codes are either commercially or academically licensed. Libraries and tools are provided by Cray as well as by HLRN staff.

TABLE 4.8: Application software, packages, and libraries.

Engineering	ABAQUS, ANSYS, ANSYS/CFX, ANSYS/FLUENT, OpenFOAM, STAR-CD, STAR-CCM+
Chemistry and *Material Sciences*	ABINIT, CP2K, CPMD, CRYSTAL, Desmond, GAMESS-US, Gaussian, GROMACS, LAMMPS, NAMD, NWChem, TURBOMOLE, VASP
Numerics	Cray Scientific and Math Libraries (SciLib), GNU Scientific Library (GSL), Intel Math Kernel Library (MKL), FFTW, PETSc, ScaLAPACK/BLACS, SLEPc, SuiteSparse, Trilinos, Cray TPSL, Numpy, Scipy
Tools and libraries *for data manipulation*	netCDF, pnetCDF, HDF5, CGNS, NCL, SPLASH, CDO Operators, NCO Tools
Visualisation tools	Ferret, GrADS, Splash, Visit, GNUplot, NcView

TABLE 4.9: Data storage systems at HLRN-III.

Name	Purpose	Availability	Properties	Backup
HOME	small data, program build	on all nodes of each complex	quotas	backup, snapshots
WORK	temporary storage, program build, simulation data	on login, compute, data, post nodes	big, fast; quotas	no backup
TMPDIR	temporary for a single job or interactive session	on login, compute, data, post nodes	big, fast; quotas	no backup
PERM	permanent long-term storage of large data	on archive nodes	very big, slow; limited file number, tape quotas	no backup, storage on tapes

4.7 Storage Strategy and Pre- and Post-Processing

On each HLRN complex (Berlin and Hanover) the HLRN supports four data storage systems which differ in terms of available disk space, enforced usage model, access time, and backup support. Table 4.9 gives an overview over the storage systems and their relevant properties.

Besides the login nodes for program development and job steering, both complexes have four data mover nodes for data transfer operations and data intensive pre- and post-processing tasks.

The two pre- and post-processing nodes are installed on each site for very memory-intensive data processing and pre-/post-processing work. These machines have four CPU sockets per node, 768 GB of memory and 4 TB of local disk space. For visualization steps each of them is equipped with a Nvidia Quadro K4000 graphics card.

4.8 Data Center Facility

The HLRN-III is operated at two sites, ZIB/Berlin and LUIS/Hanover, which are linked via a 10 Gbps dedicated fiber optics cable of approximately 300 km. Fault tolerance is provided by a separate XWIN link which is leased at the German National Research and Education Network (DFN). While this redundant link is slightly longer than 300 km, the latency stays almost the same, because both sites are level-1 nodes of the DFN.

TABLE 4.10: Conversion rate of resources utilization to NPL currency.

Resource Utilization	NPL
1 MPP node (IvyBridge, 24 cores, 64 GB) * 1 h	2
1 SMP node (SandyBridge, 32 cores, 256 GB) * 1 h	4
1 Pre-/Post-processing node (SandyBridge, 32 cores, 768 GB) * 1 h	6

The system is operated 24/7 in a high-security room with an automatic fire extinguishing system and an uninterruptable power supply which sustains the support servers and the file systems. The Cray XC30 is completely water cooled and it accepts a wide range of temperatures. This facilitates the installation, and it also allows to operate the system with a high ΔT, which in turn reduces the PUE.

4.9 Accounting and User Management: Single System View over Two Sites

Currently about 700 users in more than 130 projects are using the two HLRN-III installations[4]. Access to the HLRN resources is granted by the *Scientific Board* (see Section 4.2.1) which meets four times a year to decide on the allocation of resources to projects. Usually quarterly allocations are granted for one year with a possibility to request a prolongation at the next deadline.

The challenge for the HLRN user and project management including accounting results from the need to support various resource types on a coherent level and to provide a single system view for the user regarding resource allocation and utilization (accounting).

The HLRN offers different kinds of resource types: MPP, SMP, pre- and post-processing nodes. To establish a single metric across these different node types including past and future HLRN architectures, it was decided that the granting/accounting is not based on CPU hours but on an own currency called *NPL* for "North-German parallel computer processing unit." With that, we are able to decouple the granting of resources from specific technical hardware details (see Table 4.10).

By means of a *central user and project management, accounting and authorization* a single system view is provided. It allows, for example, to submit jobs to any site, independent of the current user's login site (see Fig. 4.13).

---

[4]See https://www.hlrn.de/home/view/Service/Projects for the list of projects.

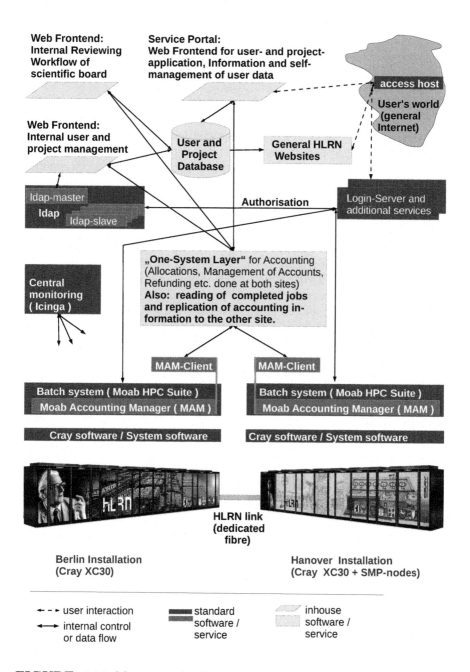

FIGURE 4.13: Managing the Berlin and Hanover installations as a single HPC system.

The batch and accounting systems (Moab HPC Suite Enterprise Edition) provide on both sites raw accounting data. Our self-developed software layer manages both installations as a single system (*single-system layer*). The user and project management is based on in-house software using a *central* MySQL database. All authorization requests are managed by one *central LDAP server* which is supported by several slave-instances for redundancy.

The *single-system layer* is a suite of HLRN-developed programs using the client software to interact with the two local accounting systems. It allows to fulfill tasks like creation of project accounts or depositing an allocation into a specific fund at both sites with a single command, hiding the real nature of two separated system installations and guaranteeing consistent user/accounting information at both sides. Completed jobs at one site are charged also at the other site with a deferment of up to twelve hours – this limits communication overhead and turned out to be acceptable in the past as limited overdrawing of the given allocations is tolerable within our scientific community.

Web interfaces allow the users to inform themselves in a convenient way, e.g., about used and remaining NPL, as well as managing their data, e.g., membership of projects (with respect to their privileges implemented by a role concept of "users," "project members," "project administrators" and "project leaders"). For convenience, unused allocations are automatically forwarded from one quarter to the next. But this is done only once, as otherwise the system might become unpredictable as real usage and granted resources could drift apart too widely.

Our user and project management was deliberately implemented in an architecture-independent way. This allowed the users to keep their well-known workflow with only minor adaptations when moving from HLRN-I over HLRN-II to HLRN-III.

4.10   Preparing for the Future

4.10.1   Second Phase Installation of HLRN-III

At the time of writing (November 2014), the second phase of the HLRN-III system has just been installed. The system now comprises a total of 3552 XC30 compute nodes, each with two sockets. The date of the upgrade was carefully chosen so that we could benefit by the newly available Haswell chip. While this means that there will be two different CPU types in the XC30 (Ivy Bridge and Haswell), the differences in their microarchitecture are less impacting on the systems operation.

In our view, two-staged HPC installations are advantageous for technological and economical reasons. The HLRN-III users benefited from the early availability of a relatively small XC30 system with a peak performance of 686

FIGURE 4.14: Cray XC30 "Konrad" at ZIB in its final installation.

TFlop/s in September 2013, which was almost quadrupled to a peak performance of 2.589 TFlop/s in November 2014. The upgrade is accompanied by a doubling in the number of SMP servers, pre- and post-processing servers, login servers and disk space. For an overview on the hardware specs see Tables 4.4 and 4.5.

Figure 4.14 illustrates the ten XC30 cabinets of the final configuration of the "Konrad" system at ZIB. With nine racks the Hanover "Gottfried" system is slightly smaller, but it is complemented by 64 SMP nodes which are exclusively available at the Hanover site. Apart from the easier system administration, this has the advantage of cheaper license costs for ISV software packages.

Furthermore, an eleventh XC30 cabinet is available at ZIB for early experiments with innovative many-core devices and solid state memory. We regard both as important architectural innovations for future computer systems: the former will pave the way towards exascale computers with millions of computing nodes, while the latter will become vital for the expected fusion of high-performance computing with big data processing.

4.10.2 Many-Core in HPC

The Cray XC30 architecture has at its heart an interconnect infrastructure which enables scalability at today's application requirements level. Furthermore, many-core devices (Nvidia GPU, Intel MIC) can be integrated to build a heterogeneous system which is attractive for certain compute-bound applications with sufficient parallelism. We believe that within the next few years, heterogeneous compute and storage architectures will become more and more mainstream in HPC to leverage compute and storage resources without sacrificing the power envelope.

With the HLRN-III infrastructure we want to address the challenge of developing and optimizing workloads for many-core platforms. One key element to foster activities in that matter is an interdisciplinary collaboration between developers of scientific simulation and analysis methods and computer scientists.

With respect to the envisaged growing importance of many-core computing in HPC, we evaluated in the *Parallel and Distributed Computing* group at ZIB disruptive processing technologies, including FPGAs, ClearSpeed, and Cell BE processors [22, 20, 19, 16], as well as general-purpose GPUs [21, 13, 25, 14], and recently the MIC architecture [27, 26].

Our research work in the area of many-core computing is continued in the context of the *Research Center for Many-core High-Performance Computing*, which was founded in 2013 as one of the first five Intel Parallel Computing Centers (IPCC). This research center aims at porting and improving HPC workloads on many-core technologies. Additionally, we provide best-practice experiences for many-core code developers and we develop low-level system software, e.g., faster offloading of HPC code on many-core devices.

4.10.3   HLRN-IV and Beyond

It does not require much clairvoyance to predict that we will be witnessing a major paradigm change in high-performance computing in the next few years. Due to physical, technical, and economical reasons the design of faster supercomputers is only possible by bundling millions of processors. Future HPC systems will have a reasonably fast interconnection network for asynchronous process communication. Full bisection bandwidth may not be expected—again for physical, technological, and economical reasons. The system memory will be split into different levels with different access latencies, throughput and consistency guarantees.

Perhaps the biggest challenge will be the fact that the whole system, which is made up of numerous single components, will have a low mean time between failure (MTBF). Hence, mechanisms for fault-tolerance are needed, either at the system or the application level. Traditional disk-based checkpoint strategies are insufficient because the secondary storage is too slow.

On the software side, such systems will require a rethinking in the way that HPC code is designed today. Since HPC systems are targeted for capability computing rather than capacity computing, users expect *strong scaling*, that is, they expect their code to run faster with increasing utilized resources (system size). This cannot be achieved by just porting the code onto a new system, but the code must be re-engineered to take full advantage of the abundance of CPUs, the faster network and the distributed memories.

System models are getting more complicated compared to former times. Today, it is no longer sufficient for code developers to be experts in their respective application fields, but they also need to have a good understanding on technical and theoretical issues of computer science. We therefore believe that it is of prime importance to extend our HPC consulting staff at ZIB—both in the application domain and in computer science. Small expert groups must be brought together to aid the users in rethinking their scientific methods, enhancing or replacing their algorithms, and improving their HPC codes. Our increasingly tightened collaboration with colleagues in applied mathematics, in various application domains and in innovative HPC architecture is just a first step.

Bibliography

[1] Adaptive Computing, Inc. http://www.adaptivecomputing.com.

[2] Bright Computing, Inc. http://www.brightcomputing.com.

[3] Environment Modules Project. http://modules.sourceforge.net.

[4] Finite-Volume Navier-Stokes procedure FreSCo. http://www.tuhh.de/alt/fds/research/current-projects/fresco.html.

[5] Icinga: Open Source Monitoring. http://www.icinga.org.

[6] IOR HPC Benchmark. http://sourceforge.net/projects/ior-sio/.

[7] mdtest HPC Benchmark. http://sourceforge.net/projects/mdtest/.

[8] Nucleus for European Modelling of the Ocean (NEMO). http://www.nemo-ocean.eu.

[9] OpenFOAM. http://www.openfoam.org.

[10] PArallelized Large-eddy simulation Model for atmospheric and oceanic flows (PALM). http://palm.muk.uni-hannover.de.

[11] PHOENIX. http://www.hs.uni-hamburg.de/EN/For/ThA/phoenix.

[12] Peter Deuflhard and Jürgen Gottschewski. Das Konrad-Zuse-Zentrum für Informationstechnik Berlin. Struktur, wissenschaftliches Konzept und Einbettung in die Region. *ZIB Technical Report TR 95-12*, Oct. 1995.

[13] Sebastian Dressler and Thomas Steinke. Energy consumption of CUDA kernels with varying thread topology. *Computer Science - Research and Development*, pages 1–9, 2012.

[14] Sebastian Dressler and Thomas Steinke. An Automated Approach for Estimating the Memory Footprint of Non-linear Data Objects. In *Euro-Par 2013: Parallel Processing Workshops*, volume 8374 of *Lecture Notes in Computer Science*, pages 249–258. Springer, 2014.

[15] Piotr R Luszczek, David H Bailey, Jack J Dongarra, Jeremy Kepner, Robert F Lucas, Rolf Rabenseifner, and Daisuke Takahashi. The HPC Challenge (HPCC) Benchmark Suite. In *Proceedings of the 2006 ACM/IEEE Conference on Supercomputing*, SC '06, New York, NY, USA, 2006. ACM.

[16] Patrick May, Gunnar W. Klau, Markus Bauer, and Thomas Steinke. Accelerated microRNA-precursor detection using the Smith-Waterman algorithm on FPGAs. In Werner Dubitzky, Assaf Schuster, Peter M. A. Sloot, Michael Schroeder, and Mathilde Romberg, editors, *GCCB*, volume 4360 of *Lecture Notes in Computer Science*, pages 19–32. Springer, 2006.

[17] Yoshifumi Nakamura and Hinnerk Stüben. BQCD - Berlin quantum chromodynamics program. In *PoS - LATTICE2010*, page 40, 2010.

[18] S. Raasch and M. Schröter. PALM - a large-eddy simulation model performing on massively parallel computers. *Meteorol. Z.*, 10:363–372, 2001.

[19] Eric Stahlberg, Michael Babst, Daryl Popig, and Thomas Steinke. Molecular Dynamics with FPGAs: A Portable API Molecular Simulations with Hardware Accelerators: A Portable Interface Definition for FPGA Supported Acceleration. In *International Supercomputing Conference 2007 (ISC 2007)*, 2007.

[20] Eric Stahlberg, Daryl Popig, Debie Ryle, Michael Babst, Mohammed Anderson, and Thomas Steinke. Molecular simulations with hardware accelerators. In *Reconfigurable Systems Summer Institute 2007 (RSSI 2007)*, 2007.

[21] Thomas Steinke, Kathrin Peter, and Sebastian Borchert. Efficiency Considerations of Cauchy Reed-Solomon Implementations on Accelerator and Multi-Core Platforms. In *Symposium on Application Accelerators in High Performance Computing (SAAHPC)*, 2010.

[22] Thomas Steinke, Alexander Reinefeld, and Thorsten Schütt. Experiences with High–Level Programming of FPGAs on Cray XD1. In *Cray Users Group (CUG 2006)*, May 2006.

[23] Joost VandeVondele, Matthias Krack, Fawzi Mohamed, Michele Parrinello, Thomas Chassaing, and Jürg Hutter. Quickstep: Fast and accurate density functional calculations using a mixed Gaussian and plane waves approach. *Computer Physics Communications*, 167(2):103–128, 2005.

[24] Q. Wang, S. Danilov, D. Sidorenko, R. Timmermann, C. Wekerle, X. Wang, T. Jung, and J. Schröter. The Finite Element Sea Ice-Ocean Model (FESOM): formulation of an unstructured-mesh ocean general circulation model. *Geoscientific Model Development Discussions*, 6(3):3893–3976, 2013.

[25] Florian Wende, Frank Cordes, and Thomas Steinke. On Improving the Performance of Multi-threaded CUDA Applications with Concurrent Kernel Execution by Kernel Reordering. *Symposium on Application Accelerators in High-Performance Computing (SAAHPC)*, 74–83, 2012.

[26] Florian Wende, Frank Cordes, and Thomas Steinke. Concurrent Kernel Execution on Xeon Phi within Parallel Heterogeneous Workloads. In F. Silva, I. Dutra, and V.S. Costa, editors, *Euro-Par 2014 Parallel Processing*, LNCS. 8632. Springer, 2014.

[27] Florian Wende and Thomas Steinke. Swendsen-Wang Multi-cluster Algorithm for the 2D/3D Ising Model on Xeon Phi and GPU. In *Proceedings of SC13: International Conference for High Performance Computing, Networking, Storage and Analysis*, SC '13, pages 83:1–83:12, New York, NY, USA, 2013. ACM.

Chapter 5

The K Computer

Mitsuo Yokokawa

*Graduate School of System Informatics, Kobe University and
Operations and Computer Technologies Division,
RIKEN Advanced Institute for Computational Science*

Fumiyoshi Shoji

*Operations and Computer Technologies Division,
RIKEN Advanced Institute for Computational Science*

Yukihiro Hasegawa

Research Organization for Information Science and Technology

5.1 Overview

Computer simulations are essential to elucidate natural phenomena such as global circulation of atmosphere, and to analyze artificial structures such as automobiles and buildings. Supercomputers which have powerful computational capability in scientific and engineering calculations are extremely important tools for such simulations. Therefore, many countries are committed to have supercomputers as a fundamental tool for national competitiveness. The performance of supercomputers has been increased during the past two decades; however, it is still insufficient to generate precise and accurate high-resolutions of simulations. Thus, the development of a supercomputer with much higher computational capability is required.

The Japanese government determined that supercomputing technology is one of the key technologies of national importance in the third Science and Technology Basic Plan, which was published in 2006. The Next-Generation Supercomputer Research and Development Project was initiated by the Ministry of Education, Culture, Sports, Science and Technology (MEXT) in 2006 as a seven-year project. RIKEN, Japan's largest comprehensive research institution [18], played a key role in the project. In cooperation with Fujitsu Ltd., RIKEN developed a next-generation supercomputer system.

We named the next-generation supercomputer "京" in Japanese and "K computer" in English after the target performance of 10 petaflops (one quadrillion floating-point operations per second or PFLOPS) in the LINPACK benchmark program. The name "京" was selected from approximately 2,000 public applications, because this kanji character stands for a Japanese prefix number indicating 10^{16} or 10 *peta* and was considered as an appropriate name for the system. The English name "K" was also determined after the same pronunciation of the kanji. Incidentally, a logo image of the K computer was written with a calligraphy-brush by a famous kanji artist, Sooun Takeda (Figure 5.1).

In October 2011, the K computer broke the 10 PFLOPS wall for the first time during the development. Development was completed successfully in June 2012, and the K computer was fully operational and officially released to the public in September 2012 (Figure 5.2).

5.1.1 Development Targets and Schedule

The objectives of the project are to develop the most advanced and high performance supercomputer system in the world and to develop and deploy its usage technologies including development of application software for various computational sciences.

Target requirements for the K computer were determined in the beginning of the project in 2006. The target requirements include the followings:

FIGURE 5.1: Logo image of the K computer.

FIGURE 5.2: A view of the K computer.

- 10 PFLOPS sustained performance in the LINPACK benchmark.

- petaflops-sustained performance in real applications.

- low power consumption and high reliablity.

- applicability to a broad range of computational science and engineering simulations.

The project schedule is shown in Figure 5.3. We started the project in 2006 with the conceptual design, which was followed by a detailed design process. A prototype system was constructed to determine if the system design could achieve the performance requirement. Production of the K computer began in 2010. The racks of the system were installed in the computer building located in Kobe, Hyogo Prefecture, Japan, in September 2010. The system

TABLE 5.1: Development history.

Date	K computer	Others
January 1, 2006		Establishment of Next-Generation Supercomputing R&D Center at RIKEN
September 19, 2006	Conceptual design was started.	
March 28, 2007		Site location was determined.
March 30, 2007		Basic design of facilities was started.
April 24, 2007	System configuration of a complex system with both scalar and vector systems was determined by RIKEN.	
July 4, 2007	Detailed design was started.	
July 31, 2007		Execution design of a computer building was started.
September 13, 2007	System configuration was approved by Council for Science and Technology Policy.	
March 21, 2008		Construction of the computer building was started.
May 13, 2009	System configuration was revised from the complex system to a scalar singly-system.	
July 17, 2009		The revised configuration was confirmed by a committee of MEXT.
May 31, 2010		Computer building finished to be built.
September 29, 2010	The first rack was installed in the computer building.	
October 2010		Logo image of the K computer was selected.

TABLE 5.1: Development history (cont'd).

Date	K computer	Others
March 31, 2011	Part of the K computer began to operate.	
June 20, 2011	LINPACK performace 8.162 PFLOPS was achieved with 672 racks and TOP 1 in TOP500 was taken.	
November 14, 2011	LINPACK performance 10.51 PFLOPS was achieved on full system and TOP 1 in TOP500 was taken again.	
November 15, 2011	TOP1 in HPCC benchmark (class 1) was awarded.	
November 17, 2011	Gordon Bell award was given for an electron state calculation of silicon nanowires.	
June 29, 2012	System development was completed.	
September 28, 2012	K computer was officially released to the public.	
November 2012	Gordon Bell award was given for simulation of gravitational evolution of dark matter.	

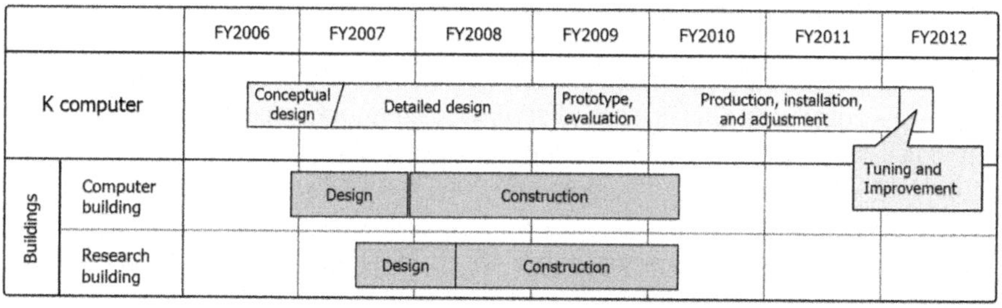

FIGURE 5.3: Development schedule of the K computer.

hardware was installed at the end of August 2011, and then system software components were developed after installation was complete. The complete system was finished in June 2012.

5.1.2 Application Software Development Programs

In 2006, two projects, the "Nano-science Grand Challenge" and the "Life-science Grand Challenge," were formed to develop large-scale, massively parallel applications (codes) in conjunction with the development of the K computer. The application codes have been released and are available for public use.

The Strategic Program for Innovative Research (SPIRE) was also established to contribute to determining solutions to urgent scientific and social issues. The objectives of SPIRE were to bear scientific results as soon as the K computer began operation and to establish several core organizations for computational science. Five strategic application fields were selected for SPIRE by MEXT:

- Field 1: Predictive life sciences, healthcare, and drug design infrastructure.
- Field 2: Creating new materials and energy sources.
- Field 3: Global nature change prediction for disaster prevention and mitigation.
- Field 4: Next-generation manufacturing technology (*MONO-ZUKURI in Japanese*).
- Field 5: Origin and structure of space and space materials.

Numerous applications were developed and are presently being executed on the K computer.

5.2   System Overview

5.2.1   Hardware

The K computer [17, 8] is a distributed-memory supercomputer system that consists of a set of 82,944 compute nodes and 5,184 I/O nodes, a hierarchical file system, control and management servers, and front-end servers (Figure 5.4).

Each node is mainly composed of a CPU, 16 GB memory, and an LSI chip that interconnects the nodes (Figure 5.5).

Each node has a SPARC64 VIIIfx made by 45 nm semiconductor process technology by Fujitsu Ltd. [14]. This CPU has 8 cores on the LSI chip and 6 MB L2 cache, which is shared by the cores. The CPU operates at a clock frequency of 2 GHz. Its peak performance and performance per electricity unit are 128 gigaflops and 2.2 gigaflops/watt, respectively. Each core has four floating-point multiply-and-add execution units, two of which are operated concurrently by an SIMD instruction, and 256 double-precision floating-point data registers to facilitate scientific and engineering computations. The architecture is an extended version of the original SPARC architecture [9, 13]. Each core also has a 32 KB L1 data cache. The system has a hardware barrier synchronization function among the cores in a CPU, allowing execution and

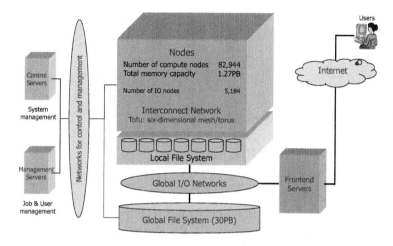

FIGURE 5.4: Configuration of the K computer.

rapid synchronization of multiple threads among the cores. A sector cache function enables software-based allocation of data to the L1 and L2 caches. If iterative and contiguous access to data is required during execution of some parts of a program, the programmer can specify which data is to be allocated and stored on a sector of the L1 or L2 cache to avoid purging of data from the cache as a result of compulsory cache miss-hits.

The newly developed Tofu network, which is a six-dimensional mesh/torus network, is implemented in the K computer for data communication among

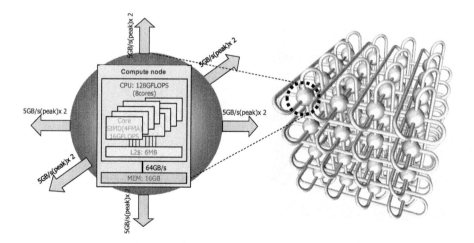

FIGURE 5.5: A node and logical 3-dimensional torus network.

FIGURE 5.6: System board.

the compute nodes [3, 2]. The LSI chip for the Tofu network has 10 routes connected to 10 adjacent nodes, and several routing paths can be employed for communication among nodes. From a programming perspective, one-, two-, or three-dimensional torus network topologies can be employed. Such network topologies can be configured dynamically when a task is assigned to a portion of the K computer by specifying the required topology in a job script. Additionally, Tofu is highly reliable against single-point failures due to its redundant routing configuration.

The entire system consists of 864 compute node racks and each rack has 96 compute nodes and 6 I/O nodes. Four compute nodes are mounted on a system board (Figure 5.6), and 24 system boards are installed in the compute rack (Figure 5.7). Installation of the entire K computer system was finished in August 2011 (Figure 5.2), and the system was operational at the end of September 2012.

FIGURE 5.7: K computer rack.

5.2.2   System Software

A system software configuration is shown in Figure 5.8.

The operating system for the nodes is Linux. The Fortran, C, and C++ programming languages are available for users as the conventional programming environment.

The K computer employs a three-level parallel programming model to attain highly sustainable performance. The first level of parallel processing is SIMD processing in the core, and the second level is thread programming in a compute node supported by automatic parallelization and OpenMP directives. Any compiler can automatically generate a binary code that is executable concurrently by threads in the CPU. The third level is distributed-memory parallel programming with a message passing interface (MPI). The MPI library is provided for communication processes among compute nodes. It is based on an implementation of Open MPI in which several functions are customized to exploit several features of the Tofu network to achieve higher performance [1].

Two file systems, a global file system and a local file system, are implemented as a hierarchical file system to support a file-staging function. A user's permanent files are always placed in the global file system. If the user assigns a job to the K computer that requires files stored in the global file system, the files are copied to the local file system before the job starts (staging in). After the job is completed, the files created in the local file system during the job are moved to the global file system (staging out). These file-staging operations are managed automatically by a job scheduler (Figure 5.9).

All user jobs submitted to the K computer are placed in appropriate queues and are processed sequentially in a first-come, first-served (FCFS) manner. The job queue accepts various job sizes ranging from a single compute node

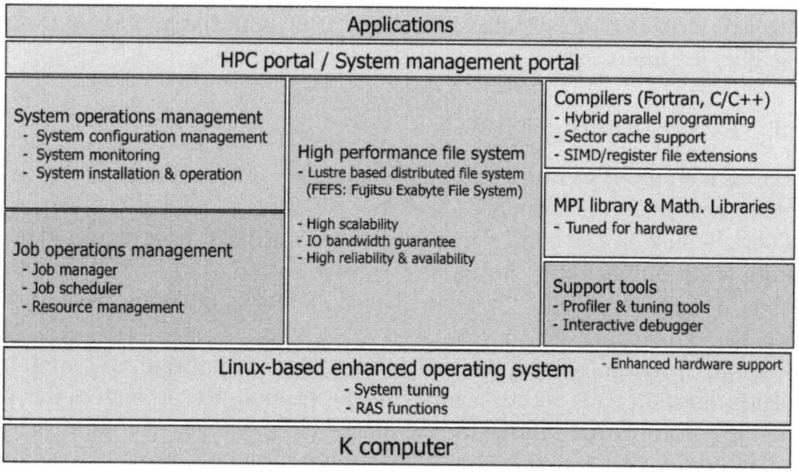

FIGURE 5.8: Software stack of the K computer.

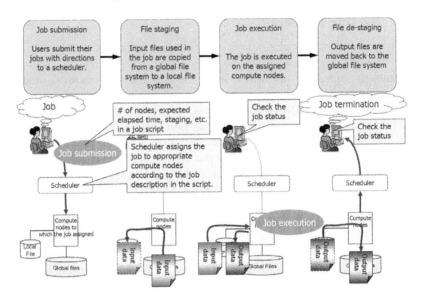

FIGURE 5.9: Batch job flow on the K computer.

job to a full-node job that requires the entire system. An application user can specify the number of compute nodes, estimated elapsed time, and files to be staged from/to the global file system and to/from the local file system that the application requires in the job script. The specification of the estimated elapsed time is essential to facilitate back-fill scheduling.

If a compute node fails during the execution of a job, the job running on the nodes, including the failed node, is aborted. Then, if indicated by the job script, the same job is requeued. The K computer does not maintain check-point states at the system level at any time, and the application user is responsible for intermediate saving of simulation results.

5.2.3 Programming Models

The K computer provides three-level parallel programming model to attain high sustained performance. The first level of parallel processing is an SIMD processing on the core, the second one is a thread programming on the compute node supported by automatic parallelization or OpenMP directives, and the third one is a model for a distributed memory parallel processing with MPI.

A hybrid programming model with both thread programming and MPI parallel programming is recommended on the K computer, though a flat programming with only MPI parallel programming is possible. This means that a large number of MPI processes by the flat programming cause a lack of memory space assigned to users, because the MPI library requests some buffer area for each MPI process.

TABLE 5.2: System configuration summary.

Compute node and I/O node	
CPU	Fujitsu SPARC64^{TM} VIIIfx
Performance	128 GFLOPS
Clock frequency	2.0 GHz
# of cores	8 cores
L1 cache/core	32 kiB (I-cache, D-cache)/core
L2 cache	6 MiB/socket
Technology	45 nm CMOS
Size	22.7 mm × 22.6 mm
Power consumption	58 WABS
Memory capacity	16 GiB
Compute node board	4 compute nodes
I/O node board	1 I/O node
	(Chilled water and air cooling system)
Rack	24 node boards
	6 I/O boards
System	82,944 compute nodes
	5,184 I/O nodes
	864 racks
Performance	10.6 PFLOPS
Memory capacity	1.27 PiB
Interconnect network	Tofu interconnect
	6-dimensional Torus/mesh topology
	24 × 18 × 17 × 2 × 3 × 2

5.2.4 Summary

The system configuration is summarized in Table 5.2 and Figure 5.10.

5.3 Early Results

5.3.1 Benchmark Results

We measured the LINPACK benchmark performance on the K computer and obtained performance of 10.51 PFLOPS, which is approximately 92.3% of the peak performance. Furthermore, in terms of LINPACK performance per unit of power consumption (flops/watt), the value for a rack ranked sixth in the Green500 list in June 2011.

Another benchmark program, the "HPC challenge," was performed on all K computer nodes. The measured values from four categories were

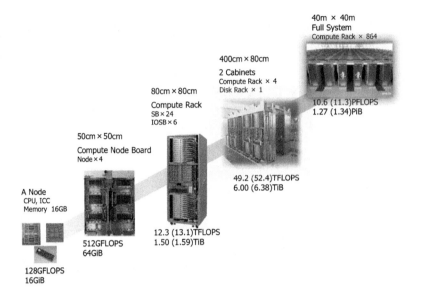

FIGURE 5.10: Configuration: From chip to system.

9.796 TFLOPS, 472 GUPS, 3857 TB/s, and 205.9 TFLOPS for global HPL, global random access, EP stream-triad per system, and global FFT, respectively. We graced the HPCC awards in four categories in 2011 and demonstrated the K computer as a well-balanced high-performance supercomputer system.

5.3.2   Gordon Bell Prizes

Two ACM Gordon Bell prizes were received for results calculated by the K computer for the electron states calculations of silicon nanowires and the gravitational evolution of dark matter in the early universe.

1. Electron states calculations of silicon nanowires [7]

   Silicon nanowires are potentially promising materials for electron channels of next-generation field-effect transistors. It is important to clarify electron states of silicon nanowires to understand the behavior of new devices. Silicon nanowires comprise 10,000 to 100,000 silicon atoms, measure 10 to 20 nm in diameter, and are roughly 10 nm in length.

   Simulations were performed with massively parallel real-space density functional theory (RSDFT) code [11] to compute the energy states and electron states of the matter. A sustained performance of 3.08 PFLOPS was achieved (representing execution efficiency of 43.6%) using approximately two-thirds of the full system in November 2011.

Recently, this simulation was performed using 82,944 nodes and obtained 5.48 PFLOPS sustained performance, which is 51.67% of peak performance [6].

2. Simulation of gravitational evolution of dark matter in the early universe [10]

The universe is primarily composed of dark matter and dark energy. There is approximately five times as much dark matter as baryonic matter, which is the type of matter we can see as atoms or molecules. Since dark matter dominates the gravitational evolution of the universe, it is important to understand the evolution of dark matter in order to reveal the structure formation of the universe.

A research group led by T. Ishiyama (SPIRE, Field 5) developed massively parallel code with a novel communication algorithm for the long-range calculation part of the simulation and a highly tuned gravity kernel for the short-range calculation part. They simulated the evolution of two trillion dark matter particles in the early universe using 98% of the K computer's resources (81,408 nodes) and achieved 5.67 PFLOPS execution performance, which corresponds to 55% of the theoretical peak.

5.4 Operation

5.4.1 Early Access Prior to Official Operation

Complete construction of the K computer took approximately one year. We installed 16 to 32 racks each week, and made hardware adjustments to the racks during installation. The complete K computer was too large to assemble in the vendor factory; however, part of the system was assembled and tested in the factory.

As the K computer was expected to be heavily utilized as an important infrastructure, and much of the world's most advanced computational science and engineering tasks would be performed immediately at the K computer completion, users must be well trained in the use of the system and understand how to improve their applications before the system completion.

In order to accelerate system adjustments and create remarkable results as soon as possible after the official release, we allowed early access to a part of the system in April 2011 to expert software developers. We gradually increased the available portion of the system from 500 TFLOPS to 9 PFLOPS.

Twenty-two applications were selected from the SPIRE fields at the beginning of the early access. The number of applications gradually increased and eventually reached 60. These applications could be used for simulations with good performance at the time of public release.

To allow use of a large number of K computer cores effectively, users were required to achieve a certain sustained performance for their applications. We presented simple rules to the developers to facilitate high concurrency of applications. If they wanted to use more cores for a larger simulation, they had to satisfy one of the following conditions.

1. Strong scaling α_{strong} should be satisfied by Equation (5.1) as the problem size is fixed and the number of cores increases from m to n.

$$\alpha_{strong} = \frac{\dfrac{T_m}{T_n}}{\dfrac{n}{m}} \leq 0.75, \tag{5.1}$$

where T_m and T_n are periods of execution time when the number of compute nodes used in measurements are m and n, respectively, and $2m \leq n$. Users could measure time with n compute nodes once before they were allowed to increase the number of compute nodes from m to n.

2. Weak scaling α_{weak}^{fl} should be satisfied by Equation (5.2) as the problem size of each compute node is fixed and the number of cores increases for applications of primarily floating-point number operations.

$$\alpha_{weak}^{fl} = \frac{\dfrac{F_m}{F_n}}{\dfrac{n}{m}} \leq 0.95, \tag{5.2}$$

where F_m and F_n are sustained performance in FLOPS when the number of compute nodes used in measurements are m and n, respectively, and $2m \leq n$. Users could measure time with n nodes once before they were allowed to increase the number of compute nodes from m to n.

3. Weak scaling α_{weak}^{IPS} should be satisfied by Equation (5.3) as the problem size of each compute node is fixed and the number of cores increases for applications of primarily non-floating-point number operations.

$$\alpha_{weak}^{IPS} = \frac{\dfrac{M_m}{M_n}}{\dfrac{n}{m}} \leq 0.9, \tag{5.3}$$

where M_m and M_n are the number of executed instructions per second when the number of compute nodes used in measurements are m and n, respectively, and $2m \leq n$. Users could measure the time once before they were allowed to increase the number of compute nodes from m to n.

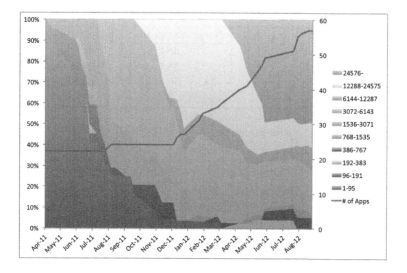

FIGURE 5.11: Progression of increasing the number of applications and the number of concurrent applications. The solid line denotes the number of applications executed. Percentage denotes the ratio of the number of concurrent applications.

Figure 5.11 shows the progression of expanding the number of compute nodes used in simulations and the number of applications for the early access period. The ratio of applications that used greater than 14,000 compute nodes increased as the system was close to the end of installation. Thirty applications achieved more than 24,000 concurrencies.

5.4.2 Operation Policy after Official Operation

The K computer officially began operation on September 28, 2012 and was open to both SPIRE users and general users chosen by a project selection committee.

As shown in Table 5.3, the system has four job queues now, though it had one queue at the release. Three of them are open in an ordinary operation mode. One-ninth of the system is allocated to interactive jobs and small jobs that use less than 384 compute nodes, and eight-ninths are allocated to jobs that use between 385 and 36,864 compute nodes. As shown in Figure 5.12, the operation mode changes for larger jobs. Huge jobs, i.e., those that use more than 36,865 compute nodes, are processed in three contiguous days per month.

FCFS job processing is a principal service policy of a job scheduling. Due to the direct connection characteristics of the Tofu network, compute nodes

TABLE 5.3: Job limitations.

Resource group (job queue)	Node size limit	Elapsed time limit
interactive	1 – 384	6 hours
small	1 – 384	24 hours
large	385 – 36,864	24 hours
huge	36,865 – 82,944	8 hours

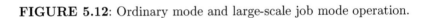

FIGURE 5.12: Ordinary mode and large-scale job mode operation.

assigned to a job are allocated such that the compute nodes are in close proximity in terms of network connections to avoid degradation of communications and imbalanced communication time. However, jobs can be inserted into the FCFS queue overtaking waiting jobs if time and compute nodes are available. The behavior is called back-fill processing and is illustrated in Figure 5.13.

To ensure fair allocation of resources in terms of periods of waiting time per node-time product, scheduling parameters, such as the number of accepted jobs per user group and elapsed time limit, are set such that job wait periods per node-time product are nearly equal.

5.4.3   Utilization Statistics

The job-filling rate is defined as ratio between the number of compute nodes used to process jobs and the total number of available compute nodes. Figure 5.14 illustrates the job-filling rate after the system was opened for shared use. During the first six months of operation, we had an opportunity to

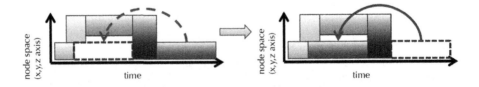

FIGURE 5.13: Back-fill job scheduling.

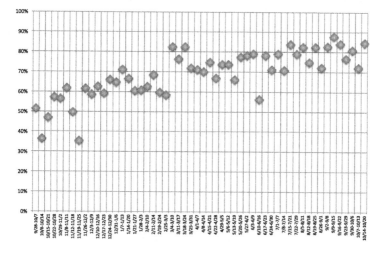

FIGURE 5.14: Job-filling rate.

assess how the job scheduler behaved in actual operation conditions. During this period the job-filling rate was 50–70%, in part because users were not familiar with the system. As of April 2013, the rate was approximately 80%, and that level has been maintained. This high rate has been achieved because users learned how to use the system effectively, we introduced a separate queue for small and iteractive jobs, and we improved the job scheduler.

We also developed a command that informs users of the expected wait time based on job attributes, such as the number of compute nodes and the estimated elapsed time.

5.5 Benchmark Applications

In addition to standard benchmarks, such as LINPACK and HPCC, six target applications employing different computational models and algorithms were selected from earth science, material science, engineering and physics to demonstrate the capability and performance of the K computer.

The applications selected were the Nonhydrostatic Icosahedral Atomspheric Model (NICAM) [16], Seism3D [5], FrontFlow/blue(FFB) [12], Lattice-QCD [4], PHASE [15], and RSDFT [11]. NICAM is used to achieve advanced simulations that capture the subtleties of tropical cumulus cloud convection activities in relation to general atmospheric circulation. The advanced simulations make it possible to explain atmospheric phenomena that have been difficult to simulate so far. Seism3D is a finite difference code which aims to evaluate earthquakes and their inducing phenomena by analyzing and predicting seismic wave propagation and strong seismic motion in a short period. FFB is an unsteady flow analysis code based on large eddy simulation that generates high performance flow predictions, including the behavior of turbulent boundary layers. LatticeQCD is a lattice QCD simulation code that identifies the origin of matter. PHASE and RSDFT are first-principle molecular dynamics codes based on density functional theory that are used to explore nanodevices and non-silicon devices. PHASE uses a plane wave expansion method and RSDFT uses a finite difference method.

Each application is a complete actual simulation program, and each employs a hybrid model that combines a thread programming model and a parallel-process programming model written in Fortran.

Application performance is closely related to both performance of a single multicore processor and parallel execution. Performance of a single multicore processor depends on the memory bandwidth between the processor and memory, which is referred to as a byte/flop value (B/F), memory access pattern, and cache miss-hit ratio. The performance of parallel executions primarily depends on message communications, such as communication type, message size, and the frequency of communications between parallel processes. If we want to optimize program and obtain higher performance, then B/F value, memory access pattern, L2 cache miss-hit ratio, and communication type, size, and frequency should be considered.

When we considered qualitative measures for each application, the applications could be classified into four types, as shown in Figure 5.15. For example, an application located on the right side of the horizontal axis indicates that higher performance is difficult to obtain in parallel execution.

Techniques for improving the performance of the applications are summarized for the four classifications.

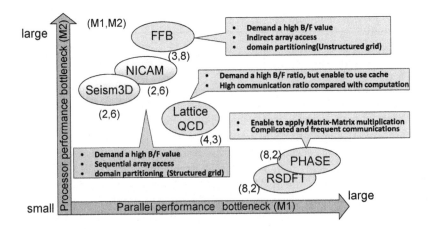

FIGURE 5.15: Categorization of the six applications.

5.5.1 NICAM and Seism3D

NICAM and Seism3D apply standard parallelization using domain decomposition, and most of the messages transferred among computational domains (a set of grids) occur through adjacent communication. This implementation is quite suitable for the Tofu network to obtain scalable performance.

Improvements for parallel implementation are not required. For example, it was found that the communication cost of Seism3D remains low as the number of parallel processes increases because Seism3D communications were limited to four adjacent compute nodes in two-dimensional network topology and the messages could be transferred effectively due to K computer's Tofu network.

However, other improvements are necessary. It is difficult to achieve high processor performance because kernel loops access many contiguous variables in the innermost loop and result in L1 cache slashing and register spills, i.e., the application requires high B/F values.

To avoid these problems, we must determine if kernel loops in hot spots use all of the available memory bandwidth which is limited to the theoretical memory bandwidth of the hardware. If the kernel loop uses all available bandwidth, either loop division or array merging should be applied. We improved the performance of the codes by such modifications.

5.5.2 FFB

FFB has some collective communications with scalar data between all processes. These collective communications are managed by a hardware barrier mechanism and do not require any improvements. Even if the number of parallel processes becomes large, FFB can maintain shorter communication times on the K computer than that on the other systems as the number of parallel processing becomes larger. Moreover, since FFB is a finite element method code, the kernel loop will access memory indirectly from list-indexed array data, and therefore a high B/F value is necessary.

An effective optimization method is to confine to the variables in a small memory address space and use cached variables as much as possible. We renumbered the finite element nodes to reduce the number of far-distance memory accesses to the memory. Renumbering is a very effective performance optimization method to obtain higher performance.

5.5.3 LatticeQCD

Although LatticeQCD has a high frequency of adjacent communications, the low latency of the K computer's MPI library improves communication delays. Therefore, degradation due to parallel execution was smaller than that of other systems. LatticeQCD is expected to have high performance because memory access can be confined to a small contiguous memory area that can be loaded to L2-cache. It was, however, difficult to obtain the expected performance without any improvement to the code.

We observed high L1 cache miss-hit rates, a large number of WAIT operations for cache access by integer operations, and a low rate of SIMD instructions in the original code. These were caused by inadequate series of instructions and because compiler analysis lacks the capability to generate a more effective sequence of instructions. However, a Fortran compiler has been improved to generate code that can be executed more quickly; thus, higher processor performance was achieved.

5.5.4   PHASE and RSDFT

PHASE and RSDFT [6] have a high frequency of collective communications for a large volume of message data and synchronization among the global communicators, such as MPI_COMM_WORLD which causes a serious performance bottleneck in large-scale parallel processing.

Computation schemes can actually have two possible parallelization spaces; however, parallelization was only implemented in one space. Therefore, an additional parallelization that the other space was incorporated to restrict collective communications to smaller computations as follows. Additional parallelization for wave numbers rather than energy bands was applied to PHASE, and additional parallelization for energy bands rather than discretized lattice grids was applied to RSDFT. These implementations allowed for collective communications to be localized to a small portion of the computations, thereby eliminating global communications. The number of code concurrencies can also be increased as a secondary effect of this improvement. As a result, larger simulations can be performed.

A collective communication algorithm called Trinaryx3 [1], which is implemented using the Tofu network, was applied to code to reduce communication costs. In addition, matrix-matrix multiplication in the kernel was replaced by a BLAS library tuned specifically for the K computer.

5.5.5   Optimized Performance

Table 5.4 shows the performance of the six target applications. A hardware monitor was used to count the number of floating-point operations, and more than 80,000 nodes were used for the measurements. We found that four applications achieved greater than one PFLOPS, and one of the development targets was accomplished.

5.6   Facilities

The facilities for housing the K computer have many features. There are four buildings at the RIKEN Advanced Institute for Computational Science

TABLE 5.4: Performance of six target applications.

Program Name	Sustained performance (PFLOPS)	Efficiency (%)	# of used nodes
NICAM	0.84	8.05	81,920
Seism3D	1.90	17.90	82,944
FrontFlow/blue	0.32	3.16	80,000
LatticeQCD	1.65	15.60	82,944
PHASE	2.14	20.15	82,944
RSDFT	5.48	51.67	82,944

(RIKEN AICS): the research building, the computer building, the chiller building, and the electricity supply substation building (Figures 5.16 and 5.17).

The research building has six stories above ground and one below. The computer building has three stories above ground and one below. These two buildings have seismically isolated structures that employ three types of seismic isolation equipment, including laminated rubber dampers, lead dampers, and stiffness steel dampers, to provide S-grade earthquake resistance (Figure 5.18).

In the chiller building, there are two types of chillers: four absorption refrigeration chillers and three centrifugal water chillers. In addition, there are two gas turbine cogeneration systems, which can generate electricity (maximum 5 MW for each) and steam for the absorption chillers. The computer room is on

FIGURE 5.16: A view of the facilities.

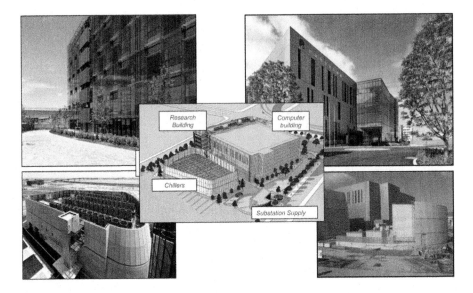

FIGURE 5.17: A view of the buildings.

the third floor and the storage system (approximately 30 petabytes) is on the first floor. These floors are raised by 5 ft. from the normal floor. The area of the computer room, which has no internal vertical supports as shown in Figure 5.19, is 3,000 m^2 (32,300 sq. ft.). Therefore, it provides considerable ease and flexibility for arranging computer racks and installing network cables.

Air handling units are located on the second floor and on the first basement, which are immediately below the computer room and storage system room floors, respectively. Cool air generated by the air-handling units travels to the above floors to cool the K computer and storage system (Figure 5.20). There are also heat exchangers between the first coolant loop from the chiller building and the second coolant loop circulating inside compute node racks of the K computer. The chilled water of the first coolant loop is generated by the refrigerators in the chiller building.

FIGURE 5.18: Seismic isolated structures: Laminated rubber damper, lead damper, and stiffness steel damper (left to right).

FIGURE 5.19: Pillar-free computer room.

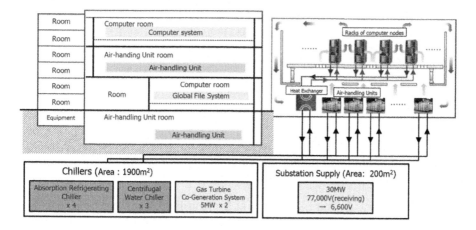

FIGURE 5.20: Cross-section of the building.

Acknowledgments

The chapter authors would like to thank all members of the Next-Generation Supercomputer Research and Development Center at RIKEN. They would especially like to thank Dr Tadashi Watanabe, the K computer development project leader, for his enthusiastic encouragement.

Bibliography

[1] T. Adachi, N. Shida, K. Miura, S. Sumimoto, A. Uno, M. Kurokawa, F. Shoji, and M. Yokokawa. The design of ultra scalable MPI collective communication on the K computer. *Computer Science - Research and Development*, 28(2-3):147–155, 2013.

[2] Y. Ajima, T. Inoue, S. Hiramoto, T. Shimizu, and Y. Takagi. The Tofu interconnect. *IEEE Micro*, 32(1):21–31, 2012.

[3] Y. Ajima, S. Sumimoto, and T. Shimizu. Tofu: A 6D mesh/torus interconnect for exascale computers. *Computer*, 42(11):36–40, 2009.

[4] S. Aoki, K.-I. Ishikawa, N. Ishizuka, T. Izubuchi, D. Kadoh, K. Kanaya, Y. Kuramashi, Y. Namekawa, M. Okawa, Y. Taniguchi, A. Ukawa, N. Ukita, and T. Yoshié. 2 + 1 flavor lattice QCD toward the physical point. *Phys. Rev. D*, 79:034503, Feb. 2009.

[5] T. Furumura and L. Chen. Parallel simulation of strong ground motions during recent and historical damaging earthquakes in Tokyo, Japan. *Parallel Computing*, 31(2):149–165, 2005.

[6] Y. Hasegawa, J. Iwata, M. Tsuji, D. Takahashi, A. Oshiyama, K. Minami, T. Boku, H. Inoue, Y. Kitazawa, I. Miyoshi, and M. Yokokawa. Performance evaluation of ultra-large scale first-principles electronic structure calculation code on the K computer. *International Journal of High Performance Computing Applications*, 2013.

[7] Y. Hasegawa, J. Iwata, M. Tsuji, D. Takahashi, A. Oshiyama, K. Minami, T. Boku, F. Shoji, A. Uno, M. Kurokawa, H. Inoue, I. Miyoshi, and M. Yokokawa. First-principles calculations of electron states of a silicon nanowire with 100,000 atoms on the K computer. In *Proceedings of 2011 International Conference for High Performance Computing, Networking, Storage and Analysis*, SC '11, pages 1–11, New York, NY, USA, 2011. IEEE Computer Society Press.

[8] M. Hoshino, editor. *Fujitsu Scientific and Technical Journal - Special Issue on the K computer*, volume 48. Fujitsu Limited, July 2012.

[9] SPARC International. *The SPARC Architecture Manual (Version 9)*. Prentice-Hall, 1994.

[10] T. Ishiyama, K. Nitadori, and J. Makino. 4.45 pflops astrophysical n-body simulation on K computer: the gravitational trillion-body problem. In *Proceedings of 2012 International Conference on High Performance Computing, Networking, Storage and Analysis*, SC '12, pages 5:1–5:10, Los Alamitos, CA, USA, 2012. IEEE Computer Society Press.

[11] J. Iwata, D. Takahashi, A. Oshiyama, T. Boku, K. Shiraishi, S. Okada, and K. Yabana. A massively-parallel electronic-structure calculations based on real-space density functional theory. *Journal of Computational Physics*, 229(6):2339–2363, 2010.

[12] K. Kumahata, S. Inoue, and K. Minami. Kernel performance improvement for the FEM-based fluid analysis code on the K computer. *Procedia Computer Science*, 18(0):2496–2499, 2013. 2013 International Conference on Computational Science.

[13] Fujitsu Ltd. SPARC64VIIIfx *Extensions (in Japanese)*, 2009.

[14] T. Maruyama, T. Yoshida, R. Kan, I. Yamazaki, S. Yamamura, N. Takahashi, M. Hondou, and H. Okano. SPARC64 VIIIfx: A new-generation octocore processor for petascale computing. *Micro, IEEE*, 30(2):30–40, 2010.

[15] T. Ohno, T. Yamamoto, T. Kokubo, A. Azami, Y. Sakaguchi, T. Uda, T. Yamasaki, D. Fukata, and J. Koga. First-principles calculations of large-scale semiconductor systems on the earth simulator. In *Proceedings of 2007 International Conference for High Performance Computing, Networking, Storage and Analysis*, SC '07, pages 1–6, 2007.

[16] M. Satoh, T. Matsuno, H. Tomita, H. Miura, T. Nasuno, and S. Iga. Nonhydrostatic icosahedral atmospheric model (NICAM) for global cloud resolving simulations. *Journal of Computational Physics*, 227(7):3486 – 3514, 2008.

[17] M. Yokokawa, F. Shoji, A. Uno, M. Kurokawa, and T. Watanabe. The K computer: Japanese next-generation supercomputer development project. In *Proceedings of 2011 International Symposium on Low Power Electronics and Design (ISLPED'11)*, pages 371–372, 2011.

[18] A. Yonezawa, T. Watanabe, M. Yokokawa, M. Sato, and K. Hirao. Advanced Institute for Computational Science (AICS): Japanese national high-performance computing research institute and its 10-petaflops supercomputer. In *Proceedings of 2011 International Conference for High Performance Computing, Networking, Storage and Analysis*, SC '11, pages 1–8, Los Alamitos, CA, USA, 2011. IEEE Computer Society Press.

Chapter 6

Lindgren—The Swedish Tier-1 System

Erwin Laure, Daniel Ahlin, Lars Malinowsky, Gert Svensson, and Jonathan Vincent

PDC Center for High-Performance Computing, KTH Royal Institute of Technology, Stockholm, Sweden

6.1 Overview

The Swedish academic computing landscape is organized under the auspices of SNIC, the Swedish National Infrastructure for Computing. SNIC coordinates investments in computing and storage infrastructure at its six national centers and manages the national process for allocating research time on its computing resources. Since its formation in 2003, SNIC has significantly increased the computational capacity available to Swedish researchers and firmly put Sweden on the international computational science map. When the Partnership for Advanced Computing in Europe (PRACE) started in 2010, SNIC joined this European HPC effort and worked with the Swedish Research

Council to allocate additional funds for a national high-end system that would also be made available to European researchers via PRACE. These efforts resulted in the installation of a CRAY XE6 supercomputer, named Lindgren, at the PDC Center for High-Performance Computing at the KTH Royal Institute of Technology in Stockholm.

In this chapter we discuss Lindgren, along with some of the main applications and projects that involve the system. Lindgren is not only a national system, but also acts as a stepping stone for Swedish researchers to access even larger European and international resources. Additionally, Lindgren is used to help in the preparation of applications geared towards future exascale systems. In this context we particularly consider two EU projects, CRESTA and EPiGRAM, which are working on smoothing the transition to exascale computing.

6.1.1   PDC Center for High-Performance Computing

The PDC Center for High-Performance Computing, which is home to the Swedish Tier-1 system, Lindgren, is part of the KTH CSC School of Computer Science and Communication in Stockholm. The center provides leading HPC services for academic and industrial research, primarily in Sweden and also more widely in Europe. PDC's services are made available to Swedish and European academic researchers, respectively via the SNIC and PRACE infrastructures. PDC also provides its services to the commercial sector via collaborative projects. PDC's activities are funded primarily by KTH, and the Swedish Research Council through SNIC, with additional support from various Nordic and European HPC research projects.

PDC, which was founded in 1990, has been providing leading HPC resources to Swedish academia since the early days of commercially available parallel systems. The first computer, which formed the basis for PDC, was an 8K Connection Machine CM2, named "Bellman" (see Figure 6.1), that was installed in late 1989. This system was followed by an IMB SP/2, which after an upgrade with national funds became the largest SP/2 system outside the U.S. at the time. This was the start of cluster solutions as the prevailing architecture at PDC with various HP and Dell solutions based on Intel and AMD. During the lifetime of the SP/2 this system was also complemented with Cray and Fujitsu vector systems. In 2005 PDC entered the terascale era with Lenngren, the first Swedish terascale system, a Dell Xeon-based cluster with 6 TFlops peak performance that was in operation from 2005 to 2009. Lindgren is the direct successor of this system as main Swedish national HPC system. In 2008 a system dedicated to Flow and Climate research was inaugurated that was then also the largest academic system in Sweden, a 89 TFlops Dell Opteron Infiniband cluster. Table 6.1 gives on overview of the main PDC systems prior to Lindgren.

PDC recognizes that being the leading national resource for high-performance computing in scientific and engineering research requires more

FIGURE 6.1: Bellman.

than just providing access to state-of-the-art HPC technology. Users need help to parallelize their code and applications, and make them run efficiently. The center therefore includes Application Experts amongst its personnel— these researchers, who have doctoral qualifications in their own academic area along with extensive HPC experience, are dedicated to offering expert support and assistance for fine-tuning and scaling applications in a number of disciplines (including fluid dynamics, molecular dynamics, computational chemistry, bioinformatics, and neuroinformatics). PDC also offers a comprehensive education and training program, including an annual summer school that provides an introduction to HPC, and more advanced seminars and workshops held throughout the year. Since the local data storage facilities of many academic departments are not sufficient to house vast quantities of measurement data or the results from large parallel programs, PDC also provides storage and data management services, including facilities for long-term archiving—

TABLE 6.1: History of main PDC systems.

Year	Name	Architecture	TPP (GFlops)
1989-1996	Bellman	CM2	0.014 (SP)
1994-2003	Strindberg	SP2	15-147
1996-2003	Selma	VPP300/VX	6.6
1996-2001	Kallsup	J90se	6.4
2000-2005	Kallsup	Power3	60
2003-2009	Lucidor	HP Itanium2	658-1,581
2005-2009	Lenngren	Dell Xeon	5,998
2007-2010	Hebb	BlueGene/L	5,734
2008-2013	Ferlin	Dell Xeon	55,910
2008-	Ekman	Dell Opteron	89,267

these can be used to store the results from computations performed on its systems or from other sources.

PDC is an active member of the major European HPC infrastructure projects (notably PRACE [8] and the European Data Infrastructure project, EUDAT) and is heavily involved in exascale research projects, such as the CRESTA [2] exascale flagship project, the PDC-led ScalaLife [1] and EPi-GRAM [4] projects, and the Human Brain Project [6]. PDC also supports a wide variety of researchers from KTH, the Karolinska Institute, Stockholm University and elsewhere in their research projects by providing HPC resources and expertise. In this capacity, PDC takes part in several projects at a national level (for example, through the Swedish e-Science Research Centre (SeRC) [10], and the Swedish Research Council), and also at the international level (for example, in relation to the European Commission and Nordforsk).

6.1.2 Why Lindgren Was Needed

For many years, Sweden lagged behind other industrialized countries in its utilization of supercomputers for academic research. The Swedish Council for High Performance Computing was formed in July 1994 to rectify this situation and substantial funding was allocated to PDC at KTH to upgrade the main system at the time (an IBM SP2 system) so as to provide a top-class parallel resource for academic research. In 2003 the various HPC efforts across the Swedish universities were bundled together to create the Swedish National Infrastructure for Computing (SNIC), thus catering for a massive increase of computational capacity in Sweden. Then, in 2010, Sweden joined PRACE—this pan-European project coordinates the largest European HPC systems (known as Tier-0 resources) and also provides a framework for smaller, national systems (known as Tier-1 resources). At the time, SNIC was providing a reasonable HPC capacity to its users, but no system in the Tier-1 range was available in Sweden, which not only impeded Swedish scientists from running large-scale simulations locally, but also made it difficult for them to access the larger European resources at the Tier-0 level. The Swedish Research Council thus created a dedicated funding line to provide a Tier-1 level system within SNIC to ensure that Swedish researchers would be on a par with their European peers. Through joint funding from SNIC and KTH, the Cray system Lindgren was made available to SNIC users in January 2011, thus doubling the HPC resources available to SNIC researchers. Since its inauguration, Lindgren has been a highly effective and productive resource for Swedish academia, contributing to the competitiveness and reputation of Swedish computational science on the European and international scenes.

6.1.3 Lindgren Project Timeline

Lindgren was installed in two stages, with the whole project spanning a total of five years. In September 2009, SNIC awarded PDC funding to

FIGURE 6.2: Lindgren phase 1.

procure a new national capability system. The system was intended to be a general-purpose capability system with a fast interconnect that could serve most of the Swedish workloads described previously. At the time, although SNIC could foresee that significant additional funding would become available for a Swedish PRACE system in the not-too distant future, the current SNIC resources were stretched thin, and thus the procurement could not be postponed until the additional funds were confirmed. PDC wisely decided to invest in a system that could be expanded when additional funding became available at a later stage. Care was therefore taken in the procurement process to purchase a system that could be easily upgraded, in addition to possessing the main requirements of having x86 CPUs and a fast interconnect. The purpose of these main requirements was to ease the process of porting applications to the new resource, which needed to be as easy as possible to maximize the effective use of the new system, while minimizing disruptions to SNIC researchers. The procurement process resulted in the installation of a 96 TF Cray XT6m system comprising 464 compute nodes, about 15 TF of main memory and a 2-D torus SeaStar-2 interconnect, which was inaugurated in June 2010. Figure 6.2 shows the first phase installation. The contract included options for a significant upgrade. So, when additional funds became available later that year and were awarded to PDC, Lindgren was upgraded to its final configuration, which is a 305 TF Cray XE6 system comprising 1516 compute nodes consisting of two 2.1 GHz AMD 12-core Magny Cours processors and 32 GB of DDR3 memory, giving a total of 36,384 cores and 47.3 TB of memory. The interconnect has also been upgraded to a 3-D torus Gemini network. An external DDN SFA10KE storage solution of 560 TB was added to the system to serve as Lustre-based scratch storage for Lindgren. The final system was inaugurated in January 2011, and will be operational until December 2014, as the whole project was established with a lifetime of five years. The final system is shown in Figure 6.3.

FIGURE 6.3: Lindgren phase 2.

6.2   Applications and Workloads on Lindgren

As PDC's facilities are used by researchers from a range of academic and industrial areas, we support a variety of applications and workloads. Since its inauguration, Lindgren has been used for the most demanding computational simulations in Swedish academia by over 300 individual users, with an overall sustained usage of over 90% of the theoretically available resources. The top 10% of the users, consuming some 60% of the resources, represent domains as diverse as Fluid Dynamics, Materials Science, Molecular Dynamics, Physics, Fusion, Climate Research, Astrophysics, Neuroinformatics and Biomolecular Modeling. These groups push the boundaries for massively parallel computing in Sweden and regularly use thousands of cores in parallel with individual jobs running on more than 20,000 cores (or two thirds of the machine). The Lindgren system is also used for industrial research, particularly Computational Fluid Dynamics (CFD) applications for truck design.

Thanks to the availability of Lindgren, Swedish researchers have been able to prepare their simulations to be used on even larger systems (such as the PRACE Tier-0 systems) and a significant number of Lindgren users have been successful in the highly competitive PRACE calls. In fact, so far there have been eight successful Tier-0 applications that involved Swedish researchers, and four of those projects had a Swedish principle investigator. There were several fluid dynamics projects looking at turbulence and instabilities in rotating flows (which has industrial applications, for example, with turbines) and simulating turbulent flows (which is relevant to the aircraft and other industries). A couple of projects are simulating the process of premixed charge compression ignition in internal combustion engines (so as to produce engines with lower emissions of greenhouse gases). Climate modeling is being used in some projects, for example, one group is working on increasing the resolution of current long-range climate modeling, so we have more accurate estimates of future climate variability and can thus better assess the likelihood of events that will have significant impact on us, such as floods and cyclones. A different group of climate researchers are participating in the Fifth Coupled Model Intercomparison Project to improve current climate models and thus produce more accurate climate projections for the rest of this century. Another project is in the area of Astronomy and aims to produce the first full numerical simulation of the Epoch of Reionization (EoR) survey by the European radio interferometer array LOFAR, while at the same time including all essential types of ionizing sources, from normal galaxies to quasars.

Despite the impressive scale of the huge PRACE Tier-0 systems in the multi-petaflops range, even they will be counted as smallish systems in the future when exascale systems appear on the market. To use such systems efficiently, significant efforts are needed to scale up existing application codes so they run effectively and efficiently on the new exascale systems. We are therefore working particularly with two applications that are highly used on Lindgren in order to improve their scaling towards exascale. These are the Computational Fluid Dynamics (CFD) application, Nek5000 [5], and the Molecular Dynamics (MD) application, GROMACS [9]. For scaling these codes, we have joined European efforts through the European Commission Seventh Framework Programme (EC FP7) exascale flagship project, *Collaborative Research into Exascale Systemware, Tools and Applications (CRESTA)*, and we are also building on national efforts through the Swedish e-Science Research Center (SeRC). CRESTA, which started in 2011, brings together four of Europe's leading supercomputing centers (PDC, EPCC in the UK, the CSC-IT Center for Science in Finland and HLRS in Germany), with one of the world's major equipment vendors (Cray), and two of Europe's leading programming tools providers (Allinea, and Dresden University of Technology) to explore how the exaflop challenge can be met, namely delivering an exaflop (or a million million million calculations per second) by the end of this decade.

CRESTA is focusing on the use of six applications with exascale potential (including Nek5000 and GROMACS) and using them as co-design vehicles to develop an integrated suite of technologies to support the execution of applications at the exascale. The project aims to make it possible to successfully execute Nek5000, GROMACS and the four other applications on multi-petaflop systems in preparation for the first exascale systems towards the end of this decade.

A key feature of CRESTA is its use of dual pathways to exascale solutions. Many problems in HPC hardware and software have been solved over the years using an incremental approach. Similarly, most of today's systems have been developed incrementally, growing larger and more powerful with each product release. However, we know that some issues at the exascale, particularly on the software side, will require a completely new, disruptive approach. CRESTA will therefore employ both incremental and disruptive approaches to technical innovation, sometimes following both paths for a particular problem in order to compare and contrast the challenges and advantages associated with each approach.

In a more local effort, several research groups from the Swedish e-Science Research Centre (SeRC) have already done great work to enable applications such as Nek5000, GROMACS and DALTON to use current supercomputer systems efficiently. However SeRC (which is a consortium established in 2010 by four Swedish universities—KTH, the University of Linköping, Stockholm University and the Karolinska Institute—along with PDC, and the Linköping-based National Supercomputer Centre) is well aware of the coming challenges of exascale computing, and one of SeRC's goals is to develop effective computational methods that can be utilized on peta- and exascale computers. SeRC has therefore established SESSI (the SeRC Exascale Simulation Software Initiative) which is a new SeRC flagship program to support researchers in getting their codes to scale orders of magnitude better than they do today. In the SESSI program, a number of research teams working with computational fluid dynamics (specifically the Nek5000 code) and molecular dynamics simulations (GROMACS) have joined forces to learn more about parallelization techniques from each other. This cross-fertilization work is complemented by the establishment of the new NVIDIA Cuda Research Center at KTH. Several researchers from PDC are contributing their expertise on new parallel programming models, profiling and debugging on complex mixed hardware (for example, when a code uses both CPUs and GPUs). This means that we have a team of several people who are dedicating a large fraction of their time to scaling Nek5000 and GROMACS to run on the next generation of hardware. In addition, SESSI aims to consolidate all efforts related to high-end parallel computation in Sweden, with the goal of establishing a co-design center that will benefit the users of other highly parallel application codes.

The exascale challenge will however not be solved by simply scaling and removing bottlenecks in application codes. As pointed out in the International Exascale Software Project (IESP) report [3], a number of additional efforts are needed to deal with energy-efficient system design, new mathematical models and algorithms, new programming models, fault tolerance, and so forth. Through the FP7 project on Exascale ProGRAmming Models (EPiGRAM), we are particularly looking into programming models that could be useful for reaching exascale. EPiGRAM is working on developing programming models for next-generation supercomputers. The project is being undertaken by a consortium consisting of KTH (Sweden), the Technical University of Vienna (Austria), The University of Edinburgh (UK), Cray UK and the Fraunhofer Society (Germany). The University of Illinois at Urbana-Champaign (USA) is also involved with the project as an associate partner. The goal of the EPiGRAM project is to prepare Message Passing (MP) and Partitioned Global Address Space (PGAS) programming models for the coming exascale systems. Although the Message Passing Interface (MPI) has emerged as the de-facto standard for parallel programming on current petascale machines,

PGAS languages and libraries are increasingly being considered as alternatives or complements to MPI. However, there are severe problems with both of these approaches that will prevent them from attaining exascale performance. Therefore, the EPiGRAM project is addressing the main current limitations of the MP and PGAS programming models. EPiGRAM will introduce new disruptive concepts to fill the technological gap between the petascale and exascale era in two ways. First, innovative algorithms will be used in both MP and PGAS, specifically to provide fast collective communication in both MP and PGAS, to decrease the memory consumption in MP, to enable fast synchronization in PGAS, and to provide both fault tolerance mechanisms in PGAS and potential strategies for fault tolerance in MP. Secondly, we will combine the best features of MP and PGAS by developing an MP interface using a PGAS library as the communication substrate. The new concepts that EPiGRAM develops for MPI and PGAS (to enable them to reach exascale performance) will be developed and tested in relation to two particular applications chosen from the suite of codes in current EC exascale projects in the domains of engineering (the Nek5000 code) and space weather (the iPIC3D code [7]). By providing prototype implementations for both MP and PGAS concepts, EPiGRAM will contribute significantly to advancements in programming models and interfaces for ultra-scale computing systems, and provide stimuli for European research in this vital area.

6.2.1 Highlights of Lindgren's Main Applications

Although the applications running on Lindgren cover areas as diverse as modeling the human brain, materials, fusion, and climate simulations, two of the most widely used pieces of code are Nek5000 and GROMACS.

6.2.1.1 Nek5000

Nek5000 is an open-source computational fluid dynamics code that simulates unsteady incompressible fluid flow with thermal and passive scalar transport. It is based on the spectral element method and can handle general two- and three-dimensional domains described by isoparametric quad or hex elements. In addition, it can be used to compute axisymmetric flows. The code is written in Fortran77 and C and employs the MPI standard for parallelism. In fact, Nek5000 won a Gordon Bell prize for its outstanding scalability on high-performance parallel computers. Nek5000 currently has more than 160 users and is a part of the co-design effort being undertaken by the Centre for Exascale Simulation of Advanced Reactors (CESAR) at the Argonne National Laboratory.

Figure 6.4 shows the strong scaling of Nek5000 on Lindgren for a jet cross flow simulation. The mesh consists of 68,480 spectral elements with a polynomial order of N=13 and around 150.5 million number of points. Figure 6.5 shows the strong scaling for a larger turbulence pipe flow simulation. The

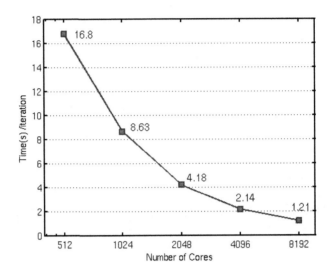

FIGURE 6.4: Nek5000 scaling on a medium-sized problem.

mesh consists of 1.26 million spectral elements with a polynomial order of N=12 and around 2182.2 million points. As can be seen from the figures, Nek5000 demonstrates excellent scaling behavior and is able to exploit over 16,000 cores efficiently for a larger problem size.

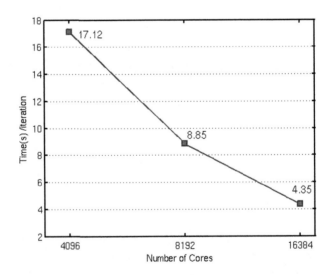

FIGURE 6.5: Nek5000 scaling on a large problem.

6.2.1.2 GROMACS

GROMACS is a highly efficient and optimized code for performing Molecular Dynamics (MD) simulations. It uses highly tuned assembly kernels for the most computationally intensive calculations and is possibly the fastest code in the MD area. GROMACS runs on all major HPC architectures including BlueGene/Q, SPARC and accelerators such as GPUs.

The MD method, which is implemented in GROMACS, solves the Newtonian equations of motions of particle systems. Thus, through sufficient simulation sampling, it is possible to observe and study the behavior of those systems at an atomic level. The software is mainly used for studies of bio-molecular systems such as proteins, membranes, and recently even whole cells. One of the application areas is the development of novel drug targets.

Some of the key features of GROMACS are that it makes it possible to perform atomic-level simulations of globular and membrane proteins such as ligand-gated ion channels and G protein-coupled receptors (GPCRs)—the latter are targets of about 40% of drugs at the moment—as well as simulations of virus capsids and also DNA systems.

Figure 6.6 shows the scaling of GROMACS in MD simulations of the envelope of a realistically sized influenza virion (84 nm diameter). The model is used to investigate the diffusion and possible aggregation of the main membrane proteins present in the envelope (hemagglutinin, neuraminidase and the influenza M2 channel). The model is courtesy of Phillip Fowler, from the University of Oxford. As can be seen from the figure, reasonable scaling behavior can be achieved up to 10,000 cores.

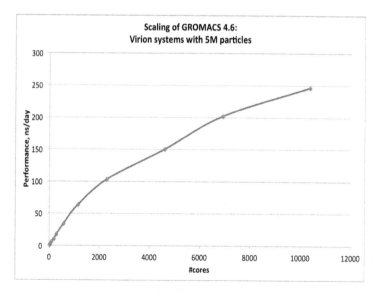

FIGURE 6.6: GROMACS scaling.

TABLE 6.2: Lindgren hardware configuration.

Feature	Phase 1 (July 2010)	Phase 2 (Jan 2011)
Node architecture	Cray XT6m Compute Node	Cray XE6 Compute Node
CPU	AMD Model 6172	AMD Model 6172
CPU microarchitecture	Magny Cours	Magny Cours
CPU frequency (GHz)	2.1	2.1
CPU count per node	2	2
Node memory capacity (GB)	32	32
Interconnection network	Cray SeaStar2	Cray Gemini
Compute racks	5	16
Total number of compute nodes	460	1516
Total number of service nodes	10	10
Peak FLOP rate (TF)	96	305

6.3 Overview of the Lindgren System

Lindgren is a 305 TF Cray XE6 system comprising 1516 compute nodes consisting of two 2.1 GHz AMD 12-core Magny Cours processors and 32 GB DDR3 memory, thus giving a total of 36.384 cores and 47.3 TB of memory. The system also features a 3-D torus Gemini network. Details of the configuration can be found in Table 6.2. The system is connected (via infiniband) to an external DDN SFE12KE solution (after an upgrade from the original SFA10KE solution) providing 900 TB of Lustre-based scratch storage. This storage system is also mounted on other PDC systems which gives us a site-wide storage solution. Additionally, we have fat node machines attached to this storage, which are used for pre- and post-processing, particularly mesh generation and rendering.

6.4 Lindgren's System Software

Lindgren features the standard Cray system software, comprising the Cray Linux Environment (CLE), based on SUSE Linux, together with Cray's compiler and performance suite, as well as compiler suites from PGI and Intel. Additional debugging and performance tools, such as Allinea's DDT, Tau, and Paraver, are provided as well. The system is managed by Adaptive Computing's Torque/Moab. Lustre is used for the parallel file system. Details can be found in Table 6.3.

TABLE 6.3: Lindgren software configuration.

Feature	Lindgren
Login node OS Compute node OS Parallel file system	SUSE Linux Enterprise Server 11 CLE3 Lustre 1.8
Compilers	Cray Compiling Environment 8.0.6 Intel 12.1 PGI 12.5 GNU 4.6
MPI	Cray MPI
Notable libraries	HDF5 netcdf MKL/ACML FFTW petsc scalapack
Job scheduler Resource manager	Moab Torque
Debugging tools Performance tools	Allinea DDT CrayPAT TAU extrae

By default, CLE is running in the Extreme Scalability Mode (ESM) that provides a low-noise kernel for scalability, along with native communication and optimized MPI, as well as application-specific performance tuning and scaling. For some ISV applications the Cluster Compatibility Mode (CCM) needs to be used that ensures compatibility with a fully standard x86/Linux, standardized communication layer, and out-of-the-box ISV installation. However, due to its reduced performance, CCM is discouraged and we work with ISV on native ports to avoid using CCM.

6.5 Lindgren's Programming System

Lindgren features the Cray HPC Suite, as indicated in Table 6.3. This suite particularly supports MPI, OpenMP, and PGAS languages. Although most applications use plain MPI, we are seeing an increasing trend towards hybrid programming using combinations of MPI and OpenMP, and also MPI and PGAS. These hybrid approaches are considered to be one of the important steps towards further scaling of applications, as discussed in Section 6.2. C and Fortran are the prevailing languages used for applications but some domains, such as neuroinformatics, also use Python and there is even some C++ usage. Additionally the Lindgren system features a number of HPC libraries, as well as productivity tools (including debuggers and performance tools) which are listed in Table 6.3. Increasing the usage of these tools is a key component of our training program, which frequently includes events focusing on how to increase the efficiency of parallel programs with the help of these particular tools.

6.6   Storage, Visualization, and Analytics on Lindgren

As we mentioned previously, a 900TB DDN SFE12KE solution is mounted to Lindgren as scratch storage and this storage is also mounted to other systems at PDC as a site-wide storage system. Of special importance is *Povel*, a 190 nodes quadcore AMD system with 32 and 64 GB RAM that is used for pre- and post-processing. Rendering applications, used for visualization purposes, are largely run on this particular system. Long-term storage is provided by the national storage infrastructure *SweStore*, a dCache- and iRODS-based distributed long-term storage infrastructure. Additional archiving is provided via an IBM TS3500 Tape Library.

6.7   Data Center Facilities Housing Lindgren

All the PDC computer systems are sited at the PDC facilities, which are part of the KTH School of Computer Science and Communication, and are located on the main campus of the KTH Royal Institute of Technology in central Stockholm. The PDC supercomputer hall is located on the ground floor of the building that houses PDC with some infrastructure on the same floor level, and some in the basement. The infrastructure and related facilities consist of the following.

- A 244 m^2 main computer room, a 36 m^2 secure room for backup and archival storage, a 63 m^2 backup computer room and rooms for UPS systems, UPS batteries, emergency power (two diesel generators), two transformers, power distribution, fiber/networking, storage, engineering/workshop, and receiving of goods give us a total area of 327 m^2. The backup room is used for storage and low heat-density equipment, while the main computer room hosts the actual computing systems.

- 3.0 MVA power feeds are available for computer and storage systems and also for cooling equipment.

- 2.1 MW UPS systems are currently installed covering all the systems at PDC. Important servers and storage systems are equipped with redundant power supplies and fed from two different UPS systems, one of which has a backup with diesel generators.

- 1.2 MW heat exchangers for energy recovery via district cooling are included, along with 0.8 MW heat exchangers for local heat re-use or district cooling when there is no local need for heating.

- 350 kW base cooling capacity is available in the main computer room, as well as 600 kW high-density in-row cooling, both with appropriate redundancy.

- An energy-efficient "heat re-use" system has been installed which takes the 600 kW of heat produced by Lindgren and efficiently re-uses that heat locally on campus. This puts PDC and KTH at the forefront of "green computing."

- PDC also has a dedicated 10 Gbit/s link to the Swedish National Research & Education Network SUNET.

In terms of challenges presented by the actual facilities, PDC is located in a listed building so it is not possible to change the exterior of the building. This made it difficult to install the usual types of cooling machines, which need to be mounted externally. Instead KTH had been using "district cooling" (as well as "district heating") from the city-wide network for a long time. This network supplies hot water (for heating) and cold water (for cooling) via underground pipes. This is a relatively economical and environmentally sound system; however, in 2010 when PDC began planning to install the Lindgren system, we wanted a more efficient method that would make good use of the extra heat produced by running Lindgren and reduce our reliance on externally supplied cooling. In consultation with KTH and the building owners, we were able to develop a way to make use of the heat generated by the new system in a manner that contributed positively to the environment. As a bonus, this approach also refunded some of the cost of the additional power needed to run Lindgren. This novel method is described further in Section 6.9.

6.8 Lindgren System Statistics

Since its upgrade to the full system Lindgren has been a very reliable and highly used resource. As can be seen in Figure 6.7, the average usage is above

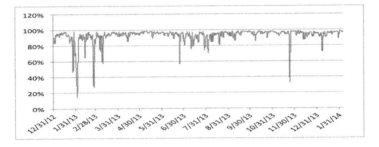

FIGURE 6.7: Lindgren usage.

90%. Allocations on the system are managed nationally by the SNIC National Allocation Committee (SNAC) that performs a scientific and technical review of allocation requests. Allocation rounds are held twice a year and allocations are typically handed out for a one-year period. All senior researchers based at Swedish research institutions are eligible to file applications.

Lindgren has some 300 users, of which about a dozen are actively using the system at any time. Users have a monthly quota, which is enforced over a sliding window of 30 days. We allow users to temporarily go over their quota; however, their priority is then very low. Once the quota is exceeded by over 50%, no further jobs are eligible to run anymore within this allocation.

Only full nodes are allocated and the maximum run-time of jobs is limited to 24 hours.

6.9   Lindgren Heat Re-Use System

When planning began at PDC to install the Lindgren system during 2010, we set ourselves a goal of re-using the heat produced by the computer system, rather than just using more district cooling. The reasons were both environmental and economic. The 16 cabinets of the new system would nearly double the power consumption at PDC from around 800 kW to 1,300 kW, and consequently produce a great deal of additional heat. Figure 6.8 shows the development of power consumption and capacity (TF) at PDC with some extrapolation for the future.

At the time, the PDC computer room was cooled using two methods: low density equipment was cooled by ambient cooling from ordinary Computer Room Air Conditioner (CRAC) units, and high-density equipment was cooled with hot aisle encapsulated cooling from APC. Both methods used cold water from the Stockholm area district cooling system. That system was already quite environmentally friendly: the company providing the water that was used for cooling actually produced local district heating by using heat pumps

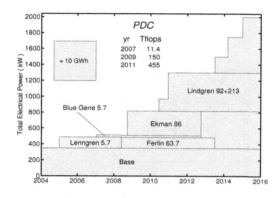

FIGURE 6.8: Power consumption and capacity at PDC over time.

to extract the additional heat from the returned (and thus heated) cooling water. If the company needed to provide additional cooling, they used sea water.

Although using district cooling was environmentally friendly, it was not financially efficient. Instead of being reimbursed for any heat that was produced, KTH would have had to pay around 0.45 SEK/kWh (at today's prices) to get rid of the excess heat energy. Moreover, during the cold season in Stockholm, KTH would have had to pay for district heating from the same energy company (currently at a rate of 0.60 SEK/kWh). Therefore we decided to try to use the excess heat from the new system to heat one of the KTH buildings close to PDC.

A major problem was that the two methods of cooling that were being used by PDC at the time produced a coolant temperature of 18°C which was too low to heat normal buildings. That temperature could have been increased using heat pumps; however, that would have involved a further increase in the use of electricity.

The air-cooled version of the Cray system takes in cold air (at less than 16°C) from under a raised floor and passes that air through the racks of computer components. The air becomes heated to temperatures of 35–45°C, and is then passed out at the top of the racks. Thus the air coming directly from Lindgren would be at a high enough temperature to heat the incoming air for another building. Since various steps in the process would each decrease the temperature somewhat, it was important to check that the final water temperature would still be high enough for heating a building. Investigations of standard industry air-water heat exchangers showed that such units could be used, and would produce final water temperatures suitable for our heating purposes.

To minimize the risk of water leakages just above the computers, we decided to hang the heat exchangers from the ceiling above Lindgren, but slightly

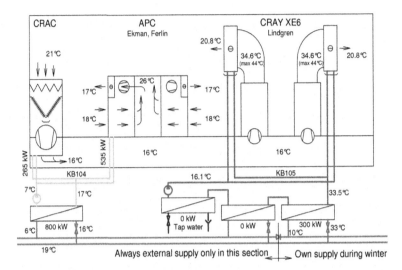

FIGURE 6.9: Layout of cooling at PDC.

displaced so the exchangers were not directly above the computer racks. Although this did not completely eliminate the possibility of problems from leakages, it reduced the consequences of a small leakage considerably. Hot air from the top of Lindgren was then fed to the suspended heat exchangers via chimney-like ducts.

Figure 6.9 shows the layout of the cooling at PDC. Ambient cooling is produced via the CRAC-units (to the left). Both the ambient cooling system and the hot aisle APC system are connected via the pipe system KB104 to the district cooling (with backup). The pipe system KB105 provides Lindgren's racks with high temperature cooling. This system has backup provided by conventional district cooling as well as tap water cooling.

Figure 6.10 shows the custom-made ducts on top of Lindgren leading the air through industrial heat exchangers.

The nearby Chemistry Laboratory at KTH was a good candidate to be the recipient of the heat from Lindgren. First of all, the building was undergoing renovations at the time, so the changes needed for using the recycled heat could be incorporated into the renovation process. Secondly, that particular building required large amounts of air to ventilate potentially dangerous fumes from the Chemistry laboratories so heated air was used more than in normal buildings at KTH.

In practical terms, the air-water heat exchangers hanging from the computer room ceiling would take the hot air from Lindgren at 35–45°C and cool it down to around 21°C. That cooled air would then be expelled from the heat exchangers back into the computer room. Meanwhile, the water in the heat exchangers would have been heated up to around 30–35°C. That heated

FIGURE 6.10: Custom-made ducts on top of Lindgren.

water would be circulated inside a closed circuit that could be cooled by a combination of three different heat exchangers that were placed in the basement outside the computer room. One of the heat exchangers was dedicated for heat re-use with the Chemistry building, another used the Stockholm district cooling system, and the final heat exchanger could use ordinary cold tap water (as a backup in case the other two heat exchangers failed to produce cold enough water).

The KTH cooling grid is actually built as a network of loops and fortunately the PDC computer room is supplied from the same loop as the Chem-

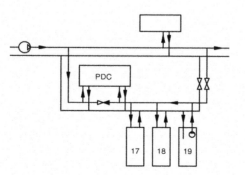

FIGURE 6.11: Ring-shaped cooling system at the KTH campus.

istry building. It is possible to close valves in the network so a section of that particular loop is isolated with the PDC computer room upstream of the Chemistry building. Figure 6.11 shows the ring-shaped cooling system at the KTH campus. The check valve closes and a self-supplying section is formed once building 19 (the Chemistry building) is capable of taking care of all waste heat in the section. This happens at about 0 °C outdoor temperature. Essentially this means that, with the addition of some components to the network, heated water can be sent from the PDC computer room to the Chemistry building via the existing cooling grid at KTH. Furthermore, cooled water (coming out of the Chemistry building) can be sent into the PDC computer room cooling system. However, just doing that is not enough as the amount of heat that the Chemistry building requires varies during the year, so under some conditions Lindgren may need more cooling than can be provided by the Chemistry building.

When the outdoor temperature is over 10°C, this heat-recycling system cannot be used at all and the Stockholm district cooling system provides all the cooling for the Cray. From 0–10°C the Chemistry building provides some cooling for the Cray with additional cooling coming from the Stockholm district cooling system through the second heat exchanger mentioned earlier. In sub-zero winter temperatures, the system really comes into its own and all cooling for the Cray is supplied by the Chemistry building.

This system for heating the Chemistry building with waste heat from Lindgren became fully operational during the winter of 2011–2012. It has been effective in providing environmentally friendly cooling for Lindgren that also offsets part of Lindgren's operational costs. During the 2012–2013 cold season 820 MWh of energy was transferred to the Chemistry building. This reduced the PDC usage of district cooling by the same amount, which corresponds to a saving of 350,000 SEK per year at current rates. On top of that, the Chemistry building saved around 250,000 SEK in district heating for the same period. However, as heating and cooling costs are expected to rise dramatically in the near future, the savings from the heat re-use system should increase significantly.

There is ongoing discussion about siting future supercomputer centers in extremely cold remote areas across Eurasia and North America, so as to take advantage of the extreme cold in the external environment to offset the cooling that is normally required for such large systems. However, the efficacy of the Lindgren heat re-use system has shown that there are actually advantages to siting large computing facilities in major metropolitan areas, aside from convenience in terms of the work force. With due planning, it would be possible to use the excess heat from such systems to provide municipal heat to surrounding areas. This has environmental advantages in that the demand for local heating would be reduced, thereby reducing the emissions of pollutants and greenhouse gases from more usual combustion-based methods of heat generation.

TABLE 6.4: Benchmarks for post-Lindgren system.

Benchmark	Domain
GROMACS	Molecular Dynamics
Nek5000	Computational Fluid Dynamics
PowerFLOW	Computational Fluid Dynamics
VASP	Materials Science
GENE	Fusion

6.10 The Future after Lindgren

Lindgren is expected to stay in operation until the end of 2014 and to provide an uninterrupted service, the process for procuring follow-up system has already been started. The new system, which will be funded jointly by SNIC and KTH together with some industrial contributions, is expected to deliver a peak performance exceeding 1.3 PFlops. A setup similar to the current Lindgren service is envisaged, combining the main HPC system with a pre- and post-processing system that will be equipped with more memory per core and GPUs. Both systems will share the same Lustre-based file system.

As the new system will again be a national system with a wide range of usage, a number of representative application benchmarks have been selected to guide the selection process. These benchmarks also mimic the typical expected job mix with job sizes ranging between 2,000 and 10,000 cores on average. Our benchmarks cover the areas of computational fluid dynamics, molecular dynamics, materials science, and fusion, and are listed in Table 6.4. These benchmarks are complemented with standard benchmarks like stream, DGEMM, HPL, FFT, and MPI benchmarks.

Bibliography

[1] R. Apostolov, H. Agren, L. Axner, et al. ScalaLife—Scalable Software Services for Life Sciences. In *Proceedings eChallenges e-2012 Conference*, 2012.

[2] CRESTA Web page. http://www.cresta-project.eu.

[3] J. Dongarra, P. Beckman, et al. The International Exascale Software Roadmap. *International Journal of High Performance Computer Applications*, 25(1), 2011.

[4] EPiGRAM Web page. http://www.epigram-project.eu.

[5] Paul F. Fischer, James W. Lottes, and Stefan G. Kerkemeier. nek5000 Web page, 2008. http://nek5000.mcs.anl.gov.

[6] The Human Brain Project Web page. http://www.humanbrainproject.eu.

[7] S. Markidis, G. Lapenta, and Rizwan-uddin. Multi-scale simulations of plasma with iPIC3D. *Mathematics and Computers in Simulation*, 80(7), 2010.

[8] PRACE Web page. http://www.prace-ri.eu.

[9] S. Pronk, S. Pall, R. Schulz, P. Larsson, P. Bjelkmar, R. Apostolov, M.R. Shirts, et al. GROMACS 4.5: a high-throughput and highly parallel open source molecular simulation toolkit. *Bioinformatics*, 29(7):845—854, 2013.

[10] SeRC Web page. http://www.e-science.se.

Chapter 7

Peregrine at the National Renewable Energy Laboratory

Kevin Regimbal, Ilene Carpenter, Christopher Chang, and Steve Hammond

National Renewable Energy Laboratory

7.1 Overview

While the focus here is typically on computer systems, the origins of this system, named Peregrine, are tightly linked to the facility and a holistic approach to energy efficient high performance computing in which the system is intimately tied to the data center and the data center is integrated in the larger research facility. The U.S. Department of Energy's National Renewable Energy Laboratory (NREL), located in Golden, Colorado, is world renowned for its commitment to green building construction and for leading by example. NREL recently completed the Energy Systems Integration Facility (ESIF), a new 182,000-square-foot research facility that includes high bay and laboratory space, office space for about 220 staff, and an ultra-efficient, showcase high performance computing (HPC) data center. This showcase facility was built in accordance with the U.S. Green Buildings Council's standards and has achieved a Leadership in Energy and Environmental Design (LEED)[1] Platinum Certification. In February 2014, the Energy Systems Integration Facility was awarded the 2014 Lab of the Year Award in R&D Magazines 2014 Laboratory of the Year Competition.

Peregrine is composed of 1440 computational nodes based on Intel Xeon processors and Intel Xeon Phi coprocessors, with a peak speed of 1.2 Petaflops, making it the world's fastest HPC system dedicated to advancing renewable energy and energy efficiency technologies. The data center itself features a chiller-less design, direct warm-water liquid cooling, and waste heat capture/re-use, and it operates at an annualized average PUE rating of 1.06 or better, making it the world's most energy-efficient data center. This data center demonstrates technologies that save energy and water, reduce CO_2 emissions, and capture/re-use waste heat with an estimated annualized average Energy Reuse Effectiveness of 0.7. Planning for the new research facility and innovative data center focused on a holistic "chips to bricks" approach to energy efficiency to ensure that the HPC system and data center would have a symbiotic relationship with the ESIF offices and laboratories, and to integrate the new facility into NREL's campus.

7.1.1   Design Features, Efficiency and Sustainability Measures

Several key design specifications have led to the data center's extreme efficiency. First, high-voltage electricity (480VAC rather than the typical 208VAC) is supplied directly to the racks, which saves on power electronics equipment (cost savings), power conversions, and electrical losses (energy savings).

Secondly, the data center uses warm-water liquid cooling supplied directly to the server racks. The decision to use liquid cooling was made several years

---

[1]The Leadership in Energy and Environmental Design (LEED) Green Building Rating System serves as a nationally accepted benchmark for the design, construction, and operation of high-performance green buildings. To achieve LEED certification, a construction project shall achieve certain prerequisites and performance benchmarks within each of the following five areas: sustainable site development, water savings, energy efficiency, materials selection, and indoor environment quality. Projects are awarded Certified, Silver, Gold or Platinum certification, depending on the number of credits achieved. For more information, see http://www.usgbc.org/leed#certification

ago, before liquid-cooled systems were routinely available. There are several advantages to this approach. Water as a heat-exchange medium is three orders of magnitude more efficient than air, and getting the heat exchange close to where the heat is generated is most efficient. Also, 75°F water supplied for cooling the computers allows the data center to use highly energy-efficient evaporative cooling towers, eliminating the need for much more expensive and more energy-demanding mechanical chillers, saving both capital and operating expenses. Using the new 2014 ASHRAE liquid cooling supply water temperature classification, the NREL data center is a class W2 facility, meaning that the cooling supply is warmer than 17°C but cooler than 27°C. Additionally, the hydronic system features "smooth piping," where a series of 45° angles replace 90° angles wherever possible to reduce pressure drops and further save pump energy. The evaporative cooling towers are paired with remote basins to eliminate the use of basin heaters, while pumps and heat exchangers efficiently transfer heat to where it is needed. Thus, the data center's high energy efficiency is achieved with best-in-class engineering practices and widely available technologies.

The ESIF data center is designed and built to capture the "waste" heat generated by the HPC system for heating within the building. By design, the hot water returned from the HPC system must be 95°F or warmer, and at least 90% of the heat load from the HPC system must be dissipated directly to the hydronic system. By focusing on direct liquid cooling, the energy needed to cool the computer systems decreases dramatically, as does fan energy use. The data center is heavily instrumented to continually monitor data center efficiency and to provide real-time optimization of energy usage.

By capturing the computer waste heat directly to liquid and integrating the data center into the ESIF, the data center serves as the primary heat source for office and laboratory space within the facility. Data center waste heat is also used to heat glycol loops located under an adjacent plaza and walkway, melting snow and making winter walks between buildings safer for laboratory staff. As the HPC system expands to meet demand, data center heat output will exceed the heating needs of the ESIF. Mechanical systems and infrastructure are planned to allow for future export of this heat to other facilities on NREL's campus. In addition to winter heating, the long-term goal is for the data center to become the summer campus water heating system, allowing central heating boilers to be shut down.

NREL's new data center features the first petascale HPC system to use warm-water liquid cooling and will be the first to reach an average PUE rating of 1.06 or better. In the long term, the computer industry trend is toward more cores per chip and continued increases in power density, making efficient cooling of large data centers increasingly difficult with air alone. While the particulars for efficient cooling of servers and heat rejection will vary depending on site-specific conditions, the fundamentals and approaches used here are widely applicable and represent a new best-in-class standard. NREL's leadership in warm-water liquid-cooled data centers coupled with waste heat re-use will pave the way for the federal government and the private sector to continue to meet increased demand for data, services, and computational capability at a much higher efficiency than has been achieved to date, reducing energy demand and saving money.

7.1.2   Sponsor/Program Background

Stewardship for Peregrine is provided by the U.S. Department of Energy's Office of Energy Efficiency and Renewable Energy (EERE), which accelerates development and facilitates deployment of energy efficiency and renewable energy technologies and market-based solutions that strengthen U.S. energy security, environmental quality, and economic vitality.

EERE is at the center of creating the clean energy economy today. It leads the U.S. Department of Energy's efforts to develop and deliver market-driven solutions for energy-saving homes, buildings, and manufacturing; sustainable transportation; and renewable electricity generation. The focus of the modeling and simulation on Peregrine is to support and advance these efforts.

7.1.3   Timeline

The timeline for this project involved an integrated construction project to build the new research facility as well as a project for the specification and acquisition of the new high performance computing system itself. The two projects were coordinated so that the new system would be delivered shortly after the data center in the new facility was commissioned. This coordinated project schedule is highlighted in Table 7.1 and major elements are described below.

Construction of the **ESIF facility** was undertaken using a Design-Build approach in which the design and construction services were contracted by a single entity known as the *design-builder* or *design-build* contractor. In contrast to *design-bid-build*, *design-build* relies on a single point of responsibility contract and is used to minimize risks for the project owner and to reduce the delivery schedule by overlapping the design phase and construction phase of a project.

The Peregrine implementation project team worked closely with the design-build team to implement the "last mile" piping and electrical distribution panels while the construction team was still on-site finishing the laboratory portion of the ESIF facility. The datacenter portion of the facility was commissioned and ready for computing hardware in October 2012.

Peregrine Phase 1a equipment was delivered in November 2012. It consisted of Peregrine's test cluster, ethernet and InfiniBand core infrastructure, NFS and Lustre filesystems, and 144 compute nodes. See Figure 7.2 for system architecture overview. The Phase 1a system enabled HP and NREL to finalize the OS stack and build the required scientific applications.

The **Phase1b** equipment delivered mid-February 2012 marked the first shipment of water-cooled equipment. Peregrine's cooling system interfaces

TABLE 7.1: Key facility and system dates for Peregrine.

ESIF Milestone	Date	Peregrine Milestone
Construction Started	Apr 2011	HPC system requirements collected
	Feb 2012	RFP released to Vendors
	Mar 2012	RFP responses due from Vendors
	Jul 2012	Contract awarded to Hewlett Packard
Peregrine *Primary* Cooling Piping Complete	Aug 2012	Detailed site preparation
HPC Datacenter Commissioned	Oct 2012	
Offices and Datacenter Complete	Nov 2012	Phase 1a delivery (air cooled nodes, infrastructure, storage)
Electrical Panels Complete	Dec 2012	
Phase 1b *Secondary* cooling loop hot work	Feb 2013	Phase 1b delivery (prototype water-cooled nodes and CDUs)
Phase 2 *Secondary* manifold installation	Aug 2013	Phase 2 Initial Delivery (first water-cooled Ivy Bridge nodes)
	Sep 2013	Phase 2 final Delivery (water-cooled Ivy Bridge and Phi nodes)
		Secretary Moniz dedicates Peregrine
	Oct 2013	Physical Installation Complete
	Nov 2013	System acceptance passed
	Jan 2014	Full production use commences

with the ESIF Energy Recover Water (ERW) loops via heat exchange and pump modules called Cooling Distribution Units (CDUs). CDUs receive water up to 75°F from the ERW Supply pipes and return that water and 95°F (or warmer) to the ERW Return side. The CDU interface with the ESIF ERW piping is called the *primary* side.

The CDUs distribute water to the compute racks via a distribution manifold built of 2.5 inch copper pipes located below the floor. The CDU interface with the compute racks is called the *secondary* side. The prototype CDU design located the primary and secondary supply and return pipes at the bottom of the rack, near the middle of the rack.

For this first of a kind system, installing the first engineering prototype CDUs required custom copper piping to be installed on-site from beneath the raised floor. The plumbing crew cut, fitted and sweated each connection to build up the cooling infrastructure. This first installation process took about three weeks and required frequent "hot" work in the datacenter as most joints needed to be soldered in place.

Phase 1b water-cooled equipment consisted of four prototype node racks and two prototype CDU racks. The compute node racks were about 8 feet tall, just tall enough to be of concern fitting onto the freight elevator and through the datacenter door. The compute racks were shipped in two pieces, designed to be stacked once on-site. Once the node racks were stacked, final plumbing network, and power connections were made and tested. Phase 1b also included a full scalable unit (288 nodes) of HP SL230 air-cooled nodes.

It is worth noting that the four engineering prototype liquid cooled racks and two CDUs were delivered to NREL on February 19, 2013. Just eight days later, the integrated system achieved 204.1 TeraFlops of HPL performance on February 27, 2013. This was just one week after prototype rack delivery to NREL.

Phase 2 delivery occurred in August and September 2013. Scalable units were shipped from HP's engineering facility in Houston, TX as they passed component and integrated testing at HP.

The biggest changes from the first engineering prototypes racks to the first product shipment were with the cooling infrastructure. HP moved the CDU inlet and outlet water connections to the back of the racks, allowing connections to be made from above the floor. Water connections were made with flexible rubber hoses with quick connect fittings rather than requiring custom-fitted copper piping. The secondary loop cooling distribution manifold, which had required weeks of custom hot work was now composed of prefabricated modular manifolds. Installation time for secondary manifolds shrank from three weeks to support six racks of equipment to three days for 17 racks of equipment, greatly accelerating site prep and installation time.

7.2   Applications and Workloads

7.2.1   Computational Tasks and Domain Examples

Peregrine is the flagship computing resource of DOE's Office of Energy Efficiency and Renewable Energy. It supports a wide variety of domain science, engineering, and analysis communities, including solar energy, bioenergy, wind and water, fuel cells, and advanced manufacturing as well as energy efficient vehicles and buildings. Some of these are model-centric, with modest computing requirements; some are simulation-centric, with either needs for traditional HPC resources in highly coupled calculations, or high capacity resources for many uncoupled calculations used for design and optimization work. Some are data-centric, requiring massive storage with high I/O bandwidth and low-latency access. Overall, the project portfolio supported on Peregrine leads to a diversity of user needs, and the system needs to provide value across the entire user community. Historically, most of the compute cycles have been utilized in applications related to materials physics and chemistry, wind energy and bioenergy applications.

1. Materials Physics and Chemistry. The discovery of new materials with better properties than the current standards is a continual challenge, and computational physics and chemistry is a foundation stone supporting the process of materials design, synthesis, testing, scaling, and ultimate commercialization. Solar photovoltaics, fuel transformation catalysis,

and reactivity in advanced fuel cell and battery architectures are several examples where computation is making an impact. Particular challenges for high-performance computing are large crystalline unit cells needed to describe low-density defects and doping as well as complex surfaces, pseudocrystalline and amorphous materials that require large numbers of atoms in simulations of dynamical processes, and characterization of chemical spaces, where explicit enumeration is required absent known relationships of continuity and smoothness between structures and properties.

2. Wind Resource Modeling. The advanced state of wind commercial penetration relative to earlier technologies makes understanding the available wind resource critical. To this end, researchers are attempting to model more complex environments over larger geographic regions, and simulate them with higher fidelity, larger couplings between model elements, for longer times. This effort creates a significant demand for performance and application scalability with respect to nodes, cores, memory, and I/O. In addition, downstream processing requires large dataset handling and extreme visualization techniques.

3. Bioenergy. Lignocellulose, a catch-all term for most plant matter not suitable for direct use as food, is a potentially important feedstock for production of fuels and chemicals at scale. Within the context of biotechnology, the focus is on transforming this diverse and heterogeneous material into sugar, which serves as a more or less universal precursor for metabolic transformations to alcohols (e.g., ethanol) or post-ethanol "advanced biofuels," as well as fine chemicals or drug precursors outside of the energy world. A primary concern for lignocellulosic feedstocks is their recalcitrance to most chemical and biochemical processes for sugar production. Much research is therefore geared to understanding the production of lignocellulose (in order to engineer less recalcitrance), the physics and chemistry of lignocellulose itself (both to understand the detailed mechanisms of recalcitrance, and to better hypothesize molecules that can transform chemical motifs within it), and the action of enzymatic catalysts on lignocellulose (to derive principles from which to engineer these enzymes via mutagenesis). Much of the application demand in this field on Peregrine is molecular dynamics, whereby a classical atomistic or coarse-grained model of the lignocellulose or LC-enzyme system is propagated in time subject to approximate Hamiltonians describing the energy and forces within the system.

7.2.2   Application Highlights

Although a wide variety of applications are supported and run on Peregrine, several constitute major shares of the overall available allocation time.

Unlike traditional HPC systems or today's leadership-class facilities, the dominant workload around these heavily used applications is not predicated on large coupled calculations with latency and bandwidth demands on the communication fabric. Rather, high-throughput calculations with substantial demands on I/O, disk capacity, and scheduling resources predominate. This usage pattern is to be expected given the greater emphasis on discovery (where spaces need to be enumerated and searched) and predictive reliability (UQ) characteristic of NREL's mission space in the world of near-commercial science and technology. Nevertheless, while these codes are usually run without an explicit requirement for traditional HPC scalability, they often carry the capacity for larger-scale runs, and/or sufficient architectural or algorithmic complexity associated with parallelism to be of interest to the computer science community.

1. The Weather Research and Forecasting Model (WRF) [3] is a mesoscale numerical weather prediction system designed to serve both atmospheric research and operational forecasting needs (see www.wrf-model.org). At NREL it is used for high resolution research forecasting to study the potential for solar and wind power generation. It has been run for both large (continental U.S.) and smaller, more limited geographical areas. WRF is one of the applications that is run on Peregrine using a large number of nodes per job. A set of simulations may be run to simulate a year or more of weather conditions, leading to a large volume of grid-based output data that must be saved for subsequent analysis.

2. The Vienna Ab Initio Simulation Program (VASP), developed by the Computational Materials Physics group at the Universität Wien [2] is a standard in the materials physics and chemistry communities. The package's multiple capabilities are centered around electronic structure and *ab initio* molecular dynamics, using plane-wave expansions of the wavefunction to solve approximately the non-relativistic time-independent Schrödinger equation. Density functional and Hartree-Fock methods are fundamental to more advanced quasiparticle and many-body perturbation theories. The analytical capabilities of the software tuned to materials science drive much of its demand, and it is a workhorse program for calculating band structures, surface reaction intermediate and transition state energies, and excited-state properties for bulk materials, in which a crystalline unit cell is periodic in three dimensions, or surfaces, where a layer of vacuum separates atomically dense images along one dimension (i.e., the material is periodic in two dimensions, with the third representing a vacuum-bounded cleavage plane).

3. Gaussian [1] is perhaps the best known package for molecular quantum chemistry. The first commercial release of this package dates back to 1970, and the legacy of hardware against which the package was optimized as well as the working models that have grown up around it may

have something to do with the software's strengths today. The current major release, Gaussian09, is capable of distributed memory paralellism via the Linda programming model. Operationally, this amounts to internode communications via shell sessions on each working node. However, the software's dominant strengths lay in a huge assembly of quantum chemical methodological implementations, large shared-memory calculations, and algorithmic adaptation to optimize the use of these resources. Shared-memory parallelism is realized via standard OpenMP threading.

7.3 System Overview

Peregrine is a Hewlett-Packard (HP) 1.2 petaflop/s cluster based on Intel Xeon E5-2670 SandyBridge processors, Intel Xeon E5-2695v2 IvyBridge processors, and Intel Xeon Phi 5120D coprocessors. Peregrine is comprised of 6 scalable units (SUs) containing a total of 1440 dual-socket computational nodes. Four types of dual-socket compute nodes are provided: (1) 16-core SandyBridge nodes, (2) 24-core IvyBridge nodes, (3) 24-core IvyBridge nodes with 64 GB of memory, and (4) 16-core SandyBridge nodes equipped with Intel Xeon Phi coprocessors. Peregrine is equipped with an InfiniBand FDR interconnect. Full bisection bandwidth is available within each SU of 144 or 288 nodes. SUs are connected to each other with an 8:1 over-subscription.

Peregrine's storage sub-system includes 2.25 petabytes of Lustre storage for scratch and shared project storage, and 40 terabytes of NFS storage for home and cluster software.

Figure 7.1 shows seven water-cooled s8500 enclosures (with blue lights visible) and 4 Cooling Distribution Units in the ESIF HPC data center. The skin applied after installation depicts Colorado landscape and Peregrine falcon.

7.4 Hardware Architecture

Figure 7.2 provides a high-level overview of the Peregrine System. The Phase 1 system includes the core InfiniBand and Ethernet network infrastructure, Network Attached Storage (NAS) subsystem, Parallel File System (PFS), system infrastructure servers (login, administration and Lustre MDS nodes), one scalable unit (SU) of SandyBridge nodes, and a test cluster. The Phase 2 system depicted with a green background includes SUs of IvyBridge

FIGURE 7.1: Picture of Peregrine.

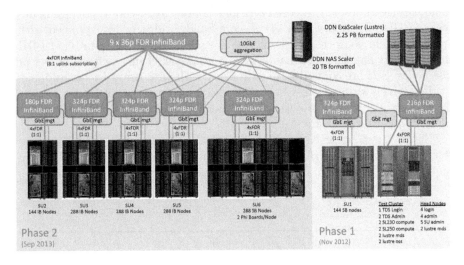

FIGURE 7.2: Peregrine architectural system overview.

nodes and 1 scalable unit of SandyBridge nodes equipped with Intel Xeon Phi coprocessors.

SU1 consists of two racks, where each rack is composed of 72 SL230G8 compute nodes. Each node is a 1U, half-width form factor with dual 8-core Xeon E5-2670 SandyBridge processors running at 2.6 Ghz and equipped with

TABLE 7.2: Peregrine hardware configuration.

Feature	SU1	SU[2-4]	SU5	SU6
Node Architecture	HP Proliant SL230	HP Proliant SE2x8530a	HP Proliant SE2x8530a	HP Proliant SE8550a
CPU	Intel Xeon E5-2670	Intel Xeon E5-2695v2	Intel Xeon E5-2695v2	Intel Xeon E5-2670
CPU microarchitecture	SandyBridge	IvyBridge	IvyBridge	SandyBridge
CPU Frequency (GHz)	2.6	2.4	2.4	2.6
CPU Count per Node	2	2	2	2
Xeon Cores per Node	16	24	24	16
Node Memory Capacity (GB)	32	32	64	32
Phi Accelerator				Intel Xeon Phi 5120D
Phi Count per Node				2
Phi Memory Capacity (GB)				8
Interconnection Network		InfiniBand 4x FDR		
Network Ports per Node		1 Mellanox Connect X-3 IB FDR HCA		
Compute Racks	2	5	2	4
Total number of nodes	144	720	288	288
Peak FLOP Rate (TF)	47.92	331.78	132.71	678.11

32 GB of 1600 Mhz DDR3 memory and Mellanox Connect X-3 FDR Infini-Band HCA and two Intel Xeon Phi coprocessors.

SU[2-5] are housed in seven rack enclosures of dual socket Intel IvyBridge based compute nodes. Each HP S8500 liquid cooled heat capture and re-use enclosure includes 144 SE2x8530a compute nodes. Each node is a 1U, half-length form factor with dual 12-core Xeon E5-2695v2 "IvyBridge" processors running at 2.4 Ghz and equipped with 32 GB (SU[2-4]) or 64 GB (SU5) 1600 Mhz DDR3 memory and Mellanox Connect X-3 FDR InfiniBand HCA.

SU6 includes four rack enclosures of dual socket Intel SandyBridge based compute nodes equipped with Intel Xeon Phi coprocessors. Each HP s8500 enclosure includes 72 SE8550a compute nodes and 144 Intel Xeon Phi 5120D coprocessors. Each node is a 1U, half-length form factor with dual 8-core Xeon E5-2670 "SandyBridge" processors running at 2.6 Ghz and equipped with 32 GB of 1600 Mhz DDR3 memory and Mellanox Connect X-3 FDR InfiniBand HCA and two Intel Xeon Phi coprocessors.

Peregrine's interconnect is based on 4x Fourteen Data Rate (FDR) Mellanox SX6518 324-Port InfiniBand Director Switches and Mellanox SX6025 36-port 56 Gb/s InfiniBand Switch Systems. Each scalable unit is equipped with a 324-port switch. This configuration provides full bisection bandwidth within each scalable unit supporting job sizes up to 6912 cores. Nine 36-port switches provide "top" connectivity. Scalable units are connected to each other at an oversubscription ratio of 8:1, which provides sufficient bandwidth so that any scalable unit can fully utilize the central Lustre filesystems.

Peregrine has two data storage subsystems. The Network Attached Storage (NAS) solution offers NFS to all peregrine nodes. NAS storage is provided by DDN based on 10K SFAs and a pair of cluster "heads" which run a software stack that offers the block storage as NFS volumes. Peregrine has two filesystems shared from the NFS solution. /home is a 10 TB filesystem which provides user home directories. /nopt is a 2 TB filesystem which is NREL's shared /opt filesystem, which contains the shared software, compilers, modules and other cluster-wide software.

The Parallel File System (PFS) cluster is a Lustre-based solution offering lustre to Peregrine compute and login nodes. The PFS solution is provided by DDN based on 12K SFAs which contain virtual Object Storage Servers that share lustre Object Storage Targets to Peregrine. PFS provides two filesystems: /scratch is a system-wide scratch filesystem, and /projects is a shared collaboration space where projects can store common data.

The **HP s8500 liquid cooled enclosure** implements a hybrid cooling approach, providing component-level liquid cooling to CPUs, Accelerators and DIMMs, and using a liquid to air heat-exchanger for the remaining parts. Peregrine includes eleven s8500 enclosures.

The s8500 has four 480/277 AC 30A 5-pin connectors, capable of providing 20 kW each for a total of 80 kW per rack. The 480AC power feed to the s8500 allows for enhanced power delivery efficiency gains, saving the 3-5% loss in the commonly deployed 480AC to 208AC transformer.

Power supplying each rack is coordinated via a lighting contactor that energizes or de-energizes all four circuits at one time. The s8500 enclosures are configured to send a 24-volt signal to coorsponding lighting contactors which remotely de-energize all 480 volt power to racks if a leak has been detected.

The **Hydronics** subsystem provides warm-water cooling waters to the s8500 enclosures. Figure 7.3 depicts the configuration of the hydronics system on Peregrine. Peregrine's Cooling Distribution Units (CDUs) are deployed in pairs in an N+1 configuration so that two CDUs provide water to four s8500 enclosures.

Water is provided to CDUs by the ESIF facility energy recovery water loop. Water returning from ESIF's main mechanical room has been cooled by water towers to a maximum of 75°F. CDUs manage primary water flow through their heat exchangers, flowing the right amount of water to ensure adequate cooling while returning water at least 95°F to the energy recovery water loop. Energy recovery water is routed to a heat exchanger that transfers heat to the building heating system before returning to the ESIF main mechanical room.

The CDUs pump water through a secondary water manifold system that distributes water to the s8500 enclosures. CDUs coordinate with each other to ensure adequate cooling is provided at all times.

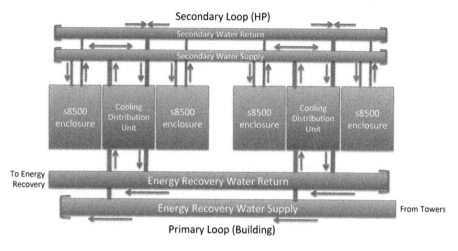

FIGURE 7.3: Peregrine hydronics sketch.

7.5 System Software

The Operating System stack on Peregrine is typical for Linux clusters. Table 7.3 summarizes the major software packages installed on Peregrine.

TABLE 7.3: Peregrine software configuration.

Feature	Software	Version
Login and Admin Node OS	RHEL	6.2
Compute Node OS	CentOS	6.2
Parallel Filesystem	Lustre	2.1
Cluster Management	HP Configuration Management Utility (CMU)	7.1
Compilers	Intel	12
	PGI	12
	GNU	4.1
MPI	IntelMPI (default)	4.1
	OpenMPI	1.7
Notable Libraries	HDF5	1.8
	netcdf/pNetCDF	4.1/1.3
	Intel MKL	13
Software Environment Management	Modules	3.2.10
Job Scheduler	Moab	7.2
Resource Manager	Torque	4.2
Debugging Tools	TotalView	8.11

Operating systems are deployed via the HP Configuration Management Utility (CMU). CMU manages provisioning of diskless node images and deployment. Node images are created on a golden master node. CMU adapts images for deployment to Peregrine's diskless nodes. At present, two node configurations are maintained. One configuration is deployed to nodes equipped with the Intel Xeon Phi coprocessors. The other configuration is deployed to all the other nodes.

Shared software is deployed to the /nopt filesystem residing on Peregrine's NAS storage. Software is made available to users via the module's software environment management system.

One acute need identified early was the ability to install additional RedHat Package Manager (RPM) packages on a regular basis. Deploying RPMs to nodes in the normal fashion would require installation on a golden node, then reboot of nodes into the new image. This approach was not flexible nor fast enough to serve user needs on Peregrine, so an alternative mechanism was developed.

The approach involves installing desired packages onto a standalone server using yum. Considerable time is saved by using RPM software installation methods instead of manually acquiring each package, tracing dependencies, building, installing and testing packages.

Once the desired software environment is installed on the standalone server, a complete copy is replicated onto the /nopt filesystem. A module is provided adding library and binary paths to a user's environment. Since many of the desired packages appear in the Extra Packages for Enterprise Linux (EPEL) RPM repository, this module was named "epel."

7.6   Programming System

Peregrine is built with Intel Xeon and Intel Xeon Phi coprocessors so the primary programming models are standards-based, including threads, OpenMP and MPI. The Xeon Phi coprocessors may also be used via Intel compiler-specific offload methods.

Because Peregrine runs standard Linux, a wide variety of languages and compilers are available, including C, C++, Fortran, Python and Java. Supported compiler suites include Intel, PGI and the GNU compilers. Intel MPI, mvapich2 and OpenMPI libraries are all available. The modules package is used to allow users to easily choose a compatible set of compilers and libraries.

The primary performance analysis tools on Peregrine are Intel VTune Amplifier XE 2013 and Intel Trace Analyzer and Intel Trace Collector. Other tools include Stat and TAU. Debuggers and correctness tools include the Rogue-Wave Totalview debugger and Intel Inspector XE 2013.

7.7 Visualization and Analysis

Peregrine supports advanced visualization and analysis both remotely and in-person. To support remote visualization and analysis, Peregrine is equipped with a large-memory data analysis and visualization (DAV) node with hardware-accelerated graphics card. The DAV node is a 4U form factor with four 8-core Xeon E5-4670 "SandyBridge" processors running at 2.6 GHz with 368 GB of 1600 MHz DDR3 memory and a Nvidia Quadro 6000 (see Table 7.4). The DAV node is used as an interactive system to support remote visualization applications as single jobs, which may contain one or more threads, potentially accessing all the memory contained within the node as a single address space. This is implemented by using *TurboVNC* to provide users the ability to run advanced visualization applications remotely on an interactive desktop. *VirtualGL* is used to provide access to the DAV graphics hardware by redirecting OpenGL rendering instructions to the DAV graphics card and copying the results to destination windows on the VNC desktop. To support in-person visualization, Peregrine is equipped with a visualization gateway node that exports the Peregrine file systems to NREL's state-of-the-art visualization laboratory, the ESIF Insight Center, which includes an immersive virtual environment and large-scale display walls (see Figure 7.4). The visualization gateway node connects to the Peregrine network with FDR InfiniBand and provides two 10 G connections to the Insight Center display systems.

The Insight Center **Visualization Room** provides meeting space that features a large, rear-projected, 14 megapixel image display. Large-scale, high-resolution visual imagery can be used to effectively convey information and illustrate research findings to stakeholders and visitors. The Visualization room also boosts the exchange of ideas among NREL researchers and their collaborating partners. Using the high-resolution, large-scale display, researchers and

TABLE 7.4: Peregrine DAV hardware configuration.

Feature	System
Node Architecture	HP Proliant DL560 Gen 8
CPU	Intel Xeon E5-4670
CPU microarchitecture	SandyBridge
CPU Frequency (GHz)	2.6
CPU Count per Node	2
Xeon Cores per Node	16
Node Memory Capacity (GB)	368
Graphics Accelerator	Nvidia Quadro 6000
Graphics Memory Capacity (GB)	6
Interconnection Network	InfiniBand 4x FDR

FIGURE 7.4: Photograph of NREL scientists analyzing a Peregrine molecular dynamics simulation in the ESIF Insight Center.

others now have the visual "real estate" to lay out a significant amount of data that will enable them to analyze large-scale simulations, ensembles of simulations, and highly detailed visual analytics displays.

The **Collaboration Room** provides multiple workspaces in which researchers and partners from all disciplines of science and engineering can interactively visualize highly complex, large-scale data, systems, and operations. In this area, researchers can view in real time the testing and simulation of equipment and technologies. The collaboration room is intended to support the analysis of a wide range of research within the EERE mission. Research areas include any that generate large-scale data. Simulation data (data that produce a representation of a spatial system or model and possibly its evolution in time), may span from the atomistic scale of a molecular dynamics simulation of new materials to the planetary boundary scales of turbine wakes and other turbulent structures in multi-turbine array simulations. Measured data (tested data as opposed to predicted or estimated data) spans from the nanostructures in 3D microscopy data of biomass pretreatments to the complex dynamics of the North American electrical power grid. The main workspace is a stereoscopic immersive virtual environment composed of six projectors that illuminate two surfaces – a wall and the floor. The projected space can be used in conjunction with an optical tracker and the visualizations respond in relation to the movement of the user. This allows users to physically explore and interact with their data as shown in Figure 7.4.

7.8   Data Center/Facility

Peregrine resides at the National Renewable Energy Laboratory (NREL), a U.S. Department of Energy laboratory, located in Golden, Colorado, dedicated to research and advancing renewable energy and energy efficiency technologies. The system is housed in NREL's new state-of-the-art, energy efficient data center described below.

7.8.1   NREL Energy Efficient Data Center

In the fall of 2012, NREL completed construction of the new Energy System Integration Facility (ESIF), providing laboratory and office space for approximately 200 NREL researchers staff. The focus of this new 182,500 ft^2 facility is research to overcome challenges related to the interconnection of distributed energy systems and the integration of renewable energy technologies into the electricity grid. Following NREL's tradition of "walking the talk," the ESIF demonstrates NREL's commitment to a sustainable energy future with its energy-saving workplace environment [2]. This showcase facility not only helps meet the nation's crucial research objectives for integrating clean and sustainable energy technologies into the grid, but was built in accordance with the U.S. Green Buildings Council's LEED Platinum Certification standards.

This new facility shown in Figure 7.5 includes a state-of-the-art data center, which is itself a showcase facility for demonstrating data center energy efficiency. The office space is shown in the front right, the energy efficient data center is the onyx black and chrome middle section of the building and research laboratory space is set back behind the data center. It is designed to achieve an annualized average power usage effectiveness (PUE) rating of

FIGURE 7.5: The Energy System Integration Facility at NREL.

1.06 or better making it the world's most energy efficient data center. The primary focus is on warm water, liquid-cooled of high power computer components. There are no mechanical or compressor-based cooling systems. The cooling liquid is supplied indirectly from cooling towers and thus the ambient temperature is warmer than typical data centers. Finally, waste heat from the HPC systems is captured and used as the primary heat source in the ESIF office, laboratory space, and to condition ventilation makeup air. The ESIF data center has approximately 10,000 ft^2 of uninterrupted, usable machine room space. Subtracting present and planned systems, there is over 7,000 ft^2 of computer-ready space.

7.8.2   ESIF Data Center Mechanical Infrastructure

The NREL data center differs from most data centers in the way it handles waste heat. As mentioned above, the primary focus is on warm water, liquid-cooling high power computer components. While both air-cooled and liquid-cooled cooling solutions can be accommodated, the data center is provisioned to air-cool up to a maximum of 10% of the total heat load. Thus, at least 90% (and up to 100%) of the total heat generated is dissipated to liquid. For liquid cooled systems, both direct liquid or indirect liquid cooling approaches are acceptable.

FIGURE 7.6: The NREL HPC data center mechanical space.

In addition to providing ultra efficient systems to reject un-needed waste heat (summer operation), it captures and re-uses the waste heat within the building to offset heating loads in office and lab space as well as condition ventilation air. As a result, there is a greater emphasis on maximizing the waste heat available and ensuring a high quality of waste heat. Some key features of the mechanical systems include: (1) Compressor-free cooling of data center equipment; (2) All pumps and fans utilize energy efficient, variable frequency drives; and (3) Central HVAC systems are designed for low velocity operation.

The energy recovery water system provides hydronic cooling for both the HPC data center and central HVAC equipment. Cooling water delivered to the computer equipment will vary between 60°F and 75°F. Using the new 2014 ASHRAE liquid cooling supply water temperature classification, the NREL data center is a class W2 facility, meaning that the cooling supply is warmer than 17°C but cooler than 27°C. This temperature variation is based primarily on outdoor conditions and the demand for waste heat within the building. Note that the ambient temperature will generally be closer to 75°F to maximize efficiency and the quality of waste heat within the building. In summer conditions, with lesser demand for waste heat, data center heat is rejected via evaporative cooling towers. During peak winter conditions, all data center waste heat can be captured and used by the building and district heating system. For any heat load not dissipated to liquid, the data center includes a full hot-aisle containment system to eliminate mixing of hot exhaust air with the cool supply air. This hot aisle air passes through a central air-to-liquid heat exchange, is filtered and recirculated.

7.8.3   ESIF Data Center Electrical Power

Power for the data center comes from the main electrical room and mechanical space on the ESIF second level and it provides for both normal and stand-by power via a central UPS system. The data center is designed to support power and cooling infrastructure up to a maximum of 10 MW with a focus on distributing 480V-3PH power directly to the racks, without the need of additional transformers and associated conversion losses. A generator provides for both emergency operations of the building as well as stand-by power for the UPS distribution board. All panel boards and circuits serving the data center are monitored and recorded to provide real-time and ongoing information on the data center performance and efficiency. At present, the data center is configured and equipped (generators, power distribution panels, cooling towers, fans, etc.) to power and cool up to 2.5 MW of electrical load.

7.8.4   Power Interruptions

NREL benefits from historically high reliability and high quality electrical supply from Xcel energy. While brief power disruptions have occurred approximately once per year on average, a UPS system provides continuity to critical components such as file systems and networks. This UPS system is supplemented with a 1 MW backup generator to ride through disruptions of significant durations.

7.8.5 Fire Suppression

Data center fire detection is accomplished by a VESDA system, an aspirating smoke detection system used for early warning applications. Fire suppression is provided by a pre-action dry stand pipe sprinkler system. The VESDA and suppression systems are deployed according to DOE guidance, applicable local and NFPA code.

7.8.6 Physical Security

Physical security to the NREL site is controlled by NREL security in accordance with DOE requirements. Access to the ESIF is key card access controlled and limited to authorized staff and escorted visitors. Data center access is key card controlled, further limited to approximately 20 people, and under video monitoring.

7.8.7 Return on Investment

Finally, we compare capital and operating costs of this new data center with those of an efficient data center. On the capital side, the data center is similar to a typical data center except that it utilizes more efficient, less expensive evaporative cooling towers rather than more expensive, energy-demanding mechanical chillers. We project that not purchasing the mechanical compressor-based chillers saved approximately \$4.5M in capital expenses. For operating expenses, compared to a state-of-the-art data center with a PUE of 1.3, and assuming approximately \$1M per year per MW of electrical load, we project that the ESIF at full build-out of 10 MW and operating with a PUE of 1.06 will save approximately \$2.4M per year in utility costs due to its efficiency. By using waste heat for office and laboratory space, NREL is able to offset another \$200K per year in heating costs. Thus, NRELs showcase HPC data center costs less to build and costs much less to operate than even an efficient, state-of-the-art data center.

7.9 System Statistics

Peregrine production operations began on January 1, 2014. At the time of this writing (May, 2014) Peregrine has about 150 users who are working on 56 projects. Peregrine is allocated in terms of node hours since a single node is the smallest unit a job can request.

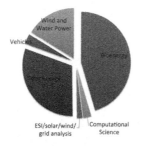

FIGURE 7.7: Peregrine use by area.

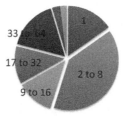

FIGURE 7.8: Peregrine utilization by node count.

Projects are binned into the six areas shown in Figure 7.7. Projects in Bioenergy, Solar, and Wind and Water Power are the largest consumers of Peregrine node hours.

Figure 7.8 shows the amount of Peregrine cycles used by jobs of different sizes. Jobs that use between 1 and 8 nodes consume the majority of time while larger node-count jobs up to 64 uniformly split the remainder.

Figure 7.9 shows the breakdown of Peregrine use by discipline. Chemistry and Materials codes consume about 60% of Peregrine node hours.

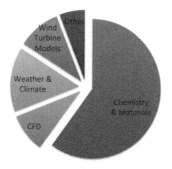

FIGURE 7.9: Peregrine utilization by node count.

Bibliography

[1] M. J. Frisch, G. W. Trucks, H. B. Schlegel, G. E. Scuseria, M. A. Robb, J. R. Cheeseman, G. Scalmani, V. Barone, B. Mennucci, G. A. Petersson, H. Nakatsuji, M. Caricato, X. Li, H. P. Hratchian, A. F. Izmaylov, J. Bloino, G. Zheng, J. L. Sonnenberg, M. Hada, M. Ehara, K. Toyota, R. Fukuda, J. Hasegawa, M. Ishida, T. Nakajima, Y. Honda, O. Kitao, H. Nakai, T. Vreven, Jr. Montgomery, J. A., J. E. Peralta, F. Ogliaro, M. Bearpark, J. J. Heyd, E. Brothers, K. N. Kudin, V. N. Staroverov, R. Kobayashi, J. Normand, K. Raghavachari, A. Rendell, J. C. Burant, S. S. Iyengar, J. Tomasi, M. Cossi, N. Rega, N. J. Millam, M. Klene, J. E. Knox, J. B. Cross, V. Bakken, C. Adamo, J. Jaramillo, R. Gomperts, R. E. Stratmann, O. Yazyev, A. J. Austin, R. Cammi, C. Pomelli, J. W. Ochterski, R. L. Martin, K. Morokuma, V. G. Zakrzewski, G. A. Voth, P. Salvador, J. J. Dannenberg, S. Dapprich, A. D. Daniels, Ö. Farkas, J. B. Foresman, J. V. Ortiz, J. Cioslowski, and D. J. Fox. Gaussian 09, rev. a.1, 2009.

[2] G. Kresse and J. Hafner. Ab initio molecular dynamics for liquid metals. *Phys. Rev. B*, 47:558–561, 1993.

[3] J. Michalakes, J. Dudhia, D. Gill, T. Henderson, J. Klemp, W. Skamarock, and W. Wang. The weather research and forecast model: Software architecture and performance. In G. Mozdzynski, editor, *Proceedings of the 11th ECMWF Workshop on the Use of High Performance Computing in Meterology*, Reading, U.K., 2004.

Chapter 8

Yellowstone: A Dedicated Resource for Earth System Science

Richard Loft, Aaron Andersen, Frank Bryan, John M. Dennis, Tom Engel, Pam Gillman, David Hart, Irfan Elahi, Siddhartha Ghosh, Rory Kelly, Anke Kamrath, Gabrielle Pfister, Matthias Rempel, Justin Small, William Skamarock, and Michael Wiltberger

National Center for Atmospheric Research

Bryan Shader and Po Chen

University of Wyoming

Ben Cash

Center for Ocean-Land-Atmosphere Studies

8.1   Overview

8.1.1   Science Motivation

Climate and weather modeling have been recognized as one of the great computational grand challenges as far back as 1950, when the ENIAC system was used to perform the first numerical simulations of a highly simplified set of nonlinear atmospheric equations [6]. Developing hand in hand with improved observational platforms such as weather satellites, computer forecasts have become steadily more skillful, saving lives and reducing property losses through earlier warning times and more accurate predictions. In 1956, scientists first began computer-based simulations of the climate using a general circulation of the atmosphere [40]. The realism of such models improved in subsequent decades as computer capabilities increased, and when combined with new observations and improved theoretical understanding, this work slowly and convincingly revealed the role of anthropogenic carbon dioxide in changing the Earth's climate.

Now, with the Yellowstone supercomputer and associated cyberinfrastructure, science is poised to take the next step in advancing the understanding of how our planet works by *dramatically accelerating* the advancement of Earth System science. When viewed in the context of the increasingly severe impacts on society of natural disasters and the catastrophic long-term implications of climate change, the sense of urgency to develop an integrated and improved understanding of our planet becomes clear.

The Yellowstone environment provides dedicated petascale computational and data resources to the U.S. atmospheric science communities, enabling dramatic improvements in resolution, better representations of physical processes, longer simulation length, and better statistics for a broad spectrum of important Earth System science applications. The deployment of Yellowstone advances three crucial scientific capabilities. First, long-term climate studies can routinely account for small-scale ocean eddies that influence atmospheric weather patterns and transport heat and nutrients throughout the world's oceans. Second, scientists can begin improving the representation of clouds – perhaps the greatest source of uncertainty remaining in climate system models. Third, scientists can study the regional impacts of climate change more effectively using simulations with nested grids at meteorological resolutions. This capability will help scientists investigate the connection between climate and hurricane frequency and strength, study the localized effects of regional climate change on agriculture and water supplies, and investigate numerous other computationally demanding Earth System processes. Solar researchers will be able to use vastly enhanced computer models of the Sun that enable the first-ever simulations of the full life cycle of sunspot assemblages, unlock the mechanisms behind the 11-year solar cycle, model coronal mass ejections, and understand the role of solar variability in climate.

Yellowstone is housed at the NCAR-Wyoming Supercomputing Center (NWSC) in Cheyenne, Wyoming. The NWSC data center is funded by the National Science Foundation (NSF) and the State of Wyoming, and is operated by the National Center for Atmospheric Research. The NWSC and Yellowstone resulted from a partnership between the University Corporation for Atmospheric Research (UCAR), the State of Wyoming, the University of Wyoming, the Wyoming Business Council, Cheyenne LEADS, and Cheyenne Light Fuel and Power Company. University of Wyoming researchers are using their share of Yellowstone to study changes in Wyoming's regional climate and hydrology, the design of proposed local wind turbine farms, seismic hazards, and the long-term stability of carbon sequestration sites in the region.

8.1.2 Sponsor and Program Background

The National Center for Atmospheric Research (NCAR) is a federally funded research and development center devoted to advancing the atmospheric and related sciences. NCAR's mission is to understand the behavior of the atmosphere and the physical, biological, and societal systems that interact with and depend on it. The NSF is NCAR's primary sponsor, and significant additional support is provided by other U.S. government agencies, other national governments, and the private sector. Beyond its core science mission, NCAR develops and maintains a variety of services and facilities used by scientists, including state-of-the-art supercomputers and databases, community-driven computer models of weather and climate, and observational platforms including aircraft, radar, and spacecraft. NCAR is managed by the University Corporation for Atmospheric Research (UCAR), a non-profit research and education institution with a mission to support, enhance, and extend the capabilities of the university community, nationally and internationally, and to foster the transfer of knowledge and technology for the betterment of life on Earth.

NCAR's supercomputing and data resources are operated by the Computational and Information Systems Laboratory (CISL), which provides HPC services to 78 UCAR member universities, 26 UCAR affiliate universities, NCAR scientists, and the larger geosciences community. Originally founded in 1964, CISL has been involved in supercomputing since the very beginning: it installed and managed a Control Data Corporation 6600 system, widely regarded as the first supercomputer. Today, CISL manages high-performance production and experimental computing systems, a High-Performance Storage System (HPSS) archival system, the Research Data Archive (RDA), networking and connectivity to the NSF's XSEDE, and information technologies that support scientific communities. CISL provides numerous services that include around-the-clock operational support of its balanced, data-centric cyberinfrastructure; curation of research dataset libraries; development and support of discipline-specific tools for the atmospheric and related sciences; the computational science expertise required to develop new algorithms needed to efficiently execute large, long-running numerical simulations and to assimilate observations for purposes of prediction; and education, outreach, and training activities to support and enhance the diversity of the user community.

8.2   Project Timeline

Because of NCAR's focus on its discipline-specific science mission, it was possible to conceive and effectively co-design both the computing facility and the computational and storage systems it would house. In its entirety, this process took nearly a decade.

8.2.1   NWSC Construction

In 2003, NCAR recognized that the demands of future high-performance computing (HPC) systems would exceed the capabilities of its facilities and infrastructure. In December 2005, after weighing its options, UCAR decided to pursue new construction. UCAR began a competitive process for prospective regional partners, ultimately selecting a partnership proposal by the State and University of Wyoming in January 2007 to build the NCAR-Wyoming Supercomputing Center (NWSC). Using the NSF's guidelines for major research equipment and facilities construction, NCAR and Wyoming developed a roadmap and preliminary plans for the facility in 2008. NCAR developed facility design criteria, and via RFI and RFP processes, selected the facility's architectural and engineering firms by February 2009. In parallel, a panel assembled to identify and articulate overarching scientific objectives, then published a science justification in September 2009. The NWSC Project Development Plan was completed and the preliminary design review was conducted in October 2009. By February 2010, the facility's design documents were completed and assessed by an external peer-review panel. A Project Execution Plan was developed and the final Facility Design Review was conducted in March 2010.

Formal groundbreaking ceremonies were held on June 15, 2010. Construction proceeded at a rapid pace and the facility's superstructure was completed

FIGURE 8.1: Nearly a decade of planning produced the 1.5-petaflops Yellowstone system and the energy-efficient NCAR-Wyoming Supercomputing Center in Cheyenne, Wyoming.

before the onset of winter. An external panel assessed the project's status in February 2011. The building underwent final inspections in August 2011, integrated systems testing in September, and UCAR accepted the facility in October. In November 2011, CISL installed the first equipment in the facility: two StorageTek SL8500 Modular Library Systems, each with a capacity of 10,000 tape cartridges. Installation of the Yellowstone equipment began in May 2012. The NWSC Grand Opening was held on October 15, 2012. The entire construction project was completed on time and under budget.

8.2.2 Yellowstone Procurement

The procurement of the first petascale HPC environment at NWSC provided a unique opportunity to design a forward-looking, data-centric system. The procurement of the Yellowstone environment began at the end of 2010 with the release of a fixed-price best-value RFP that solicited three key components: an HPC system, a centralized filesystem, and data analysis and visualization systems, each to be maintained and operated over at least a four-year lifetime. The NCAR HPSS data archive and Ethernet networking infrastructure were enhanced via separate subcontracts.

The benchmark suite used during the Yellowstone procurement process was designed to mirror the science needs of the NCAR user community [27]. To assemble the benchmark suite, CISL convened a Scientific Advisory Panel and a Technical Evaluation Team. These two groups worked together to identify a set of application and synthetic benchmarks capable of measuring the machine performance characteristics relevant to our science code base. The suite was based primarily on prominent applications, although a set of synthetic interconnect and I/O benchmarks were included to help interpret application benchmark results.

Initial vendor proposals were received in April 2011, and the procurement team began an intensive evaluation of the proposed solutions and benchmark results. After reaching a consensus, UCAR negotiated terms, obtained NSF approval, and awarded the Yellowstone subcontract to IBM in November 2011 [47]. At the time of the award, the two key technologies of the Yellowstone environment had not been released: the Intel Xeon E5 processor and Mellanox FDR InfiniBand. CISL and UCAR made the strategic decision to wait for these technologies to gain their performance advantages. Equipment delivery began in May 2012 and was completed by the end of June. IBM, Mellanox, and CISL engineers assembled the systems then performed software installation and configuration through the summer. Acceptance testing began in August, and the system received provisional acceptance in September 2012.

8.3   System Overview

The Yellowstone environment consists of end-to-end petascale cyberinfrastructure designed with the recognition that data access – not flops – is the limiting factor for the scientific disciplines it serves. Its data-centric design (a) reallocated system resources to minimize data motion, (b) increased the I/O bandwidth between system components, and (c) brought more elements of the workflow under a single job scheduling system: goals long advocated for balanced systems [5]. Four aspects of the system design were influenced by these considerations: the use of a centralized disk storage system, disk storage capacity, I/O bandwidth, and analysis system characteristics.

Figure 8.2 shows that the central storage system, called the Globally Accessible Data Environment (GLADE), is the heart of the Yellowstone environment, with the systems for supercomputing, analysis and visualization, HPSS archive, data transfer, and science gateways all connected to it. GLADE eliminates the need to copy data in scientific workflows, saving file transfer overheads and disk costs. Centralizing storage is also more flexible and easier to administer, but it comes at the expense of complicating the system interconnect design. GLADE serves as the data crossroads for the system, and it provides plentiful throughput and space for scientists to run analysis workflows without resorting to using the tape archive as a slow file server.

The size and I/O bandwidth of GLADE was dictated by several interrelated factors: the relative cost of centralized disk storage to computing nodes, the ratio of I/O bandwidth to storage volume presented by storage appliances available at the time of procurement, the anticipated data production rate of the supercomputer for the anticipated science workload in terms of sustained flops per output bytes, and the 100:1 ratio of disk storage to system memory recommended by Bell et al. [5]. While these factors are interrelated, the relationships are generally linear, permitting a reasonable estimate of a balance point. In terms of budget allocation, this estimate of a balanced system implied that 20% of the system cost would go to central storage, 75% to computing nodes, and 5% to data analysis nodes. Given the aspect ratio of high performance storage appliances, this yielded an I/O bandwidth for Yellowstone lower than that projected for our most data-intensive applications, and substantially less than that suggested by Amdahl's law [5], but adequate for most NCAR applications.

The data-centric considerations also influenced the design of Yellowstone's data analysis and visualization systems, where memory size on some nodes was increased to one terabyte to reduce the amount of disk I/O in data analysis workflows. Placing the compute and analysis resources within the scope of a single scheduler instance enabled users to implement cross-platform workflows using familiar job submission tools.

Early production experience supports many of these design choices. A tangible measure of its success was demonstrated by its immediate high utilization despite providing a 30-fold increase in capacity compared to its predecessor. The tape archive net growth rate of 250 terabytes/week is substantially lower than the projected "business as usual" rate of 450 terabytes/week, a material realization of an anticipated cost saving. Steady-state disk storage growth rates are generally tracking with the central file system size that was chosen. Synchronous I/O overheads are reportedly under 10% for many data-intensive simulations, such as the MPAS model, another desired outcome of Yellowstone's data-centric design.

The primary computation resource of the complex at NWSC is Yellowstone, a 1.5-petaflops IBM iDataPlex cluster supercomputer with 72,576 Intel Xeon E5 processor cores and a full fat tree Mellanox FDR Infiniband interconnect. The data analysis and visualization clusters Geyser and Caldera perform scientific analysis on the simulation output. Geyser is designed for big data analysis, while the Caldera analysis cluster additionally offers parallel visualization or GPGPU computation. Likewise, Pronghorn is a system with Intel Xeon Phi coprocessors available for evaluation of the applicability of Intel many-core coprocessors to Earth System science applications. Important subsets of post-processed simulation results can be shared with the scientific community via allocated storage on GLADE's "projects" filesystem, either through direct access from the analysis servers or through the attached Data Transfer or Science Gateways. Data of long-term significance is stored on the HPSS data archive.

Finally, test systems have proven invaluable to CISL for refining administrative procedures and installing and testing new firmware and software before their introduction on production systems. The test systems for the Yellowstone environment are comprised of a 32-node iDataPlex computational

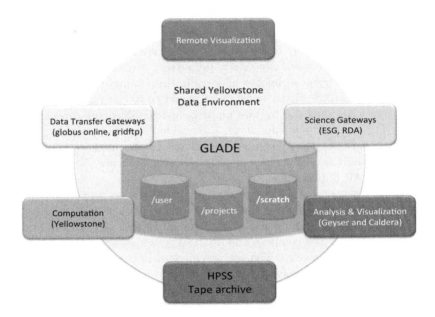

FIGURE 8.2: High-level architecture of NCAR's data-centric environment.

cluster (Yellowstone test) with two GPU-computation nodes (Caldera test), one large-memory node (Geyser test), one Phi node (Pronghorn test), two GPFS NSD servers, a DCS3700 storage subsystem, and three Mellanox SX6036 FDR InfiniBand switches.

8.4   Hardware Architecture

8.4.1   Processors and Nodes

The Yellowstone supercomputer consists of 4,536 dual-socket 1U IBM dx360 M4 diskless nodes with 2.6-GHz Intel Xeon E5-2670 8-core (Sandy Bridge EP) processors. Each node has 32 gigabytes of DDR3-1600 memory, or 2 gigabytes per core, for an aggregate memory size of 145.1 terabytes. Each node has a single-port Mellanox ConnectX-3 FDR adapter, and the nodes are interconnected via a full-bandwidth full fat tree network. Physically, Yellowstone's computational nodes and level 1 switches are housed in 63 cabinets, with an additional 9 cabinets required for the 648-port Mellanox IB director (levels 2 and 3) switches. An administrative Ethernet and about two dozen other special-purpose nodes are used for user login and interactive access and operational and administrative system management. Finally, a smaller, standalone 28-teraflops system, Erebus, is dedicated to producing twice-daily, 10-km-resolution numerical weather predictions over the Antarctic continent to support Antarctic scientific operations.

The system architecture of the 16-node Caldera and Pronghorn systems is quite similar to Yellowstone's, except that each node has 64 gigabytes of DDR3-1600 memory and dual PCIe-attached coprocessors. The nodes in each system are interconnected by a level-1 full fat tree IB network. Caldera is equipped with two NVIDIA Tesla M2070Q graphics processing units per node. Each Pronghorn node is equipped with dual Intel Xeon Phi 5110P coprocessors, each with 61 cores and 8 gigabytes of onboard memory.

Geyser is designed for big-data analysis, and is comprised of 16 IBM x3850 X5 nodes, each equipped with four, 10-core Intel Xeon E7-4870 (Westmere-EX) processors, one NVIDIA Quadro 6000 graphics processing unit, 1,024 gigabytes of DDR3-1066 memory, two single-port Mellanox ConnectX-3 FDR adapters, and a dual-port 10GigE Ethernet adapter.

The hardware component details for Yellowstone, Erebus, Caldera, Pronghorn, and Geyser are summarized in Table 8.1. Information on the Intel processors used in the complex can be found at [24, 25, 26]; background on IBM hardware at [19, 20, 21]; and information regarding NVIDIA's accelerators at [38, 39].

8.4.2   Rack-Level Packaging

The racks in the IBM iDataPlex have a unique shallow-rack design that effectively provides 100U of device-mounting space in the same floor space as a standard 42U rack [51, 18]. The shallow depth provides efficient airflow and reduces cooling costs. Each rack contains 72 compute nodes, 4 InfiniBand switches, 2 Ethernet switches, and two 60-Amp, 3-phase intelligent power distribution units. Designed for a maximum power load of 29.9 kW, each Yellowstone rack consumes 17.5 kW while running NCAR's production workload. The racks are equipped with the optional Rear Door Heat eXchanger which, using the NWSC's 18°C (65°F) chilled water at a flow rate of 8 gallons per minute, keep Yellowstone's output temperature room neutral.

8.4.3   Interconnect

Yellowstone's interconnect is a single-plane, three-tier full fat-tree topology comprised of Mellanox 56-Gbps FDR 4X InfiniBand components. This topology provides a maximum hop count of five between arbitrary nodes in the Yellowstone system and a theoretical bisection bandwidth of 30.9 terabytes/second.

The first tier of the system's interconnect topology utilizes 252, 36-port Mellanox SX6036 leaf switches, also called "top-of-rack" or TOR switches, with one copper downlink to each of 18 associated compute nodes, and 18 fiber

TABLE 8.1: Key hardware attributes of the Yellowstone environment.

	Yellowstone	Caldera	Geyser	Pronghorn	Erebus
System	IBM dx360 M4		IBM x3850 X5	IBM dx360 M4	
Compute Racks	63	0.5	2	0.5	1
Total # of Nodes	4536	16	16	16	84
Peak FLOPS Rate	1509.6 TF	21.8 TF	14.4 TF	37.7 TF	28.0 TF
CPU					
	Intel Xeon E5-2670		Intel Xeon E7-4870	Intel Xeon E5-2670	
Microarchitecture	Sandy Bridge EP		Westmere EX	Sandy Bridge EP	
Frequency (GHz)	2.6	2.6	2.4	2.6	2.6
Count per Node	2	2	4	2	2
Memory/Node	32 GB	64 GB	1024 GB	64 GB	32 GB
Memory Type	DDR3-1600	DDR3-1600	DDR3-1066	DDR3-1600	DDR3-1600
Accelerators					
Model	-	NVIDIA Tesla M2070Q	NVIDIA Quadro 6000	Intel Xeon Phi 5110P	-
Peak DP (FLOP Rate (GF))	-	515.2	515.2	1011	-
Count per Node	-	2	1	2	-
Memory Capacity	-	6 GB	6 GB	8 GB	-
Memory Type	-	GDDR5			-
Network					
Type	InfiniBand 4x FDR				InfiniBand 4x FDR-10
Topology	3-tier full fat tree	1-tier full fat tree			2-tier full fat tree
Ports per Node	1	1	2	1	1
Bisection Bandwidth (GB/sec)	30,927	109.1	91.2	109.1	409.1

uplinks to the level two switches. Nodes that share a TOR switch are termed an "A-group": there are four TOR switches (and therefore four A-groups) in a fully populated iDataPlex rack of 72 nodes, and a total of 252 A-groups in Yellowstone. The upper two tiers of the interconnect topology are housed in nine 648-port Mellanox SX6536 director switches, each of which can contain 36, 36-port SX6036 "leaf" modules, each with 18 downward-facing links. Of the 36 leaf modules available in each director switch, only 29 are populated to fill out Yellowstone's Tier 2 interconnect. Processors that are interconnected at the Tier 2 level form an association that is termed a "B-group." There are 18x18 or 324 nodes in a B-group and a total 14 B-groups in Yellowstone. In the Tier 3 layer, 18 "spine" switch modules in each director switch receive the Tier 2 uplinks and interconnect them in a crossbar.

Each TOR switch has two fiber uplinks connecting it to two different leaf modules on each director switch. In a true fat tree, both links would go to the same leaf module on each director. This small difference technically

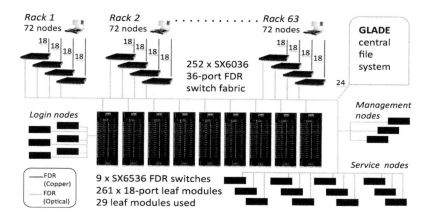

FIGURE 8.3: Conceptual diagram of Yellowstone switch hierarchy showing the compute nodes at the top, the 252 Tier 1 TOR SX6036 IB switches, and the nine SX6536 director switches that form the Tier 2 and Tier 3 of the interconnect hierarchy.

makes Yellowstone, from a routing perspective, a "quasi" fat tree (QFT). The advantage of this QFT connection strategy is that larger B-groups, i.e., 18 TOR vs. 9 TOR in size, allow more nodes to communicate through Tier 1 and 2 switches and avoid spine traffic altogether. This improves the probability that smaller jobs will be supported by localized interconnect fabric, reducing the number of hops, and lowers application interference effects of crossing the Tier-3 spine.

Figure 8.3 shows a high-level diagram of Yellowstone's switch hierarchy. NCAR is currently working with Mellanox on a new QFT routing algorithm that will deliver full fat tree performance for a Yellowstones QFT network. This is expected to be available in the second half of 2014.

Yellowstone's interconnect is not a completely symmetric fat-tree topology. A 29th leaf module in each of the director switches contains a total of 21 direct FDR IB connections to Yellowstone's login and administrative nodes and 24 connections to GLADE for I/O to the GPFS filesystems. This asymmetry complicates using the fat tree (ftree) routing algorithm in OpenSM. At the time of this writing, the ftree routing algorithm cannot be used, and Yellowstone's OpenSM system is configured to use up-down scatter ports routing, with LMC=1 (two logical channels per physical link). Mellanox is currently developing new routing engine enhancements, referred to as routing engine chains, that will optimize routing and minimize collisions for asymmetric topologies such as Yellowstone's.

GLADE contains a Mellanox SX6512 FDR InfiniBand switch with 24 FDR links providing I/O connectivity to Yellowstone's SX6536 switches and ultimately to each of Yellowstone's nodes. Geyser, Caldera, and Pronghorn share a 216-port Mellanox SX6512 FDR InfiniBand director switch. Each Caldera and Pronghorn node has one, and each Geyser node has two FDR InfiniBand links to the director switch. Six FDR links from the DAV SX6512 director switch to GLADE provide a theoretical aggregate bidirectional I/O bandwidth of 81 gigabytes/second [32, 33, 34]. As noted previously, Yellowstone's integrated IB fabric allows data to be shared across all systems, which is increasingly important for supporting complex scientific workflows.

8.4.4   Storage System

The GLADE storage cluster consists of 20 IBM x3650 M4 servers, each equipped with two 8-core Intel Xeon E5-2670 processors, a single-port Mellanox ConnectX-3 FDR adapter, either 32 gigabytes or 64 gigabytes of DDR3-1600 memory, and 76 IBM System Storage DCS3700 controller units each with a single EXP3700 expansion chassis. The DCS3700/EXP3700 is a modular, scalable disk storage controller and expansion chassis; each assembly can accommodate 60 NL-SAS drives in a 4U space. In GLADEs current configuration, four DCS3700 controllers, four EXP3700 expansion units, and an NSD server are mounted in each of a pair of neighboring 19-inch racks, while each DCS3700 controller and EXP3700 expansion chassis is twin tailed via 6 Gbps SAS to the pair of IBM x3650 M4 NSD servers and contains ninety 3-terabyte near-line SAS disk drives.

The GLADE storage cluster is designed to provide more than 90 gigabytes per second bandwidth over InfiniBand to the Yellowstone compute nodes. Figure 8.4 provides a schematic diagram of a GLADE building block. Nine storage building blocks are configured to support scratch space and dedicated project spaces. An additional half building block supports user directory spaces. Finally, GLADE provides access to additional services through a 10 Gbps IP-based network.

8.5   System Software

This section discusses important software components of the Yellowstone system, including the operating system, parallel filesystem, system monitoring software, and programming environment. Table 8.2 provides a more detailed summary of software components with current version numbers included. CISL keeps software levels consistent across the Yellowstone, Caldera, Geyser and Pronghorn clusters. Older and newer test compiler versions are made available to the user community via the Modules environment.

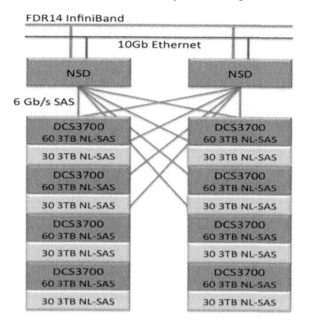

FIGURE 8.4: GLADE storage configuration.

8.5.1   Operating Systems and System Management

Yellowstone and GLADE use the Red Hat Enterprise Linux (RHEL) 6 Operating System. One variant, called RHEL Server OS, uses the traditional stateful model where the OS resides on a direct-attached hard drive and state is maintained across reboots. RHEL Server is used on all nodes of GLADE, Geyser, Caldera, and Pronghorn clusters, and on Yellowstone's login and infrastructure nodes. Yellowstone's compute nodes use a stateless operating system called RHEL for HPC that does not store the OS or its state locally. Rather, the operating system is loaded onto the node over the network when the system is booted, eliminating the OS's need for direct-attached disks. The advantages of using a stateless OS are that it ensures consistency in the operating system content across thousands of compute nodes and centralizes all OS maintenance activities for them.

The RHEL Server OS instances are maintained through three stateful management nodes, and an NFS storage appliance provides centralized storage for administrative functions. The Yellowstone environment is managed using the Extreme Cloud Administration Toolkit or xCAT, an open-source cluster management and provisioning tool that also provides an interface for hardware control, discovery, and operating system deployment. Initial installation of a consistent stateful image on the non-management nodes is achieved by updating the image definition within xCAT. Configuration management software keeps the stateful nodes consistent after deployment. Logs from

TABLE 8.2: Yellowstone software matrix.

Software	Current Installed Version
Operating System	RHEL 6.4
Parallel Filesystem	IBM GPFS 3.5.0-13
Compiler and Tools	Intel Cluster Studio 12.1.5.339 (Fortran, C, C++)
	PGI CDK Cluster Development Kit 13.3 (Fortran, C, C++)
	PGI Accelerator CDK 13.3 (OpenACC, CUDA Fortran, CUDA)
	PathScale EKOPath Compiler Suite 5.0.0 (Fortran, C, C++)
Debugger	TotalView 8.12.0-1
MPI	IBM Parallel Environment 1.3.0.7
InfiniBand	Mellanox OFED 2.0-3.0.0.3
	Mellanox Unified Fabric Manager 4.6.0-13
	OpenSM 4.0.5.MLNX20130808.c2b40b1-0.1
Job Scheduler/ Resource Manager	IBM Platform LSF 9.1.1.1
Cluster Management	xCAT 2.8.4

TABLE 8.3: GLADE filesystem configurations.

Scratch	Projects	User
5 PB total space	9.9 PB total space,	844 TB total space,
4 MB block size	4 MB block size	512 KB block size
10 TB quota per user,	500 GB allocation per user	10 GB allocation per user
90 day purge policy	Large project allocation	Small project allocation
	by request	by request
	2 PB allocated to data	10 TB home space
	collections, e.g., RDA, ESG,	Application software repository
	CDP	Snapshots, backups

stateful nodes are sent to a central system log server rather than storing them locally.

Yellowstone resources are scheduled and managed via the Load Sharing Facility (LSF), a commercial job scheduler and resource manager that provides a comprehensive set of intelligent, policy-driven scheduling features that enable the efficient use of the Yellowstone infrastructure resources.

8.5.2   Disk Filesystem and Tape Archive

The GLADE storage cluster uses IBM's GPFS parallel filesystem configured into three filesystems supporting scratch, allocatable project spaces, and user directories. Table 8.3 provides a summary of GLADE filesystem attributes. The two largest filesystems in GLADE, scratch and projects, are configured with large, 4-megabyte blocks and span 9 storage building blocks, while the third, smaller user filesystem is configured with small 512-kilobyte blocks contained within a half-sized storage building block. Storage allocations are controlled using a mixture of user/group-based quotas and a unique feature of GPFS: filesets, or virtual containers.

NCAR's HPC environment uses GPFS's Multicluster feature to provide access to the GLADE file systems for clusters external to GLADE. This provides GPFS access to clusters outside the administrative domain, GPFS access to clusters over the 10-Gbps ethernet network, and stability for GLADE while other HPC clusters are offline for maintenance.

The HPSS tape archive consists of four Oracle SL8500 robotic tape libraries, two at the NWSC in Cheyenne, Wyoming, and two at NCAR's Mesa Laboratory Computing Facility in Boulder, Colorado. These libraries have a total of over 34,000 tape cartridge slots. Using current tape technology, the total capacity of the archive is over 170 petabytes. The archives are federated with production core servers located at the NWSC and two data mover servers located at the MLCF. The long-range plan is to store nearly all of the data at the NWSC and use the MLCF for business continuity purposes. The system includes 50 T10000C tape drives, 95 T10000B tape drives, 500 terabytes of disk cache, and an aggregate I/O bandwidth greater than 6 Gbps.

8.5.3 System Monitoring

The Yellowstone system is monitored by a variety of tools [8]. The Nagios monitoring framework provides infrastructure-level monitoring, event notification, and problem resolution guidance. Splunk is a commercial product for collecting and analyzing machine data. Splunk helps correlate system logs across multiple clusters to reveal patterns that point toward system issues. Ganglia is an effective distributed monitoring system for high-performance clusters. Its scalability and hierarchical design provide significant flexibility. Ganglia is used in the GLADE environment to both monitor the GPFS servers and track the performance and usage profiles of the GPFS filesystems. The gpfsmond daemon was developed locally to monitor GPFS state on all client nodes and help system administrators identify problem nodes before widespread problems occur. Every five minutes, this daemon gathers the current GPFS state then examines the state of GPFS mount points. If any are found not mounted or stale, it will attempt to remount them and reports this status.

NCAR's HPC environment uses a tiered and scalable approach to system-level monitoring. Each cluster has its own Nagios instance that monitors its critical components. Events requiring action are fed to a central Nagios instance that is monitored 7x24. Nagios' ability to attach procedural documentation to an event allows operations staff to take the proper corrective actions. The Ganglia system had to be scaled out to handle the volume of metric updates, as a single Ganglia server could easily be saturated by the volume of metric updates in a petascale system. For Yellowstone, Ganglia and Nagios client hosts were evenly distributed over six servers using the InfiniBand fabric.

8.5.4   Programming Environment

The Yellowstone environment supports four compiler families (Intel, PGI, PathScale, and GNU), three primary languages (Fortran, C, and C++), and the Python language. The compilation and runtime environment is designed to manage the architectural differences between the Intel Xeon (Sandy Bridge and Westmere) and Xeon Phi processors. Programming of NVIDIA-based GPUs on Caldera is provided via the CUDA programming language and through OpenGL for traditional GPU-enhanced visualization applications.

The user environment is managed with the Lmod modules implementation [30], custom wrapper scripts, and settings exported into the user environment. This allows for streamlined control, automated documentation, version control, and customization, while accommodating both novice and expert users. All supported software libraries on the system are compiled with versions specific to the supported compilers. When a user loads a module, their environment is updated to use software built against the compiler currently in their environment. Furthermore, CISL automatically includes necessary Rpath information into the binaries via wrapper scripts for the compilers. This avoids users needing to locate the correct runtime library paths after they have compiled applications.

8.6   Workload and Application Performance

Yellowstone's computing resources are partitioned among the following four distinct communities: modelers participating in the Climate Simulation Laboratory (CSL) (28%); researchers at U.S. universities and scientific institutions (29%); NCAR scientists (29%); and geosciences researchers at the University of Wyoming (13%). In addition, 1% is reserved for special purposes such as benchmarking and other testing.

Each of these communities has distinct needs and usage patterns. The CSL is dedicated to large-scale and long-running simulations of Earth's climate system that produce large amounts of model data, often conducted by distributed teams of researchers. The university community allocation supports U.S.-based researchers who have NSF awards in the atmospheric or related sciences, as well as graduate student and postdoctoral research projects. These projects range from small- to large-scale and from paleoclimate to ocean modeling to weather prediction to solar physics. University users include a larger proportion of new users, as well as users of community models. NCAR staff researchers have similarly wide-ranging areas of scientific interest. While smaller in size, the NCAR community has a larger proportion of expert users and application developers. Finally, the Wyoming community encompasses a broader set of disciplines in the geosciences, notably including solid Earth physics, but

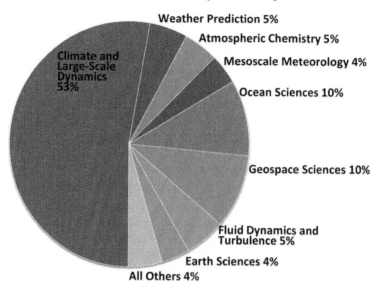

Weather Prediction 5%

Atmospheric Chemistry 5%

Climate and Large-Scale Dynamics 53%

Mesoscale Meteorology 4%

Ocean Sciences 10%

Geospace Sciences 10%

Fluid Dynamics and Turbulence 5%

Earth Sciences 4%

All Others 4%

FIGURE 8.5: Chart of current Yellowstone resource usage by discipline, illustrating the dominance of climate, atmosphere, and ocean science.

this group is concentrated in a smaller number of users. Collectively, these communities represent a much tighter disciplinary focus than is typical on other petascale systems (see Figure 8.5).

8.6.1   Application Domain Descriptions

Climate Science

Climate-related simulations represent nearly half the workload on Yellowstone. Climate models are typically run from decadal to millennial scales, and they require 64-bit precision computations for accuracy. The primary climate model used at NCAR is the Community Earth System Model (CESM), a fully coupled, community-developed, global climate model [31]. CESM couples components of the Earth System including the atmosphere, atmospheric chemistry, land surface, sea ice, land ice (glaciers), and the oceans – each of which may use different grids – by exchanging regridded fluxes and material quantities through the flux coupler application. CESM has scaled to tens of thousands of processors on a variety of platforms [12].

CESM is integrated with an ecosystem of related modeling and prediction efforts. CESM can be run in data assimilation mode using NCAR's Data Assimilation Research Testbed (DART) to study climate predictability. The Nested Regional Climate Model (NRCM) combines CESM with the Weather Research and Forecasting (WRF) model that runs embedded on a high-resolution mesh over an area of interest to better simulate regional climate variability and change. The Whole Atmosphere Community Climate Model (WACCM) is also part of the family of CESM models. WACCM spans the lower, middle, and upper atmosphere to enable investigations of atmospheric chemistry including the effects and contributions of solar variability and the solar cycle. Finally, an emerging model that bridges climate, regional climate, and weather studies is the Model for Prediction Across Scales (MPAS), a joint effort of NCAR and Los Alamos National Laboratory [42]. MPAS is well suited for global mesoscale atmosphere and ocean simulations.

Weather Prediction and Atmospheric Chemistry

Studies in the closely related areas of numerical weather prediction, atmospheric chemistry, and mesoscale meteorology together comprise the second-largest area of activity on Yellowstone. The WRF model [35] is an open-source, collaboratively developed, numerical weather forecasting model used in operational, research, and educational settings. WRF has a large user base in the environmental sciences. It features two dynamical solvers: the Advanced Research WRF (ARW) model, developed by NCAR's Mesoscale and Microscale Meteorology Division [41], and the Nonhydrostatic Mesoscale Model (NMM) solver developed by the National Centers for Environmental Prediction (NCEP). WRF has a three-dimensional variational (3DVAR) data assimilation system, and its WRF-Chem variant couples it with processes that govern the behavior of atmospheric trace gases and aerosols. WRF-Chem is used to study regional-scale air quality and cloud-scale interactions.

Ocean Sciences

A representative application from computational oceanography is the Parallel Ocean Program (POP), a flexible and widely used ocean general circulation model developed at Los Alamos National Laboratory [44]. POP solves the 3-D primitive equations for ocean dynamics under the hydrostatic and Boussinesq approximations. Spatial derivatives are computed using finite-difference discretizations that are formulated for generalized orthogonal coordinates. Time integration of the model is split into two parts. The three-dimensional vertically varying (baroclinic) tendencies are integrated explicitly using a leapfrog scheme. The fast modes of the vertically uniform (barotropic) component are integrated implicitly using a two-dimensional preconditioned conjugate gradient (PCG) solver. While the baroclinic component scales well, at high processor counts, POP is dominated by the MPI reduction operations associated with this PCG solve. The Mellanox Fabric Collective Accelerator feature can offload these MPI collective communications and significantly improve POP's scalability on Yellowstone.

Geospace Sciences

The Sun-Earth System is studied at NCAR with a set of loosely coupled models that operate at vastly different length-scales and physical conditions.

Magnetohydrodynamics (MHD) applications, such as the MPS/University of Chicago Radiative MHD (MURaM), are used for realistic simulations of solar magneto-convection and related activity in the photosphere [50]. Other aspects of solar interactions are examined via computational fluid dynamics methods, such as those embodied in ZEUS-3D [9]. The Thermosphere Ionosphere Electrodynamics General Circulation Model (TIE-GCM) is a first-principles model of the coupled thermosphere and ionosphere system [46], and the related Thermosphere Ionosphere Mesosphere Electrodynamics GCM (TIME-GCM) extends the simulation boundary down to an altitude of 30 km to include processes in the mesosphere and upper stratosphere.

Fluid Dynamics and Turbulence

Turbulence plays an important role in a variety of geophysical flows, and the large-eddy simulation (LES) and direct numerical simulation (DNS) approaches to modeling turbulence appear frequently on Yellowstone. NCAR's LES model, for example, is used to study mixing in a wide variety of physical contexts, including ocean layers, land-surface interactions with the planetary boundary layer, and in cloud physics. LES uses as its basic numerical algorithm a mixed pseudo-spectral finite difference code with third-order Runge-Kutta time stepping [36]. LES scales well to tens of thousands of cores using a hybrid MPI-OpenMP scheme in which work in the vertical (finite difference) direction is partitioned across MPI processes, and the horizontal (pseudo-spectral) dimension is distributed across OpenMP threads.

Earth Sciences

Early research by University of Wyoming researchers has focused on seismology. For instance, the Anelastic Wave Propagation - Olsen, Day, Cui (AWP-ODC) model is a portable, highly scalable application that simulates the dynamic ruptures and wave propagation through the Earth's crust during an earthquake using a staggered-grid finite difference scheme [3]. The widely used SPECFEM3D code [45], which uses a continuous Galerkin spectral-element method, was used to study earthquake wave propagation through sedimentary basins.

Data Assimilation Systems

Yellowstone allowed NCAR user communities to expand their models in two dimensions: (a) running at higher resolutions and (b) increasing ensemble size to improve statistics or apply ensemble-based data assimilation methods to achieve better forecasts. NCAR's DART is a framework that provides ensemble-based data assimilation capabilities to geophysical models through a set of specified interfaces. DART works with a growing number of models, including WRF and CESM's atmospheric component CAM, combining them with a diverse and growing set of observation types [2]. Other models running on Yellowstone also have data assimilation capabilities. For example, WRFDA provides variational data assimilation capabilities for the WRF model [52]. Another example is the FWSDA model, described below, for studying earthquake hazards and mitigation.

8.6.2 Application Performance

This section describes the performance of CESM and WRF benchmarks, which represent the largest components of Yellowstone's application workload.

High-Resolution CESM on Yellowstone

The simulation rate and scaling efficiency of high-resolution CESM are shown in Figure 8.6, which was generated by version 1.1.0 rel4 of CESM configured with the 0.25°-resolution CAM-SE (atmosphere) and CLM3.5 (land surface) models and the 0.1°-resolution POP (ocean) and CICE (sea ice) models. The timings measured the cost to perform a five-day simulation of this configuration and excluded any initialization or I/O time.

Shown in the top panel of Figure 8.6 is the simulation rate in years per wall-clock day (SYPD) as a function of processor count. Depending on the particular science question, climate simulations can range in length from decades to several hundred years. As can be seen below, Yellowstone attained a simulation rate of 1.16 SYPD on 11,274 cores, while 1.95 SYPD were achieved on 23,404 cores. A minimum simulation rate of 1 SYPD is generally considered necessary to perform a climate experiment within a reasonable time.

The bottom panel of Figure 8.6 is the cost in thousands of CPU-hours per simulated year (KCPU/yr) as a function of core count. Considering only those configurations that achieve at least 1 SYPD, the minimum cost of 229 KCPU/yr is achieved at 14,276 cores with an integration rate of 1.49 SYPD, while the 23,404-core configuration costs 290 KCPU/yr integrating at 1.95 SYPD. The scalability of CESM on Yellowstone is illustrated by this performance measurement: the configuration with the greatest simulation rate, 23,404 cores, was only 26% more expensive than the 11,274-core configuration.

WRF Scaling

The scaling and performance of the WRF Version 3.5 meteorological model was studied on Yellowstone in both MPI-only and MPI-OpenMP hybrid modes. The benchmark simulated weather events leading up to hurricane Katrina and ran for one hour or 1,200 time steps. The 1 km North American problem domain included the Gulf of Mexico, and contained 3,665 x 2,894 grid points and 35 terrain-following vertical levels. No initialization or disk I/O times were measured in this benchmark.

On Yellowstone, hybrid runs gave some marginal performance benefits vs. MPI-only. In most cases, however, run-to-run variability increased substantially compared to MPI-only runs. The benchmark measures the simulation speed, defined as the ratio between simulated and wall clock time. Only speeds

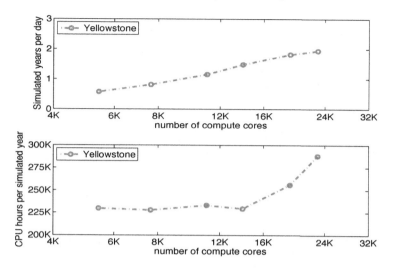

FIGURE 8.6: These charts show (a) the simulation rate and (b) the CPU-hours cost as a function of core count for high-resolution CESM on Yellowstone.

significantly greater than 10 are considered useful for forecasting purposes. The results in Figure 8.7 show that WRF scaled well on Yellowstone for this problem up to about 20,000 cores, achieving an integration rate nearly 50 times wall clock at 65,536 cores. See [28, 10, 53] for further details.

8.7 System Statistics

8.7.1 System Usage Patterns

When Yellowstone entered production in December 2012, more than 1,800 user accounts and 424 projects had already been established. These included active users migrated from NCAR's previous system, Bluefire, as well as projects reviewed and allocated prior to Yellowstone's arrival. By July 2013, the user community had grown by a third, to more than 2,400 users and 651 projects.

The system's normal production workload includes a spectrum of job sizes. As can be seen in Figure 8.8, a small but demanding set of capability-oriented projects consumed more than 70% of Yellowstone's delivered core-hours for high-resolution climate and weather models, while 80% of projects on Yellowstone completed their science objectives with smaller-scale jobs using fewer

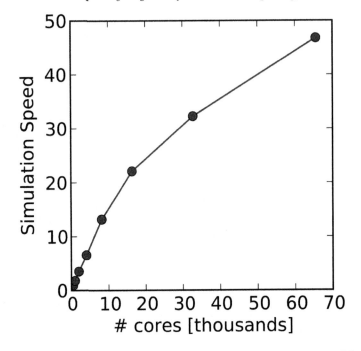

FIGURE 8.7: Strong scaling of WRF for the 1 km Katrina problem from 512 to 65,536 cores on Yellowstone.

than 2,048 cores. This pattern is expected to persist throughout the system's lifetime [16].

The data-intensive components of the Yellowstone environment have also been instrumented to better understand their usage patterns [17]. This data includes job accounting statistics for the Geyser and Caldera analysis clusters and weekly storage accounting data for the GLADE central file systems and the HPSS tape archive. While trailing HPC use, HPSS growth seems to have stabilized at 200-300 terabytes per week (Figure 8.9). Prior to the Yellowstone procurement, CISL estimated an archive growth rate of approximately 450 terabytes per week.

The growth in disk storage usage is also being tracked (Figure 8.10). Ignoring transients that occurred before March 2013, GLADE storage use across all filesystems has been growing steadily at a rate of 350 terabytes per month, and it surpassed 5 petabytes total by November 2013. Roughly half of this growth is in the /project filesystem, which serves as longer-term storage of high-value datasets to increase science impact. If this trend continues, the GLADE system could be full by the middle of 2016, even with the planned capacity increases. In response, modifications to future storage allocation and retention policies may be required.

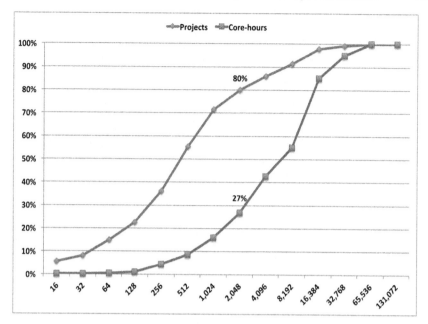

FIGURE 8.8: Distribution of projects and Yellowstone usage, according to project's largest jobs.

8.7.2   Reliability, Uptime, and Utilization

From a contractual standpoint, the key reliability metrics for the systems in the Yellowstone environment are availability and mean time between system failure (MTBSF). The target thresholds were 99% and 24 days for GLADE; and 98% and 16 days for Yellowstone, Caldera, and Geyser.

During the early months of production, NCAR, IBM, and Mellanox collaborated closely to identify and resolve key reliability issues that often accompany the deployment of petascale systems. Perhaps the most challenging were those surrounding Yellowstone's FDR InfiniBand fabric, including fabric instability and routing engine reconfiguration and refinement, which affected early-user job success rates and application performance reproducibility. The end-user impact was mitigated by extensive efforts by Mellanox and IBM to optimize the OpenSM configuration. Fabric reliability issues were found to be the result of an early manufacturing problem with the FDR optical cables that caused some links to run at sub-FDR speeds and to experience higher-than-expected cable failure rates. To address these issues, a complete replacement of Yellowstone's optical cables was performed between September 30 and October 9, 2013.

Other system reliability issues included: refinement of the routing engine configuration; management of application-induced out-of-memory conditions; and scaling and start-up issues with the IBM Parallel Environment runtime

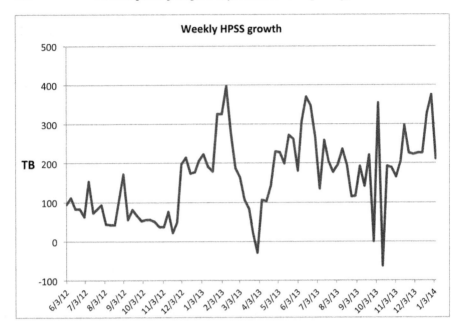

FIGURE 8.9: Weekly growth of CISL's HPSS archive. The downward trend in March and April was caused by a major data deletion effort unrelated to Yellowstone use.

system and its interaction with the LSF workload management system. Despite these issues, by spring 2013, Yellowstone was maintaining an availability in excess of 99% with daily-average user utilization generally over 90%.

8.8   Early Science Results

As with past NCAR systems, early access to Yellowstone was provided to large-scale Accelerated Scientific Discovery (ASD) projects selected from the university and NCAR communities based on their potential to produce scientific breakthroughs. These 11 projects exhibited a diversity of scientific problems, algorithms, and computational scales that also served to stress-test the Yellowstone system, as would be typical in a "friendly user" period. This section describes some of these projects with their preliminary scientific findings and their computational experiences.

Regional-Scale Prediction of Future Climate and Air Quality

As modern society becomes increasingly complex, it becomes increasingly vulnerable to changes in air quality, weather, and climate. These changes

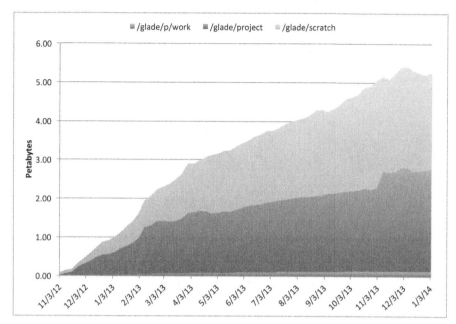

FIGURE 8.10: Growth in GLADE file systems usage since the start of Yellowstone. Data shown is cumulative across filesystems.

emphasize the need for reliable projections of future climate and air quality on regional to local scales. Reliable projections require the use of regional models with a horizontal resolution consistent with the scale of the processes of interest. They also require simulations spanning multiple years to quantify the interannual variability and provide statistically significant projections. Simulations of this type are thus an enormous challenge to supercomputing systems.

With support of NCAR's Accelerated Scientific Discovery program, a set of high-resolution (12-km) simulations was run using the fully coupled nested regional climate model with chemistry (NRCM-Chem) to predict changes in air quality and climate over the U.S. between present time and the 2050s. NRCM-Chem is based on the regional WRF Model with Chemistry (WRF-Chem) version 3.3, which is a fully coupled chemical transport model [15], and has been updated to include all climate-relevant processes and feedbacks. The simulations follow the IPCC A2 climate and RCP8.5 precursor emission scenario with about 8 W/m^2 radiative forcing by 2100, but large reductions in short-lived pollutant emissions in the developed world.

As shown in Figure 8.11, these simulations provide in-depth analysis of future air quality and chemistry-climate feedbacks. They supplement the global simulations performed in recent assessments of future climate and composition and, in particular, quantify the ability of global models at moderate

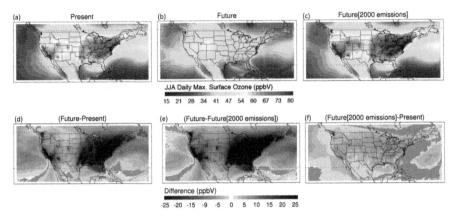

FIGURE 8.11: Average daily maximum surface ozone during summertime over the U.S. for present day (a), a future climate and pollutant emission scenario (b), and a future climate scenario with emissions kept at present-day levels (c). Difference plots are shown in (d)-(f). Results indicate that a warming climate will aggravate ozone pollution over the United States in the middle of the century (see panels a, c, and f). However, if emissions of pollutants continue to decline, U.S. ozone levels should improve even as temperatures rise (panels a, b, and d).

horizontal resolution to capture regional air quality characteristics. In addition, these high-resolution simulations are used to identify how specific local meteorological flows, e.g., in the vicinity of topography, affect local to regional chemistry. They will also contrast the chemical importance of specific events such as heat waves in present and future climate conditions. To assess the impacts of changes in emissions versus changes in climate on air quality, sensitivity simulations for the 2050s were run where anthropogenic emissions were held at present-time levels. Future simulations without chemistry are used to quantify changes in weather patterns and climate associated with atmospheric composition.

A High-Resolution Coupled Climate Experiment

The current generation of coupled general circulation models (CGCMs) is designed to perform century and multi-century simulations, including ensembles that span the uncertainty associated with natural variability or parameter sensitivity. With previous computing capabilities, models have been limited to grid spacings of around 1° (∼100 km). These models adequately resolve large-scale modes of climate variability (such as the El-Niño Southern Oscillation), but do not capture smaller-scale features that have important local impacts and may feed back to the large-scale climate. For example, it would

FIGURE 8.12: Snapshot showing latent heat flux overlaid on sea surface temperature from year 14 of the high resolution CESM run. Note the influence of Gulf Stream meanders on a cold-air outbreak in the Northwest Atlantic (upper left) and a cold temperature wake beneath a tropical cyclone in the Indian Ocean (lower right). Previously, neither feature has been well simulated by lower-resolution climate models.

be useful to know how the statistics of tropical cyclones and polar lows change over time in response to changes in the large-scale climate state.

The deployment of Yellowstone presented an opportunity to perform a multi-decadal run of a much higher-resolution CGCM. As shown in Figure 8.12, such a simulation can be used to study climate interactions at all scales down to oceanic and atmospheric mesoscale (i.e., tens of kilometers). It can also potentially act as a benchmark for comparing various high-resolution regional modeling approaches. In this ASD experiment, the CESM was used for a century-long climate simulation under present-day (year 2000) greenhouse gas conditions. The experiment coupled a 25-km-resolution land surface and atmosphere based on the Community Atmosphere Model (CAM5), and 10-km-resolution sea ice and ocean models based on the Parallel Ocean Program (POP2) – perhaps the longest run with CAM5-enabled CESM at this resolution of ocean and atmosphere – allowing analysis of variability on seasonal to decadal timescales.

The experiment was more computationally intensive than many previous high-resolution simulations, largely because of the additional computational cost of adding prognostic aerosol equations in the CAM5 model. Use of the highly scalable spectral element atmospheric dynamical core within CAM5 allowed for faster throughput than was possible with previous dynamical cores [11]. The experiment ran on 23,404 cores of Yellowstone and the first 60 simulated years consumed 25 million CPU-hours over three months. The core count was chosen to maximize the model throughput while also keeping the computational cost reasonable. A throughput of 2.0 SYPD was obtained by carefully load-balancing between the model components, some of which can run concurrently. The I/O for this run was substantial, adding an approximately 6.5% overhead to the run, and generating approximately one terabyte of data per wall-clock day. The simulation output is now being examined by climate scientists specializing in atmospheric, oceanic, and sea-ice processes. Results from a preliminary analysis show that the high-resolution simulation captures more cases where the ocean drives atmospheric variability than previous low-resolution runs. Amongst the scientific results, there is a better spectrum of El-Niño variability in the high-resolution model, compared to a complementary run at lower resolution [43]. To assist collaborative analysis, these data are made available to the community via NCAR's Earth System Grid portal [14].

Resolving Mesoscale Features in Coupled Climate Simulations

On Yellowstone, an international project led by the Center for Ocean-Land-Atmosphere Studies has been exploring the effect of explicitly resolving mesoscale features in the atmosphere on coupled climate predictions for lead-times of a few days to several seasons. Coupling allows testing of the hypothesis that the insensitivity of certain climate features to changes in resolution seen in Project Athena [23] – such as intraseasonal variability in the tropical Indian and Pacific Ocean sectors – is due to the absence of an air-sea feedback. Similarly, increasing atmospheric model resolution in the coupled prediction system can improve forecast accuracy and reliability of known deficiencies in the operational forecasts. As an example, the simulation and prediction of the Madden-Julian Oscillation remains a challenge in operational coupled prediction systems (e.g., Kim et al. 2014) which may be due in part to insufficient horizontal and vertical resolution in the atmosphere [22]. Additionally, the high data storage capacity of Yellowstone's central file system, GLADE, has allowed researchers to retain a far more extensive suite of variables. This capability has already paid important dividends scientifically, as retaining hourly rainfall rates for the highest-resolution simulations (16 km) has allowed investigation of the detailed structure of tropical cyclones, demonstrating the clear presence of an eye, a fact that was not apparent in earlier work.

Full Wave Seismic Data Assimilation

Earthquake hazard analysis and mitigation depends on seismology to quantify ground motion and failure due to earthquakes. Scientists have developed and tested a new physics-based seismic wave propagation model, known as full-wave seismic data assimilation (FWSDA), that assimilates increasingly high-quality broadband seismic waveform observations [7]. The study performed on Yellowstone is part of a collaborative project between the University of Wyoming and the Southern California Earthquake Center (SCEC)

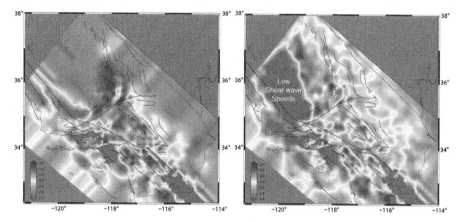

FIGURE 8.13: Shearwave speeds at 2 miles below the surface using conventional seismology (left) and FWSDA (right), showing new areas of vulnerability farther from the fault, on the left side of the simulated domain.

with the goal of refining the seismic velocity and attenuation structure of the San Andreas Fault Near Parkfield, California. It was carried out at several supercomputer centers in the U.S., including the NWSC.

The project demonstrated the ability of the new model to make significantly more reliable predictions of ground shaking, especially in regions with complex 3D geological structures. For example, the shear-wave speed of the subsurface is highly correlated with shaking: regions with lower shear-wave speed often experience stronger shaking during a large earthquake. The plots in Figure 8.13 indicate the predicted shear-wave speed at 2 miles below the surface near Parkfield in Southern California. Here, the light and dark areas indicate the distribution of high and low shear-wave speeds. The plot on the left shows predicted shear-wave speeds using conventional seismology techniques that are only accurate near the faults. The plot on the right uses the new model that assimilates numerous waveform observations and more accurately predicts shear-wave speeds farther away from the faults. The model and its outputs are now being used to more precisely constrain the plate-tectonic processes of lithospheric creation, deformation, magmatism, and destruction to improve imaging of seismic sources.

The FWSDA model used a tetrahedral mesh with 1.4 million elements that conforms to the irregular surface topography in the Parkfield area. The mesh was refined in regions around the San Andreas Fault zone and in regions close to the surface where the seismic velocity is low and the wavelength is short. A 5,000-time-step simulation costs approximately 45 minutes on 2,400 cores of Yellowstone. Data from 600 earthquakes in the Parkfield area was assimilated and required 2,400 simulations per iteration, costing approximately 4 million core-hours per iteration. A total of 3 iterations were run in the first year, requiring approximately 12 million core-hours on Yellowstone. The experiment's storage requirement is proportional to the total number of tetrahedral elements, the number of time steps, and the number of earthquakes. For this experiment, the space-time storage for a single earthquake required 2.6 terabytes of disk space. Volume renderings of the 3D Earth structure model were generated using the NWSC's data analysis and visualization clusters equipped with the open-source software Paraview and the Visualization Toolkit by Kitware Inc.

Toward Global Cloud-Resolving Models

The Model for Prediction Across Scales (MPAS), collaboratively developed by NCAR and Los Alamos National Laboratory, is designed to perform global cloud-resolving atmosphere simulations. It is comprised of geophysical fluid-flow solvers for the atmosphere and ocean that use unstructured spherical centroidal Voronoi meshes to tile the globe. The meshes, nominally hexagons, allow for both quasi-uniform tiling of the sphere in an icosahedral-mesh configuration, or a variable-resolution tiling where the change in resolution is gradual and in which there are no hanging nodes. This contrasts with traditional nested grid or adaptive mesh refinement (AMR) techniques that use cell division for refinement.

Three weather events were studied using global MPAS simulations: (a) a very intense extratropical cyclone (see Figure 8.14) and an associated series of isolated tornadic storms that occurred over North America during the period of 23-30 October, 2010; (b) the period of 27 August through 2 September, 2010, during which several hurricanes occurred in the Atlantic Basin; and (c) a very strong Madden-Julian Oscillation (MJO) event observed in the Indian Ocean and maritime continent region during 15 January through 4 February, 2009.

Simulations of each event were performed on meshes with 3, 7.5, 15, and 30 km cell spacing. The most ambitious component of these experiments is the 3 km simulations where convection is explicitly resolved to produce fine-scale convective structures similar to those observed in nature. Specifically, isolated severe convective cells were produced in the warm sector ahead of the strong cold front in the October 2010 simulation; the observed hurricanes (Daniel, Earl, and Fiona) were well simulated in the August case; and a strong MJO was produced in the longer (20-day) simulation of the 2009 MJO. Observed mountain-wave activity was also reproduced. The fine-scale convective structures were resolved at a level commensurate with state-of-the-art cloud models using similar mesh resolution. The MJO simulation provides further evidence that convective-scale dynamics play an important role in MJO dynamics: the coarser mesh simulations using parameterized convection produced much poorer representations of the MJO. Further analysis is underway to understand the connection between the convective systems and the larger-scale MJO signal.

On Yellowstone, the 3 km simulations were typically performed on either 16K or 32K cores with an integration rate of somewhat greater than 2 and

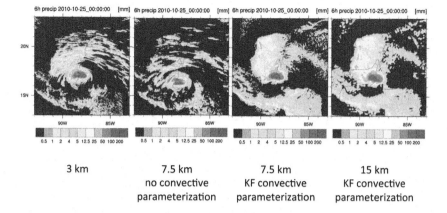

FIGURE 8.14: The panels show 6-hour precipitation totals for Tropical Cyclone Richard (25 October, 2010) for four experiments with MPAS that test the effects of resolution and physics parameterization choices. In variable-resolution grids, a challenge is to design convective schemes that turn off in refined regions where their assumptions become poor. In this case it seems that the Kain-Fritsch (KF) convective scheme is not too dependent on grid size between 7.5 and 15 km, which is promising. At 3 km resolution, no convective parameterization is needed because the dynamics resolve the deep convection.

4 simulated days per wall clock day, respectively. This mesh is composed of about 2.7 billion cells, and 144,000 time steps were required for the 20-day simulation of the MJO event. These high-resolution variable mesh simulations, along with the lower-resolution uniform-mesh results, will be used to evaluate the suitability of the variable-resolution meshes for future weather prediction and climate applications.

The Magnetic Field of the Quiet Sun

While sunspots are the most prominent manifestation of solar magnetism, they cover only a small fraction of the solar surface: the remainder is not free from magnetic field, but it is organized on very small scales below the resolving power of current solar telescopes. These regions of the solar surface are referred to as the "Quiet Sun," and their properties are mostly independent of the solar cycle, in contrast to the "Active Sun" that shows a strong modulation of area occupied by sunspots throughout the 11-year solar cycle. A series of high-resolution numerical simulations of the solar photosphere has been run on Yellowstone to study the origin and properties of the Quiet Sun's magnetic field (see Figure 8.15). In these simulations, a mixed-polarity magnetic field is maintained through a small-scale dynamo process that involves magnetic field amplification in chaotic flows. Using large eddy simulations of radiative magnetohydrodynamics, these models for the first time reached an overall

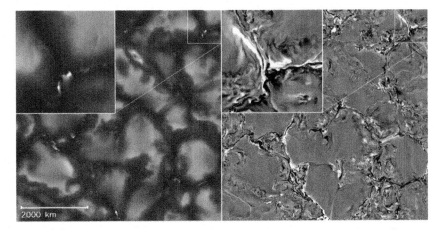

FIGURE 8.15: Results from a 4 km simulation of the Quiet Sun, with a domain size of 6,144 x 6,144 x 3,072 km. Left: Emergent intensity showing the solar granulation pattern. Right: Vertical magnetic field at the visible surface of the sun (optical depth of unity). Magnetic field is organized in mostly sheet-like features and even in the Quiet Sun can reach a field strength exceeding 2,000 G. These regions typically show a brightness enhancement.

magnetization of the photosphere that is consistent with the level inferred from observations. The downward extrapolation of these photospheric models into the solar convection zone implies that even during phases of low solar activity, the magnetic field is close to having an equipartition of kinetic and magnetic energy throughout most of the solar convection zone.

8.9   The NWSC Facility

8.9.1   Overview and Design

The Yellowstone supercomputer is located in the NCAR Wyoming Super-computing Center (NWSC), five miles west of Cheyenne, Wyoming. Three key goals drove the NWSC's design: flexibility, sustainability, and energy efficiency. Flexibility is important because the future directions of IT heat loads and system design are difficult to predict. Sustainability and energy efficiency not only make sense financially, but also align with the environmental mission of the research center. The success of this design approach can be measured in part by the outside recognition of the NWSC. The facility has been certified at a Leadership in Energy Efficiency and Design (LEED) Gold level, which is difficult for a computing facility to achieve. The NWSC's "green" design won the Uptime Institute's Green Enterprise IT first-place award for Facility

FIGURE 8.16: The NCAR-Wyoming Supercomputing Center (NWSC), located in Cheyenne, Wyoming, houses supercomputers and equipment dedicated to research in atmospheric and related science. The facility opened its doors in October 2012, and has garnered numerous awards for its sustainable design and energy efficiency.

Design Implementation [48], Best Project award in the Green Project Category from Engineering News Record [37], and received the top award in the "Green" Data Center category from Data Center Dynamics [4].

The NSF required a facility design for NWSC with a minimum useful life of 20 years. So a modular and flexible design strategy was adopted to minimize risk. A site was selected with sufficient room to accommodate potential expansion over the facility's lifetime. The initial building shell was made large enough to accommodate a conservative 10-year system power growth projection, the longest that could be made with any confidence. The initial electrical and mechanical components were provisioned for only a 5-year time horizon.

The flexibility of the NWSC was enhanced by several important design details. Conduits and equipment pads were installed to accommodate future equipment expansions and avoid expensive alterations. Pathways between loading docks and the machine room were designed to eliminate installation bottlenecks. The 10-foot raised floor in NWSC's dual computer rooms simplifies the installation and maintenance of liquid cooling systems and electrical components without disrupting production systems.

The NWSC was constructed with a holistic approach to sustainability: materials selection, construction practices, and water conservation all played key roles. The project made extensive use of regionally sourced concrete and precast panel systems. More than 510 tons of recycled concrete, 60 tons of recycled wood, and 26 tons of recycled metals were used in the facility's construction. More than 70% of all construction waste was recycled. Construction techniques such as continuous insulation on steel and precast concrete panel systems ensured a tight building envelope, and along with rigorous testing [49], reduced the amount of energy required for heating, cooling, and humidification.

Further, the building design reduced power needed for lighting by optimizing all relevant factors: building placement, ratio of windows to insulated walls, atrium space, skylights, exterior solar shades, and daylight-responsive electric lighting controls.

Water conservation and run-off management are critical elements of sustainability in Wyoming's arid environment. The facility's cooling towers employ a zero liquid discharge approach that reduces water use by 40% [13]. Plantings around the facility are primarily native grasses and xeric plants that eliminate the need for irrigation. And the facility makes extensive use of bioswales [29], shallow, sloping landscape features that safely transport water during rainstorms or snow melts. These effective features blend in with the rolling prairie that surrounds the facility.

The facility design team systematically evaluated the efficiency and cost of mechanical cooling systems, water and air delivery methods, and electrical distribution strategies. It was clear that future HPC systems would employ various forms of liquid cooling, so indirect evaporative cooling was a particularly efficient, flexible, and cost-effective choice as Wyoming's cool, dry climate supports the use of evaporative cooling techniques for most of the year. Evaporative cooling was key to the NWSC achieving a projected Power Use Efficiency (PUE) [4] as low as 1.1, while staying within recommended ASHRAE TC9.9 [1] conditions.

Eliminating flow restrictions in the system and reducing pressure drops was another important efficiency strategy. Fan-wall technology and ductless, air-based cooling provide large air flow volume with very low pressure drops. Oversized piping and using $45°$ pipe bends achieved efficiency gains in the chilled water system. Variable frequency drive (VFD) fans and pumps, used throughout, provided two significant benefits. First, when coupled with the building automation system, VFD cooling components can dynamically meet the variable demands of modern computing systems. Second, the power consumed by fans and pumps has a cubic relationship to velocity: there is a distinct power advantage to operating at low speeds.

Energy losses in the facility's electrical distribution systems were reduced by using high-efficiency oil-immersed transformers and by stepping the voltage directly down from the 24,900-volt utility supply to the 480 volts required at the rack level. The uninterruptible power supply at the NWSC was sized to protect only the systems sensitive to power interruptions, such as disks.

Finally, the efficiency of the facility design was modeled and validated at a 4 MW building load using eQuest DOE version 2.2 software, then compared to a traditional facility design. This modeling effort showed that the facility design would consume 29.8% less energy and cost 28.9% less to operate than a conventionally designed data center.

8.9.2   Early Experience in Operation

Yellowstone is the first HPC system installed at NWSC, and its selection occurred as the computing facility was nearing completion. This allowed CISL to manage the system fit-up costs while completing the building. As Yellowstone came online, operations staff tuned the efficiency of the facility. The PUE has trended below 1.2 during this tuning process, and appears to be approaching ∼1.1. Given that the NWSC was designed for a worst-case initial load as high as 4 MW, and that Yellowstone normally operates at or below 1.2 MW, achieving a low PUE is a significant achievement. Additionally, the facility responds directly to both changes in outside conditions and considerable changes in IT load. Yellowstone incorporates a number of energy-saving features that can impact PUE: during idle times, Yellowstone's power consumption can drop to 300 KW.

The construction and provisioning of NWSC offered a unique opportunity to provide research and education opportunities for electrical and mechanical engineering students through CISL's Summer Internships in Parallel Computational Science (SIParCS) program. While the facility was under construction, one student created an energy model of the facility, while another evaluated vendors' proposals using a computational fluid dynamics (CFD) model of the computer room floor. The next summer two SIParCS interns compared the results of the energy model to actual facility data and verified the CFD model with measurements. During summer 2013, a graduate student provided both engineering and statistical analyses of facility performance using a full year of operational data.

8.10   Future Challenges

As scientists strive to model and understand the physical, chemical, biological, and human components that govern the climate system in ever-greater detail across a range of timescales, the HPC community must continue to provide increasingly powerful cyber-resources tailored to these objectives. Contained within the Yellowstone experience are some clues to the future challenges facing the HPC community. The sheer number of components in modern large-scale supercomputers requires a relentless focus on scalability and fault-tolerance at the application, system software, and hardware levels.

Rising power requirements and utility costs tax the ability to deploy systems at the necessary scale and put an increasing premium on energy efficiency in all areas. HPC architecture changes, including many-core systems and new classes of memory and storage, provide both opportunities and challenges, requiring innovation in both system and application design.

Future systems may be so complex and costly that scientists may need to modify how they approach basic issues such as calculation correctness and reproducibility. New metrics of system performance that capture the growing importance of bandwidth and energy consumption relative to flops will be critical in advancing system designs. Regardless, the scientific adventure in numerical atmospheric science that began with ENIAC and continued through the CDC6600, the Cray 1A, and down to Yellowstone today, is in some ways, only just beginning.

8.11 Acknowledgments and Contributions

No decade-long project like this can be accomplished without the contribution of too many people and organizations to list conveniently. However, we especially want to acknowledge all the NSF, NCAR, and State and University of Wyoming people, past and present, who were tireless in their commitment to making the dream of NWSC and Yellowstone a reality. We include those who went on to operate it and push it toward its design goals, and also those at other organizations who provided their enthusiasm, oversight, critiques, and advice throughout the project's duration. Further, the authors want to acknowledge the hard work of our private sector colleagues for their contributions to making the project a success, and the many authors and contributors who, either through writing or editing, helped shape this chapter. Some of the work presented here was performed under National Science Foundation award numbers M0856145, ATM-0830068, AGS-1134932, EAR-0944206, and ACI-0941735.

Bibliography

[1] American Society of Heating, Refrigeration and Air-Conditioning Engineers, Inc. *ASHRAE Environmental Guidelines for Datacom Equipment*, 2008. http://www.ashrae.org.

[2] J. Anderson, T. Hoar, H. Liu K. Raeder, N. Collins, R. Torn, and A. Arellano. The data assimilation research testbed: A community facility. *Bulletin of the American Meteorological Society*, 90:1283–1296, 2009. doi:10.1175/2009BAMS2618.1.

[3] AWP-ODC. http://hpgeoc.sdsc.edu/AWPODC/, August 2013.

[4] C. Belady, A. Rawson, J. Pfleuger, and T. Cader. The green grid data center power efficiency metrics: PUE and DCiE. White Paper No. 6, 2008.

[5] G. Bell, J. Gray, and A. Szalay. Petascale computational systems. *Computer*, 39(110-112):1337–1351, 2006.

[6] J. Charney, R. Fjörtoft, and J. Von Neumann. Numerical integration of the barotropic vorticity equation. *Tellus*, 2(4):237–254, 1950.

[7] P. Chen. Full-wave seismic data assimilation: A unified methodology for seismic waveform inversion. In Y.G. Li, editor, *Imaging, Modeling and Assimilation in Seismology*, pages 19–64. Higher Education Press and Walter de Gruyter GmbH & Co., 2012.

[8] Yellowstone. http://www2.cisl.ucar.edu/resources/yellowstone/, 2013.

[9] D. Clarke. What is ZEUS-3D? http://www.ica.smu.ca/zeus3d/documents/whatiszeus.pdf, August 2013. Saint Mary's University.

[10] D. Del Vento and C. G. Kruse. Optimizing performance of the weather research and forecasting model at large core counts: an investigation into hybrid parallelism and domain decomposition. In *Proceedings of AMS 2014*, 2014.

[11] J. M. Dennis, J. Edwards, K. J. Evans, O. Guba, P. Lauritzen, A. Mirin, A. St-Cyr, M. A. Taylor, and P. Worley. CAM-SE: A scalable spectral element dynamical core for the community atmosphere model. *International Journal of High Performance Computing Applications*, 26(1):74–89, 2012.

[12] J. M. Dennis, M. Vertenstein, P. Worley, A. Mirin, A. Craig, R. Jacob, and S. Mickelson. Computational performance of ultra-high-resolution capability in the community earth system model. *International Journal of High Performance Computing Applications*, 26(1):5–16, 2012.

[13] D. Duke. ZLD: New silica based inhibitor chemistry permits cost effective water conservation for HVAC and industrial cooling towers. International Water Conference IWC Report 07-11, 2011.

[14] Earth System Grid website. http://www.earthsystemgrid.org, 2013.

[15] G. Grell, S. Peckham, R. Schmitz, S. McKeen, G. Frost, W. Skamarock, and B. Eder. Fully coupled "online" chemistry within the wrf model. *Atmospheric Environment*, 39(37):6957–6975, 2005.

[16] D. L. Hart. Deep and wide metrics for HPC resource capability and project usage. In *SC'11 State of the Practice Reports*, Seattle, WA, 2011. doi:10.1145/2063348.2063350.

[17] D. L. Hart, P. Gillman, and E. Thanhardt. Concurrency Computat.: Pract. Experiences (26) 2210–2224, 2014. doi: 10.1002/cpe.3228.

[18] IBM rear door heat eXchanger for the iDataPlex rack, installation and maintenance guide. Technical Report P/N 49Y2134, IBM Corporation, March 2009.

[19] IBM x3650 M4. http://www-03.ibm.com/systems/x/hardware/rack/x3650m4/, Aug. 2013.

[20] IBM x3850 X5. http://www-03.ibm.com/systems/x/hardware/enterprise/x3850x5/, Aug. 2013.

[21] IBM system x iDataPlex dx360 M4. IBM Redbooks Product Guide, Aug. 2013.

[22] Hye-Mi Kim, Peter J. Webster, Violeta E. Toma, and Daehyun Kim, 2014: Predictability and prediction skill of the MJO in two operational forecasting systems. *J. Climate*, 27, 5364–5378. doi: 10.1175.JCLI-D-13-00480.1.

[23] J. L. Kinter III, D. Achuthavarier, J. M. Adams, E. L. Altshuler, B. A. Cash, P. Dirmeyer, B. Doty, B. Huang, L. Marx, J. Manganello, C. Stan, T. Wakefield, E. K. Jin, T. Palmer, M. Hamrud, T. Jung, M. Miller, P. Towers, N. Wedi, M. Satoh, H. Tomita, C. Kodama, Y. Yamada, P. Andrews, T. Baer, M. Ezell, C. Halloy, D. John, B. Loftis, and K. Wong. Revolutionizing climate modeling– project athena: A multi-institutional, international collaboration. *Bull. Amer. Met. Soc.*, 94:231–245, 2013.

[24] Intel Xeon E5-2670 (Sandy Bridge EP). http://ark.intel.com/products/64595/Intel-Xeon-Processor-E5-2670-20M-Cache-2_60-GHz-8_00-GTs-Intel-QPI, Aug. 2013.

[25] Intel Xeon E7-4870 (Westmere EX). http://ark.intel.com/products/53579/Intel-Xeon-Processor-E7-4870-30M-Cache-2_40-GHz-6_40-GTs-Intel-QPI, Aug. 2013.

[26] Intel xeon Phi 5110P coprocessor. http://ark.intel.com/products/71992/Intel-Xeon-Phi-Coprocessor-5110P-8GB-1_053-GHz-60-core, Aug. 2013.

[27] R. C. Kelly, S. S. Ghosh, S. Liu, D. Del Vento, and R. A. Valent. The NWSC benchmark suite using scientific throughput to measure super-computer performance. In *SC'11 State of the Practice Reports*, Seattle, WA, 2011. doi: 10.1145/2063348.2063358.

[28] C. G. Kruse, D. Del Vento, R. Montuoro, M. Lubin, and S. McMillian. Evaluation of WRF scaling to several thousand cores on the yellowstone supercomputer. Work presented at FRCRC HPC Symposium 2013, Laramie, WY.

[29] P. M. Loechl et al. Design schematics for a sustainable parking lot. Technical Report ERDC/CERL TR-03-12, US Army Corps of Engineers, Research and Developing Center, Construction Engineering Research Laboratory, Champaign, IL, 2003.

[30] R. McLay, K. W. Schulz, W. L. Barth, and T. Minyard. Best practices for the deployment and management of production HPC clusters. In *SC'11 State of the Practice Reports*, page 11, New York, NY, 2011. ACM. doi:10.1145/2063348.2063360.

[31] G. Meehl, W. Washington, J. Arblaster, A. Hu, H. Teng, J. Kay, A. Gettelman, D. Lawrence, B. Sanderson, and W. Strand. Climate change projections in cesm1 (cam5) compared to ccsm4. *J. Climate*, volume 26, issue 17, pp.6287–6308. doi:10.1175/JCLI-D-12-00572.1.

[32] SX6536. http://www.mellanox.com/page/products_dyn ?product_family= 122&menu_section=49, Aug. 2013.

[33] SX6512. http://www.mellanox.com/page/products_dyn ?product_family= 137&mtag=sx6512, Aug. 2013.

[34] SX6036. http://www.mellanox.com/page/products_dyn ?product_family= 132&menu_section=49, Aug. 2013.

[35] J. Michalakes, J. Dudhia, D. Gill, T. Henderson, J. Klemp, W. Skamarock, and W. Wang. The weather research and forecast model: software architecture and performance. In *Proceedings of the 11th ECMWF Workshop on the Use of High Performance Computing In Meteorology*, volume 25. World Scientific, 2004.

[36] C-H. Moeng and P.P. Sullivan. Large eddy simulation. Encyclopedia of Atmospheric Sciences, http://www.mmm.ucar.edu/applications/ les/les.php.

[37] Climate Research Spurred by Green Design of Supercomputing Center. http://mountainstates.construction.com/mountainstates_construction_ projects/2012/1022-climate-research-will-be-spurred-by-green-design-of-new-supercomputing-center.asp, 2013.

[38] NVIDIA Quadro 6000. http://www.nvidia.com/object/product-quadro-6000-us.html, Aug. 2013.

[39] NVIDIA M2070Q. http://www.nvidia.com/docs/IO/43395/ NV_DS_Tesla_M2050_M2070_Apr10_LowRes.pdf, Apr. 2010.

[40] N. A. Phillips. The general circulation of the atmosphere: A numerical experiment. *Quarterly J. Royal Meteorological Society*, 82:123–164, 1956.

[41] W. C. Skamarock and J. B. Klemp. A time-split nonhydrostatic atmospheric model for weather research and forecasting applications. *Journal of Computational Physics*, 227(7):3465–3485, 2008.

[42] W.C. Skamarock, J.B. Klemp, M.G. Duda, L. Fowler, S-H. Park, and T.D. Ringler. A multi-scale nonhydrostatic atmospheric model using centroidal voronoi tesselations and c-grid staggering. *Monthly Weather Review*, 240:3090–3105, 2012. doi:10.1175/MWR-D-11-00215.1.

[43] Small, R.J. et al. (2014), A new synoptic scale resolving global climate simulation using the Community Earth System Model, *J. Adv. Model. Earth Sys.*, 06. doi: 10.1002/2014 MS000363.

[44] R. Smith, P. Jones, B. Briegleb, F. Bryan, G. Danabasoglu, J. Dennis, J. Dukowicz, C. Eden, B. Fox-Kemper, P. Gent, M. Hecht, S. Jayne, M. Jochum, W. Large, K. Lindsay, M. Maltrud, N. Norton, S. Peacock, M. Vertenstein, and S. Yeager. The Parallel Ocean Program (POP) reference manual: Ocean component of the Community Climate System Model (CCSM). Technical Report LAUR-10-01853, Los Alamos National Laboratory, March 2010.

[45] SPECFEM3D. http://www.geodynamics.org/cig/software/specfem3d, August 2013.

[46] TIEGCM v1.94 model description. http://www.hao.ucar.edu/modeling/ tgcm/doc/description/model_description.pdf, Aug. 2013.

[47] NCAR selects IBM for key components of new supercomputing center. http://www2.ucar.edu/atmosnews/news/5662/ncar-selects-ibm-key-components-new-supercomputing-center, Nov. 2011.

[48] 2013 Green Enterprise IT award honorees. http://symposium. uptimeinstitute.com/geit-awards, 2013.

[49] U.S. Army Corps of Engineers air leakage test protocol for building envelopes.

[50] A. Vögler, S. Shelyag, M. Schüssler, F. Cattaneo, T. Emonet, and T. Linde. Simulations of magneto-convection in the solar photosphere: Equations, methods, and results of the MURaM code. *Astron. & Astrophys.*, 429:335–351, 2005.

[51] D. Watts and M. Bachmaier. Implementing an IBM system x iDataPlex solution. Technical Report SG24-7629-04, IBM International Technical Support Organization, June 2012.

[52] WRFDA users page. http://www.mmm.ucar.edu/wrf/users/wrfda/, Aug. 2013.

[53] Optimizing WRF performance. https://www2.cisl.ucar.edu/resources/ software/models/wrf_optimization.

Index

A

Accelerated Scientific Discovery (ASD) projects, 208

ACF, *see* Advanced Computer Facility

ACTA, *see* Advanced Complex Trait Analysis

Active Sun, 215

Adaptive mesh refinement (AMR), 214

Advanced Complex Trait Analysis (ACTA), 13

Advanced Computer Facility (ACF), 31

Advanced Research WRF (ARW) model, 202

Allocation unit, 34

ALPS, *see* Application Level Placement Scheduler

Amdahl's law, 191

AMR, *see* Adaptive mesh refinement

Application Level Placement Scheduler (ALPS), 103

ARCHER, 7–40

    applications and workloads, 11–14

        Advanced Complex Trait Analysis open-source software, 13

        big data/data intensive computing, 13

        computational fluid dynamics, 13

        earth sciences, 12

        Fluidity ocean modelling application, 12

        highlights of main applications, 13–14

        Lattice-Boltzmann approach, 12

        Ludwig, 14

        materials science and chemistry, 12

        nanoscience, 12

        physical life sciences, 13

        plasma physics, 12

        R statistical language, 13

        soft matter physics, 12

        SPRINT, 14

        Unified Model MicroMag, 12

        VASP, 14

    data center/facility, 31–34

        Advanced Computer Facility, 31

        infrastructure, 31–33

        innovations and challenges, 33–34

        location and history, 31

        Power Usage Effectiveness, 33

    hardware architecture, 16–19

        Aries router, 17

        compute node architecture, 16–17

        Dragony topology, 17

        external login nodes, 17–18

        home filesystems, 18–19

        interconnect, 17

        non-uniform access, 17

        pre- and post-processing nodes, 18

        QuickPath Interconnect, 16

        service node architecture, 17

        storage systems, 18–19